When the student is ready the teacher appears.
When the student is truly ready the teacher disappears.
~Lao Tzu

TEACHING

DANCE

THE SPECTRUM
OF STYLES
SECOND EDITION

ELIZABETH GOODLING

authorHOUSE®

AuthorHouse™
1663 Liberty Drive
Bloomington, IN 47403
www.authorhouse.com
Phone: 1 (800) 839-8640

Dance photo at the back cover is credited to **East Stroudsburg University Photo/Office of University Relations**

Published by AuthorHouse 02/23/2019

ISBN: 978-1-5462-6374-6 (sc)
ISBN: 978-1-5462-6373-9 (e)

Library of Congress Control Number: 2018912177

Print information available on the last page.

This book is printed on acid-free paper.

Dedication

This book is dedicated to my family, with measureless thanks for their constant love, healing, support, patience, and humor. They continue to teach me what is truly valuable in life and make it all worthwhile.

o   To my daughter Emily for her vibrant energy and laughter.
o   To Harry, for his patience, love and support.

Acknowledgements

o To Betsy Blair, who started it all with her enthusiasm, artistry, love and support;

o To the children at the Edison Johnson Arts & Athletics Center in Durham, NC, where I first started teaching;

o To my professors at the University of North Carolina at Greensboro, Texas Woman's University, and the Laban Centre;

o To Sara Ashworth and the late Muska Mosston, who conceived and developed the Spectrum in the first place; and more thanks than I can possibly express to Sara for her many emails, expressmails, and conversations of encouragement to help expand and apply the amazing structure of the Spectrum to dance;

o To the faculty and administration at Broadway Dance Center for allowing me to observe classes, especially Jamie Salmon, Sue Samuels, Tracie Stanfield, and Samantha Mortorano; and Dariusz Hochman, Joy Karley, Dorit Koppel, Peter Schabel, and Andrey Silantyev for keeping me literally on my toes;

o To the following for their help in the editing process: Jessica Batha, Tess Edwards, Jennie McNelis Frey, Steven Martinez, Nicole Field Susko, Noelle Martin Zagorski.

o To the members of Dance Teacher Network online who shared suggestions for keeping healthy;

o And to my students at East Stroudsburg University, who provided ideas and energy as I applied these principles to my teaching and who continue to amaze, surprise, delight, humble and inform me.

About this book

The old adage, "If all you have is a hammer, then you tend to treat everything as a nail" means that the successful teacher must have many tools available. Every teaching situation doesn't require a hammer, so our pedagogical tool belt must be well-stocked.

Throughout the years, from the time I first encountered the Spectrum, I've realized more and more what an amazing pedagogical tool it is, for all ages, forms, and levels of dance as an art form. My main reason for writing this book is to share the Spectrum with as many current and prospective dance teachers as possible, and to help you to benefit from all it has to offer.

Teaching dance is an activity that is both a rigorous discipline which involves many years of study and a deeply personal expression. Bringing these two extremes together on the printed page has involved years of writing, thinking, researching, re-thinking, and re-writing. One of the challenges in writing this text has been balancing the first-, second- and third-person aspects of writing. On one hand, maintaining the rigor and integrity of any field of study requires a certain detachment. On the other hand, I want to write to *you, the reader*; to share, on a personal level, first-hand experiences to illustrate the information. I love both types of writing: the objective approach of the third person, and the passion and personal touch of the first person. So I've tried to keep most of the writing in the theory section in the third person, application in second person, with personal illustrations, first-person anecdotes, and tangential or background information, to clarify or augment the text, in shaded boxes inserted throughout.

It is important for me to recognize the solid foundation of the Spectrum, built by Muska Mosston and Sara Ashworth, without which this present work would not exist. I have been working with, living and breathing the Spectrum for many years, and it is difficult to identify the exact lines where the original work of Muska and Sara leaves off and my work begins. My work in dance pedagogy is so thoroughly infused with the Spectrum that it is sometimes difficult to know the boundaries. However, I have tried to make sure that terminology or concepts specific to the Spectrum as developed by Mosston and Ashworth (found in many Spectrum books and articles) are referenced with "MM/SA".

Notes to readers

You may be using this book for personal and professional growth or for a dance pedagogy or dance education class; you may be functioning in the role of student or teacher. I have included suggestions for activity in the form of "To Do" boxes throughout the text, questions for discussion at the end of every chapter, and a variety of worksheets, criteria and task sheets, lesson plans and other material for you to use as you feel is appropriate.

Over the years I've developed many forms, checklists, task and criteria sheets, hand-outs, etc., and you are welcomed to download them from the website, *teachingdancespectrum.com*, in keeping with the viewpoint that teaching is a dynamic, creative, personal act, you are welcomed to email *teachingdancespectrum@gmail.com* to ask questions, share ideas and offer suggestions concerning application of the Spectrum. It is an evolving, growing phenomenon.

Liz Goodling

The Spectrum of Teaching Styles

Reproduction Cluster	A	Cued Response
	B	Practice
	C	Reciprocal
	D	Self-Check
	E	Inclusion

Discovery Threshold

Production Cluster	F	Guided Discovery
	G	Convergent Discovery
	H	Divergent Discovery
	I	Learner-Designed Individual Program
	J	Learner-Initiated
	K	Self-Teaching

Teacher

Learner

Decision-Makers

The Spectrum of Teaching Styles[1]

Reproduction Cluster

A. Cued Response
<u>Essence</u>: The immediate and precise response by the students to a cue from the teacher.
<u>Purpose</u>: To learn to do a dance movement or phrase accurately and within a short period of time.

B. Practice
<u>Essence</u>: Time is provided for students to rehearse a movement or phrase individually and privately, and for the teacher to provide individual and private feedback to each student.
<u>Purpose</u>: To take the first step in shifting specific decisions from the teacher to the learner.

C. Reciprocal
<u>Essence</u>: Using criteria provided by the teacher, students work in pairs to offers and receive immediate and personal feedback.
<u>Purpose</u>: To shift decisions concerning feedback to the students.

D. Self-Check
<u>Essence</u>: Learners work individually and provide self-feedback using criteria provided by the teacher.
<u>Purpose</u>: For students to develop an awareness of personal performance, enhancing kinesthetic awareness and becoming more able to accurately assess performance.

E. Inclusion
<u>Essence:</u> The teacher designs different degrees of difficulty for a single step or dance phrase, and learners decide what level to choose.
<u>Purpose</u>: For students to select a level of entry to successfully accomplish the task.

DISCOVERY THRESHOLD

Production Cluster

F. Guided Discovery
<u>Essence</u>: The teacher uses a sequence of questions designed to bring the learner along a path of discovery to a single correct answer.
<u>Purpose</u>: For students to discover a predetermined target concept, or principle by following a sequenced set of questions designed by the teacher.

G. Convergent Discovery
<u>Essence</u>: The teacher presents a task whose intrinsic structure requires a single correct answer.
<u>Purpose</u>: For learners to discover, using a logical process, the solution to a problem. This Style enables learners' greater independence but still focuses on one discovered answer, move, response or solution.

H. Divergent Discovery
<u>Essence</u>: Learners are engaged in producing multiple discovered responses to a single question, or movement problem.
<u>Purpose</u>: For learners to discover or create multiple responses to a problem or question.

I. Learner-Designed Individual Program
<u>Essence</u>: The learner designs, develops and performs an organized personal program.
<u>Purpose</u>: For learners to design, develop, and perform the personal program in association with the teacher. The learner now discovers and designs specific questions or problems, then seeks the solutions.

J. Learner-Initiated
<u>Essence</u>: The learner initiates the Style for the episode or series of episodes, selecting any Style on the Spectrum.
<u>Purpose</u>: For the learner to initiate a learning experience, design it, perform it, and evaluate it, together with the teacher based on agreed-upon criteria; for first time the individual learner initiates the Style.

K. Self-Teaching
<u>Essence</u>: The learner initiates a learning experience, designs it, performs it, and evaluates it.
<u>Purpose</u>: To provide the learner the opportunity to make maximum decisions about the learning experience without any direct involvement from the teacher.

The Spectrum will help dance teachers address many issues, including the following:

For the beginning teacher,
1. Did I meet my objectives? How can I tell how well I did?
2. How can I continue to grow and improve as a teacher?

For the advanced teacher,
1. How can I encourage initiative and make students more responsible and self-motivated?
2. How can I teach the same basic information in my elementary classes, year after year, without going nuts?

For the college or university teacher,
1. How do I help my colleagues in other disciplines and my administration understand dance as an academic discipline?
2. Grading often seems so subjective; what can I use as the basis for assigning grades? How do I document evidence to support assigning a particular grade to a student?
3. How can I engage students cognitively and encourage critical thinking?

When teaching children,
1. How can I focus on the creative possibilities of movement for each child and harness their love of discovery?
2. How can I make this class part of a comprehensive curriculum that takes my students from being creative children to independent adult dancers who take responsibility for their learning, seek initiative, and who are able to master technique, improvise and choreograph?

For teachers with adult community classes or ballroom dance,
1. How do I create an environment that is conducive to social interaction and self-confidence as well as learning?
2. How do I help my adult students learn basic movement material without "teaching down" to them, to recognize their cognitive level and maturity?

For teachers in private studios,
1. The students in my class are at several different levels! How can I coax the beginners and still challenge the more advanced students?
2. How can I get the children (and parents) to take dance classes more seriously?
3. How can I teach so that I reach every student, keep students coming back for more classes, and thus keep enrollment (and my business) up?

When teaching large classes,
1. How can I provide individualized feedback for every student in the class and still keep the class moving?
2. The students are so diverse—how can I make sure that I teach all students optimally?

For any teacher,
1. What do I do about those students who always stand in the back and just follow everyone else?
2. I always seem to have some students who I never get to know, who tend to get lost and might not take another dance class. How can I reach them?
3. How can I really focus on students?

Table of Contents

1 Introduction

> "If a child can't learn the way we teach, maybe we should teach the way they learn." ~Ignacio Estrada

Many of us started in dance because we loved the act of dancing, and teaching was something that came later: it was necessary to teach dance if we wanted to continue dancing and making a living doing it. I started my life in dance intending to choreograph and perform, but teaching dance has become one of the great passions of my life.

Dance is recognized as uniquely able to apply to all seven of the multiple intelligences identified by Howard Gardner.

Two important concepts are at the heart of teaching dance: enabling students to educate themselves through the art and medium of motion, and dance's capacity for the self- transformation of the dancer. Howard Gardner's Theory of Multiple Intelligences has reshaped the way intelligence is viewed and assessed, and dance is recognized as uniquely able to apply to all seven of Gardner's proposed intelligences.[2] Dance is an intimate art, a physical art, a conceptual art, a spiritual art. The medium of dance uses the human body; according to Havelock Ellis, "Dance is the only art form wherein we, ourselves, are the stuff of which it is made."

The capacity for the self-transformation of the individual through dance is very powerful. Whereas many of life's experiences will affect us, there is an ineffable power and mystery inherent in dance that can profoundly change the life of an individual. Consider how different your own life would be if you hadn't found dance! Dance, when done for its own sake, can substantially alter the dancer's being. It shapes us in metaphysical as well as physical ways; shapes who we are, how we relate to others, how we conceive of the world. However, this capacity for self-transformation through dance is not always recognized or reflected by teachers in the way that they approach teaching.

I had a university student who waited until her junior year to fulfill her fitness requirement by taking a folk dance class. Deborah enjoyed it and enrolled in a ballroom dance class for the second of the two required fitness classes. She enjoyed that and enrolled in a basic dance technique class, telling me, "I can't believe that I'm taking more than the two required fitness classes!" At the conclusion of the class she shared with me how she felt transformed through dance: originally somewhat shy, she had become bubbly and more outgoing; while she didn't have the typical dancer's physique, she nonetheless participated with lively gusto and enjoyed discovering her movement potential.

Deborah graduated, married, and a year later, returned to enroll in an elementary ballet class that I taught through the university continuing education program. She told me that, while she felt busy with her new job and marriage, her husband had urged her to take another dance class because, he said, "You look taller when you dance. And you're happier!"

Teaching is also self-transformative. For me, teaching, choreographing and performing are creative acts that feed each other. I have found out who I am, and helped students find themselves, through these three facets of dance. Teaching is a connection between the teacher and the learner. If there is no connection, there is no learning. Mosston and Ashworth defined teaching as "the ability to be aware of and utilize the possible connections with the learner—in all domains" (1994 p. 3).

Three domains that are usually associated with learning are the cognitive, affective, and psychomotor domains. Another organization of the domains includes five: physical, social, emotional, cognitive, and ethical, and other ways of organizing the domains are possible as well.

In dance, the relationship of the student to the teacher is very special.[3] We come to know our students, they come to know us, and they come to know themselves, in profound ways due to the very personal, non-verbal nature of this art form. As teachers, we have the capacity to learn from every class. Teaching is a dynamic, creative act: The work of art it produces, the dancer, is alive, and takes on a life of its own. Furthermore, this work of art will continue to live and develop for years.

The material, ideas, content, and terms that present and explain the Spectrum are those of Muska Mosston and Sara Ashworth. Muska has said that he didn't invent the Spectrum but rather *discovered* it; that the relationship between teacher, learner, and content existed before him and will always continue. However, it was important to Muska to have the Spectrum properly implemented and thus avoid trivialization or misunderstanding. In the time that our teaching careers overlapped, he was enthusiastic about applying the Spectrum to dance and encouraged me in this work.

Muska was a creative, powerful, lively person; his biography, listed at the end of the book, makes for fascinating reading. A rebel, he was once kicked out of a theatre for entertaining the audience, when the film broke, by doing a handstand and walking across the stage on his hands. In addition to being a well-loved, internationally-known and highly respected educator, he was also a parachutist and a concert violinist.

Integrity to the essence of the Spectrum is also important to Sara, who describes herself as "keeper of the flame," and she strives to maintain an honesty and purity for the Spectrum. Writing this book has meant working closely with Sara to keep the theory of the Spectrum clear and intact while focusing on dance. I have gained so much insight through our correspondence, and helping dance students and teachers explore the Spectrum is foremost in my work.

We must be willing to change who we are in order to become what we want to be. Just as we encourage our students to study a variety of dance styles with a variety of different teachers in order to gain breadth and depth in their dancing, as teachers we need to continue to learn and grow. Being unshakably anchored in one's own idiosyncrasies, regardless of the level of success, limits one's options and contributions to the learning potential of one's students. We must ask, "What is there to teaching beyond my own methods, present experience, successes (and failures)? Am I willing to continue to learn and expand?" The balance between conservation of the tradition and breaking new ground is always an adventure.

Many arts education programs are in the process of questioning how the arts should be taught and are far from agreeing on the best method even within a single arts discipline. This book attempts to present and encourage diversity of teaching style and change. The Spectrum approaches the concept of dance pedagogy from the viewpoint that all teachers can be reflective and intentive decision-makers, who choose and plan teaching-learning interactions by considering the relationship that includes the teacher, the learner, and objectives to be reached. In planning classes, each teacher will consider a personal philosophy, priorities, and criteria that cover a wide range of possibilities that can include movement qualities, skills, and other aspects of dance as a multi-faceted art form.

Format of the Book
- Chapter 1 is an introduction.
- Chapter 2 is an overview of the Spectrum with information on each Style including the shift of decisions and the nature of the Impact Sets in each Style.
- Chapter 3 is focuses on the concept of dance pedagogical knowledge and what the Spectrum offers for a new paradigm for dance pedagogy.
- Chapters 4 presents the basics of dance including the vocabulary used to describe time, space, and qualities of movement, parts of the dance class and the function of a warm-up, and choosing material which is safe for your students.
- Chapter 5 defines aspects of the teaching-learning interaction in dance: a course, unit, lesson and episode; structuring the lesson, and writing unit and lesson plans.
- Chapter 6 provides information on feedback and observation strategies in the dance studio, tailoring feedback, and addresses touch as feedback.
- Chapters 7 and 8 detail application. The Reproduction Cluster (Styles A-E) is presented in Chapter 7. The Discovery Threshold and Production Cluster (Styles F-K) are presented in Chapter 8. These chapters apply the theory of previous chapters to dance teaching, and include many tips, suggestions, activities, lesson plans and criteria sheets.
- Chapter 9 discusses the nature of discovery, creativity and artistic process in dance, bringing together the groundbreaking work of Getzels and Csikszentmihalyi in creativity and flow, my research in artistic process, and Mosston and Ashworth's Spectrum. This section will likely be more useful for teaching technique, improvisation, choreography and theory than for other applications, but can be informative and applicable to all teachers and educators. It includes quotes and information by and about choreographers, performers and writers as a way of gaining insight into the creative process, so that we may gain insight into how we, as artists and teachers, can continue to learn and create, and how we can guide our students.

- Chapter 10 is a special chapter on self-care for the dance teacher, how to maintain body, mind, spirit, and voice at their optimum.
- Chapter 11 is a summary.

The Spectrum is presented twice. First, in Chapter 2 a quick *overview* of the Spectrum is provided, defining the *essence* and *purpose* of each of the eleven Styles. The *application* of each Style is presented in Chapters 7 and 8, with many examples and suggestions for how to use these Styles in different classes. This repetition is important for two reasons. First, dance and the Spectrum are both multifaceted entities. Each presentation gives a different facet of each Style and how they fit into the gestalt of the Spectrum as a whole. Second, even with careful attention it is easy to miss key elements. Repetition is at the heart of learning dance, because it is through repetition that deeper understanding grows, and it is not until a certain level of understanding and familiarity is reached that we can really *use* what we are learning.

Chapter Summary

Teaching is a discipline; it is also personal, creative, transformative. Dance educators who are willing to broaden their approach may reach more objectives, be more effective in reaching more students, and be more likely to produce self-directed learners who can ultimately become better dancers. We will all be rewarded with more active learners, more competent teachers, and better dance artists if we are willing to invest in a little extra time to fully engage our students in the learning process and enable them to discover.

Questions for reflection and discussion

1. Reflect on and discuss what it means to **educate yourself**, or enable students to educate themselves, through the art and medium of motion.

2. Reflect on and discuss what is meant by the phrase, "dance's capacity for the **self-transformation** of the dancer." How has it been transformative for you?

3. If you are unfamiliar with the following words, look them up and discuss, particularly in reference to dance: **ineffable, metaphysical, idiosyncratic, intentive, multi-faceted**. What does each mean for you, for dance, for teaching?

4. Discuss ways that you have felt teaching and learning as a **connection** between the teacher and the learner(s). Do you feel that dance provides unique connections between teacher and learners? If so, how?

5. Discuss how teaching can be a **dynamic and creative act**.

Ahead

Now let's look at the overall structure of the Spectrum: the Reproduction cluster of Styles, the Discovery Threshold, and the Production cluster of Styles; the planning, implementation, and decision-making involved with each Style, and how the Spectrum can solve teaching problems in the dance studio and enhance learning and retention.

2 The Spectrum: An Overview

> "There is nothing like teaching to help one learn." ~Dalai Lama XIV

What is the Spectrum of Teaching Styles?

The Spectrum of Teaching Styles,[4] developed by Muska Mosston in 1966 and later with Sara Ashworth, is a non-versus paradigm for teaching which explains a variety of teaching- learning possibilities, and is rich for dance pedagogy. Its non-versus nature means that no single teaching strategy is more important than any other; no single Style is necessarily better than any other.

The Spectrum is a non-versus paradigm: no single teaching strategy is more important than any other.

The Spectrum brings an integrated, comprehensive approach to teaching that can be used for any subject including theory or lecture classes as well as technique or activity classes; it can be utilized for all ages and in all dance classes including ballet, modern, jazz, tap, ballroom, international folk or character dance, aerobics, improvisation, composition, creative dance, notation, and history classes.

The structure of the Spectrum is based on three key premises. First, teaching is governed by *decision-making*. Every deliberate act of teaching is governed by a previously and consciously made decision. Second, it is possible for *both the teacher and the learner* to make decisions, and these decisions shift from teacher to learner throughout the Spectrum. Third, teachers and learners can demonstrate *mobility* among a variety of teaching Styles. The Spectrum delineates the range of decision-making, from the teacher making decisions about content, choices for learning and providing feedback, to the learners making decisions and choices for learning and providing their own feedback.

The structure of the Spectrum is based on key premises:
1. *Teaching is governed by decision making.*
2. *Both teacher and student can make decisions.*
3. *Teachers and learners can demonstrate mobility among a variety of teaching Styles.*

Parents want their children to grow up to be capable and independent, able to make their own decisions about important aspects of life. We know that children need to learn how to make decisions, and give them practice and parameters in decision-making, moving from small choices with limited parameters ("Which shirt do you want to wear today, the green or the blue?") to bigger, more open-ended ones ("What would you like for dinner?"), to important life choices ("Let's discuss college options"). The Spectrum provides a structure for giving students practice in decision-making, from small decisions with clear parameters to more complex and open-ended, student-generated ideas.

Shifting responsibility to make decisions does not mean that the students determine the direction of class or that "anything goes" in the classroom, but that students gradually learn how to make certain decisions. Learning to make decisions enables students to become active learners, able to pull the maximum amount of information from the lesson themselves.

The teacher determines which choices are appropriate to be shifted to students. At first, the decisions shifted to the student are minor, such as what direction to face when practicing individually, or the order for practice of assigned tasks. The student gradually gains the knowledge necessary to make more decisions, such as determining an achievable level of complexity in a dance phrase, or which of several self-generated phrases or movements would be an appropriate conclusion to a study, or how to set criteria for an independent project. The Spectrum covers the range of decision-making in the teaching-learning relationship.

> *Muska has said that he did not "invent" the Spectrum, the Spectrum was waiting for someone to discover it. "I did not invent any of the Styles. They always existed as possible behaviors for people. I discovered the specific decisions which defined each Style, their relationship one to another, and delineated their impact on human development" (Uriel, n.d.).*

The eleven Styles of the Spectrum delineate the range from the teacher making all decisions to the learner making all decisions:
- Style A: Cued Response: the teacher makes the decisions concerning what students will do, when to do it and how to look doing it; students learn how to respond by immediately recalling a movement or phrase;
- Styles B: Practice: students learn to make decisions concerned with practicing, such as when to start, pace, and when to stop;
- Style C: Reciprocal and Style D: Self-Check: students learn to make decisions concerning feedback, given teacher-generated criteria;
- Style E: Inclusion: students learn to choose an appropriate level of difficulty;
- Style F: Guided Discovery, Style G: Convergent Discovery: students learn to use logic and reasoning to discover ideas and concepts;
- Style H: Divergent Discovery: students learn to generate or create new movement or ideas;
- Style I: Learner-Designed Individual Program: students learn to develop criteria for assessing a personal program of study;
- Style J: Learner-Initiated: students learn to initiate the topic and Style for a personal program of study;
- Style K: Self-Teaching: the learner makes all decisions.

> *In Mosston and Ashworth's work, Style A is referred to as Command Style. The word "command" often has such a negative connotation that most dancers have a very strong reaction to it (though, in some classes, that negative response is well-earned). It took many conversations with Sara Ashworth to realize the beauty and power in the synchronicity that is the hallmark of this Style. However I felt the need to find another name for this Style. "Cued Response" is not intended to imply too much behaviorism, but is used as a description of the teacher-learner relationship in this Style, in which the teacher gives a cue, such as the ubiquitous "5, 6, 7, 8" and students respond by starting to dance.*

The Styles of the Spectrum can be clustered to reflect two basic human capacities: for *reproduction* of knowledge or ideas, which includes replication and practice skills, and *production* of new ideas, new movements, and new models. Styles A-E represent teaching options that foster reproduction in which learners seek to reproduce known information or practice codified skills; F-K are options that invite production, discovering or generating new information. Between these is the Discovery Threshold.

Reproduction Cluster	Style A: Cued Response Style B: Practice Style C: Reciprocal Style D: Self-Check Style E: Inclusion	Teacher
DISCOVERY THRESHOLD		
Production Cluster	Style F: Guided Discovery Style G: Convergent Discovery Style H: Divergent Discovery Style I: Learner-Designed Individual Program Style J: Learner-Initiated Style K: Self-Teaching	Learner

Responsibility for Decision-Making

Decision-making is the key aspect of the Spectrum. The teaching Styles flowing along the Spectrum range from the *teacher* having maximum decision-making responsibility to the *learner* having the maximum decision-making responsibility. In Style A, the teacher makes all decisions. Styles B-E present a shift of decisions from teacher to student; this gradual shift is not to suggest that the teacher is no longer responsible for the learning environment, but rather that the students are provided deliberate opportunities to make certain decisions in the classroom.

The Opposition and Interdependency of Reproduction and Production: Conservation vs. Change
Both clusters of the Spectrum offer excitement and reward for teachers and learners. Reproduction and production are both necessary for dance as an art form, because any art form depends on the two opposing and interdependent factors of conservation and change.

Reproduction: Conservation	*Production: Change*

Reproduction: Conservation
Dance is often an unrecorded and completely ephemeral part of history and culture. Reproduction is how rich cultural and historical traditions are passed on: it is by learning, copying, and following movement and gesture that these patterns of thought as well as movement are preserved for the centuries. Learning and reproducing the history, religious practices and social cultures of a nation or ethnic group through movement can forge powerful bonds. Students who engage in any form of dance can feel that they are part of a living tradition whether learning ballet, tap, an Irish reel, or the Argentine tango.

Using Styles A-E enables learners to experience reproduction of existing movement patterns and cultural traditions and their accompanying rules and strategies, and at the same time learning the decision-making that will enable the stretching and breaking of those rules which is the nature of change and growth.

<u>Production: Change</u>

Crossing "The Discovery Threshold" with students can be very exciting and challenging for both you and your students, as they learn to leave the known and develop artistic process skills, and as you learn to design tasks conducive to discovery and encourage behavior which facilitates creative processes. Crossing the Discovery Threshold is essential to educate active learners who take initiative and seek to discover. Such students will thus be cognitively equipped not only to find their own solutions but also to develop their own questions. In addition, Jerome Bruner (1961) proposes that memory is greatly enhanced when a student makes the discovery; learning by discovery commits a concept or phenomenon to memory for a long period of time. It is essential, when using Styles beyond the Discovery Threshold, to provide a special and private time for each learner to engage in the cognitive operation, to produce or discover one's own movements, and to examine the validity of each response in reference to the problem.

When using F-K, the application of the element of discovery engages the learner actively in the search for the solution; however, you must be patient and wait for the student to discover the answer. Even though it seems much easier just to show and/or tell the student the answer or proper way to do something, Guided Discovery and Convergent Discovery have other important applications. Guided Discovery and Convergent Discovery are two Styles that develop and reinforce a thinking process using logic. Application of these Styles enables the student apply reasoning, logic, and exploration to discover solutions to problems such as those in technique, composition, kinesiology and prevention and management of dance injuries.

The Structure of the Spectrum

One way to envision the Spectrum is as a Zen garden. Stepping stones lead to a stream traversed by a bridge. Each stepping stone affords a new and different view of the garden. The bridge represents the Discovery Threshold. On one side of the stream, it is the teacher who makes the decisions regarding specific content; as one crosses the bridge to the other side of the stream, it is the learner who is invited to actively participate in content decisions.

> *Each Style of the Spectrum has a unique structure, which defines the role of the teacher and the role of the learner.*

This is not a one-way path. Walking through this garden is not a goal-oriented event. Since every stepping stone affords one a different view of the garden, all stones are equal; it just depends on what one wants to see or experience. One may walk along the path in any direction or even skip from one stone to another depending on where one wants to go. Teachers and learners may move to any step along the path depending on the goals for the class or lesson at that moment.

When planning to use a Style, ask yourself, "What kind of relationship do I want between teacher and student at this point? How do I determine if the objectives of this Style are reached?" Each Style of the Spectrum has a unique decision structure that defines the role of the teacher and the role of the learner. This decision structure also identifies the purpose or objective of this relationship.

The Landmarks and Boundaries of Each Style

Implementation of a given Style is flexible within the boundaries of what each Style is designed to accomplish. As long as you recognize the essence of a particular Style, you have certain latitude for using that Style. Certain landmark features define the exclusive decision-making structure and specific teacher-learner relationships in each Style. When teaching, situations arise that will seem to fall between these landmarks. For example, if the teacher has set up stations for different tasks, the location of the stations seems to take away from students their decision to choose location; however, students may choose which direction to face or where, within a certain area, they stand. For another example, in most dance technique classes, shape or position is intrinsic to the task or activity; therefore this decision is generally not shifted to the learner. These distinctions may seem minor, but they identify different realities in terms of the theoretical structure of decision-making that is the basis of the Spectrum.

The "City Limits" of the Spectrum Styles
Another way to picture these landmarks and boundaries, which Mosston and Ashworth described as the "canopy" of a Style, is as the geographical distinctions of city limits and counties. I lived for a while within the city limits of Durham, North Carolina, after living outside the city limits in more rural Durham County. Within the Spectrum, you can be within the "city limits" of a particular Style, or you can be a little outside the city but still be in the broader county.

Thus the parameters of each Style can be identified while recognizing that some teaching-learning situations will fall outside the strict definition or "city limits" of a Style but within the "county" of that Style.

Mobility Along the Spectrum and a Non-Versus Reality

Pedagogical agility: the ability to switch Styles depending on what you want to accomplish.

As you become more skilled in using each Style of the Spectrum, you'll find that you are able to shift Styles as needed. You will become better able to adapt your teaching Styles to the needs of your students. You will become better able to develop various educational objectives, to reach more objectives and thus reach more students. When you feel that one teaching Style is not working at any particular moment, you'll be able to switch to another Style. Remember that the Spectrum is based on a non-versus reality. Deliberate mobility along the Spectrum enables the teacher to achieve a variety of pedagogical goals. This viewpoint solves two important problems. First, if a teacher is "wedded" to a single idiosyncratic or personal teaching style or method and it isn't "working" or if students or teachers are having a problem or hitting a roadblock, it often feels like utter and complete failure; both teacher and students become frustrated. When applying the Spectrum, if an episode in one Style isn't successful or appropriate at the moment, you make a decision to select a more appropriate teaching-learning experience and move to another Style. The second problem solved by this non-versus reality is that it helps both you and your students to understand the many ways that you can connect in the teacher-learner relationship. If a student doesn't particularly like one Style, he or she knows that in a few minutes the class will likely be involved in another Style.

An episode is a unit of time during which teacher and learner are engaged in the same Style with the same objectives. Episodes may vary in length from a few minutes to an hour or more. A single dance class or lesson typically comprises several episodes (more in Chapter 5).

Each Style has unique characteristics or an essence that is shown by the teacher-learner relationships and the nature of the decisions made by the teacher and learner. Each Style represents a different reality, a different teacher-student relationship, a different set of "guidelines," a different set of potential problems. Teachers who are aware of these unique qualities can work proactively to troubleshoot for problems.

The Reproduction Cluster
Replication of Known Information, Practice of Skills

This cluster of Styles is for *reproduction of known information, knowledge or ideas,* which includes *practicing skills.* Whenever the content of the class includes delivering existing concepts, movements or ideas to students, Styles within the Reproduction Cluster are appropriate to use. Dance technique such as ballet, modern, jazz, and tap; aerobics; national, character or international folk dance, and ballroom dance, Labanotation and theory classes such as dance history are some of the classes which can benefit from application of Styles A-E.

For each Style, the following will be presented:
1. Essence, or unique characteristics.
2. Decisions: Planning and implementation of the following three aspects of planning, teaching, and evaluating:
   - **Pre-Impact**, or the planning that occurs prior to the face-to-face interaction between teacher and learner(s). It includes *objectives* or *intent.*
   - **Impact**, or the face-to-face interaction in the studio or classroom: *action,*
   - **Post-Impact**, or the assessment of what happened: *outcomes.*

(The application of each of these Styles will be detailed next, in Styles A-E.)

Style A: Cued Response

Essence

The beauty of Style A: Cued Response lies in the power of a group moving in unison.

The essence of Cued Response Style is the immediate and precise response by the learner to a stimulus from the teacher. The purpose of this Style is to learn to perform the task accurately and within a short period of time; the objective is for students to copy and memorize movement quickly and precisely. The role of the teacher is to make all decisions in the Pre-Impact, Impact, and Post-Impact Sets: decisions concerning what to do, when to do it, where to do it, and how to look while doing it. The role of the learner is to perform the task precisely. This Style is for replication or reproduction of a model, and is almost universally used in dance technique classes.

The objectives for Cued Response(MM/SA)
1. *Immediate, precise and accurate response to a stimulus,*
2. *Uniformity and conformity*
3. *Synchronized performance*
4. *Adherence to and replication of a predetermined model*
5. *Perpetuation of cultural traditions*
6. *Maintenance of aesthetic standards*
7. *Enhancement of esprit de corps*
8. *Efficiency in time use*

Decisions: Planning and Implementation

The teacher is the decision-maker. The learners perform and follow exactly. The essence of this Style is the direct and immediate relationship between the teacher's stimulus (cue) and the learner's response. An episode planned in the Cued Response Style must reflect the essence of this relationship. In Style A: Cued Response, one person makes all the decisions for others, who follow exactly. When this relationship exists, the objectives for Cued Response Style are reached.

Pre-Impact
In the Pre-Impact set of decisions, you plan the interaction between yourself and your students. Plans may be written or may be kept only in your head. Beginning teachers will want to consider and write down each aspect, and even advanced teachers benefit from reconsidering each part of a lesson plan.

Impact
This is the face-to-face interaction in which you present the expectations, and learners are engaged in active participation, implementing your planned Pre-Impact decisions. In Cued Response Style, it is imperative that the students know and understand the expectations of this episode. When expectations are known, in any of the Styles, both teacher and students can be held accountable for their behaviors. You make a sequence of decisions to "set the stage" for expectations in the Impact Set.

1. Expectations: Behaviors and roles. Because Cued Response is so universally used in dance classes, teachers usually assume that students are familiar with the expected behaviors and roles. However, teachers vary in certain expectations and must be aware that any unspoken expectations of teacher and student might not be the same, and expectations should be explained. In Cued Response, typical expectations are that the teacher will provide a model or demonstration and students will respond in unison. Expectations such as those mentioned in the previous chapter should be identified by the teacher and conveyed to the students.

   Making expectations clear is important, especially in elementary classes.

2. Expectations: Subject matter delivery or demonstration. You present the task or phrase. This can be a physical and/or visual demonstration by the teacher or an assistant, a film, notation, a "talk-through," etc. You can also give more specifics concerning the task.

3. Expectations: Logistics. This includes spatial organization and equipment. Spatial organization may include, "Find a place where you can see me and you're not touching anyone or anything," "Juanita, please go in the group with Anna and Don," and "Please sit in your assigned seat." Equipment will typically include the accompaniment such as drum, piano or acoustic equipment; overhead projector, posters, or video camera used for demonstration. This explanation is important for several reasons. First, it tells the students clearly what behaviors are expected of them and why. Second, it lets the students know that this is one of several ways to learn, one of several relationships between teacher and learners. Third, it lets the students know that you are applying a specific teaching Style, that this is one Style in a Spectrum of Styles which are used for certain tasks, and that other Styles and behaviors will be used in class.

4. Putting expectations into action. The cue or stimulus can be directly by the teacher, in terms of a verbal cue such as "Ready, go," "5-6-7-8," your drumbeat, clap or nod, the musical introduction played by a live accompanist or recorded music.

Post-Impact
This set of decisions offers feedback to the learner about the performance of the task, and about the learner's role in following the teacher's decisions. This Style is one of action: repeating

the movements and replicating the model. Feedback in Cued Response can be delivered to the group as a whole or to an individual. Since the purpose of this Style is *performance according to a model*, your feedback will be primarily *corrective* and *value* (the nature of feedback will be detailed in Chapter 6).

Style B: Practice

Essence

Practice is a new reality in which learners practice not only a particular dance task, but actually also practice deliberately making decisions.

The essence of Practice is that time is provided for the learner to rehearse the task individually and privately, and for you to circulate throughout the studio or classroom to provide feedback individually and privately to each student. The purpose of Practice Style is to take the first step in shifting decisions from the teacher to the learner.

The nine decisions made by learners in the Impact Set[5]

1. *Location.* Students may choose where to practice and which direction to face.
2. *Posture.**
3. *Order of tasks practiced.*
4. When to *start*
5. *Pace* and *rhythm.***
6. When to *stop* each task
7. *Interval* or what to do between each activity.
8. Attire and *appearance*.
9. Initiating *questions* for clarification.

While posture and alignment are codified and standardized for many dance forms, students may be given the choice to alter some aspects of posture. If choices are allowed, they are limited to a particular few alternatives, such as, "You may have the arms en avant or en haut for the pirouette," or "Followers may do one or two turns under the leader's arm." This will be discussed further in Application, Chapter 7.
**Unless the music specifically directs the tempo.*

Decisions

Your role is to make decisions in the Pre-Impact Set and Post-Impact Set. The role of the learner is to make the decisions in the Impact Set. Like Cued Response, Practice enables very efficient time management: every student can be working the entire time while you circulate to observe and give feedback. However, using Practice means creating a new reality in which learners practice not only a particular dance task, but actually also practice deliberately making decisions.

Planning and Implementation

Pre-Impact

Just as in Cued Response Style, you make all decisions in the Pre-Impact set. However, you must be fully aware of the deliberate shift of decisions to the learner that will occur during the Impact set, and select tasks that are appropriate for this Style. Appropriate tasks are:

Appropriate tasks for Practice Style are fixed tasks performed according to a specific model that can be assessed by correct/ incorrect criteria.

1. Fixed tasks that must be performed according to a specific model; no alternatives are sought. Ballet enchâinements, tap steps, modern or jazz combinations, ballroom steps, folk dances are all appropriate.

2. Skills that can be assessed by correct/incorrect criteria. You should be able to say what is correct or incorrect about a student's performance. Criteria can include which foot to step on, body design, rhythm or timing, qualitative features such as Efforts (e.g, lightness, free flow, suddenness), or any other criteria that you feel are important.

This is not to say that alternatives are forbidden; for example, giving the students the option of two different arm positions. Creating or discovering alternatives, especially in dance, is how new movements and genres are developed. However, these criteria will serve to emphasize the importance of precise performance when it is called for in class; it is fixed for this particular episode. Other Styles along the Spectrum can be implemented for students to generate divergent alternatives.

> *Dance is an art form, and teaching dance is very subjective; it's often not a black/white, yes/no issue. However, having parameters will help you guide your students. The words "right" and "wrong" are value-laden, and many dance teachers don't want to polarize human movement to imply that a particular movement should never be done. It's OK to tell students, "That sense of lightness is appropriate in ballet, but since the style we're working with is Limón modern dance, we need more a sense of weight...." or work with degrees of correctness such as, "Pull your elbows back just a little farther, because...." When it's your class or your rehearsal, it is appropriate to tell students that a particular movement or quality is inappropriate in a certain context: "That's not appropriate in this dance, but you might remember that for another work," or "That wouldn't be appropriate in Cecchetti, but in the French school of ballet...." One important purpose of the individual feedback in Practice is for you to be able to give students this one-on-one coaching or explain an aspect in detail.*

Impact

In this Style, certain decisions are deliberately shifted from the teacher to the learner. Select tasks that are conducive to this Style or select this Style following the decision to work on certain tasks. Also explain the nature of Style B to learners the first time it is introduced; procedures and expectations may need to be reinforced when this Style is implemented again. The main task in the Impact Set is for you to make clear the expectations for the new roles and relationships for this Style:

1. Expectations: Behaviors and Roles. Introduce a different way of working by gathering students near you. Then state the objectives of this Style: To offer time for students to work on their own, and to provide time for you to offer individual and private feedback to each student. Describe your role as teacher: to observe each student, offer private feedback and be available for questions. Describe the shift in decision-making for the learner by naming all or just some of the decisions, writing them on a blackboard or using a poster or wall chart (see the wall charts at the end of this book) and clearly identifying the decisions for which the learner is responsible.
2. Expectations: Subject Matter Delivery or Demonstration. Present the task or phrase. This can be a physical and/or visual demonstration by you or an assistant, a film, notation, a "talk-through," etc. You can also give more specifics concerning the task.
3. Expectations: Logistics. Tell the quantity of each task to be done (how many repetitions, say 8 on each side, or the length of time, say 10 minutes) and the order of the tasks (sequence or random). An *interval decision* must be made to let students know what to do if they finish the task before the designated time. This might include writing in a journal, working on another suggested step or phrase, stretching, reading ahead in a text, working with weights or elastic bands or completing a hand-out.

4. <u>Action</u>. Address any questions for clarification, then tell the students to begin when ready. The class will then disperse and proceed. Observe the class as a whole for the first few moments of this initial episode, and then circulate to initiate individual feedback and questions. If the entire class is having trouble with a particular aspect of the task, you can stop the Practice session, make a correction to the class as a whole, and then let the class proceed again.

Post-Impact

In Practice Style, the Post-Impact set begins when you move from student to student offering individual and private feedback. Observe the decision-making process of each learner as well as the performance of the task, and then offer feedback and comments. At this time, keep in mind the following:

> *In Post-Impact, you identify errors and offer private feedback to each student.*

1. Identify the learners who need immediate feedback because they are making errors in either the decision-making process or performance of the task or both.
2. Offer corrective feedback to each student individually, then stay, usually a few seconds, to verify performance.
3. Be sure to observe and offer feedback to those who are practicing the task correctly as well as those who need correction. All students deserve your attention and feedback, not just those who are making mistakes.
4. For some tasks, it may take two or three episodes to observe every individual, but both you and your students will develop the patience. In beginning episodes make it a point to speak with every student.
5. Be aware of the options for feedback. Various kinds are available, depending on the impact that you feel is needed for a particular student in a given instance (more on feedback in Chapter 6).

Style C: Reciprocal

> *Reciprocal represents the first time that you shift the decision of feedback to a learner.*

Essence

The essence of Reciprocal is to receive immediate feedback from a peer ("Observer") who has a teacher-prepared criteria while the other student ("Doer") is practicing the task. Doer and Observer trade roles so that each student is provided the opportunity to practice each role. A partner relationship develops socialization skills. The purpose of Reciprocal is to shift the decision of feedback from the teacher to the learner. The roles of the learners involve working in pairs; one student (the "Doer") performs the task, the other (the "Observer") observes the Doer and offers feedback by following criteria supplied by the teacher. In the Impact Set, it is the role of the Doer to make the same nine decisions as in Style B: Practice while performing the task, and it is the role of the Observer to make certain decisions in the Post-Impact Set and offer feedback. Your role as teacher is to make all decisions in the Pre-Impact Set, and then circulate around the classroom to answer questions by and communicate only with the Observers.

<u>Decisions</u>
This Style represents the first time that you shift the decision of feedback to a learner. It creates a new reality with new roles for the students, and new social and psychological demands on teacher and learners. It also offers immediate and personal feedback for every student.

Two main conditions are hallmarks of this Style. First is the social relationship between peers. The socializing process is unique to this Style, in which students give and receive feedback with a peer. Partners engage in several steps, which include observing the peer's performance, analyzing the performance in terms of established criteria, formulating conclusions, and giving constructive feedback to the partner. This involves developing the patience, tolerance, caring attitude, and confidence to work with another learner. It also

> *Two main aspects of Reciprocal:*
> 1. *The opportunity for immediate feedback,*
> 2. *The social relationship between peers.*

involves experiencing the rewards of seeing a peer succeed and developing social bonds among students that endure beyond the task and often beyond the class.

The second condition is the opportunity for immediate feedback. This includes the opportunity to have repeated chances to practice with a personal observer and to discuss the specific aspects of the task or phrase. It also means that students can practice without the teacher necessarily knowing when mistakes were made and corrected.

A diagram of the interaction in this Style looks like this:

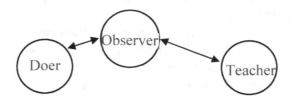

The Teacher-Observer-Doer Triad

> **_"Transparent Teaching" gives students a window to the teaching process._** *Typically in class, the focus of the teacher is on teaching, and the focus of the student is on learning. However, sometimes you want to invite students to "the other side of the mirror" by making them aware of the teaching process. This is often called "transparent teaching." The following are some examples:*
>
> *"The reason I've asked you all to face the same direction for the curl-up sequence is so that I can easily see how you are using your spine on the floor."*
>
> *"Even though the class is engaged in an episode of Style C: Reciprocal, since we have an odd number of students, I'll have Jacki do Practice (or Self-Check, or Inclusion)."*
>
> *This is especially good when your students include prospective or student teachers.*

Planning and Implementation
<u>Impact</u>
The main task in the Impact Set is for you to make clear the expectations for the new roles and relationships for this Style.

1. <u>Expectations: Behaviors or Roles</u>. State the objectives of this Style: To work with a partner and learn to offer feedback to that partner. Identify the Teacher-Observer-Doer triad, explain each role and that each learner will be both the Doer and the Observer. The role of the Doer is to perform the task and make the same decisions as in Practice Style. The Doer will only communicate with the Observer. The role of the Observer is to offer feedback to the Doer, based on the criteria sheet prepared by the teacher, during the performance and after the completion of each task. Thus, while the Doer is making decisions in the Impact Set, the Observer is making decisions in the Post- Impact Set.

> *In Style D: Self-Check students develop an awareness of their own performance and become better able to accurately assess performance based on set criteria.*

2. <u>Expectations: Subject Matter Delivery or Demonstration</u>. As in Practice Style, you present the task or phrase and address any questions for clarification.
3. <u>Expectations: Logistics</u>. Reciprocal uses many of the same logistics as in the previous Style. A new aspect is the use of a list of criteria for the task, which may be in the form of a single-sheet handout for each student or pair of students, a poster, or a transparency projected on the wall.
4. <u>Action</u>. The class will then disperse and proceed. Observe the class as a whole for the first few moments of this initial episode, and then circulate throughout the room.

Post-Impact

Unlike the previous two Styles, in Style C: Reciprocal the learners are also involved in decisions in the Post-Impact Set. The role of the Observer is to complete the following steps:
1. Receive the criteria for correct performance, usually a criteria sheet,
2. Observe the Doer's performance,
3. Compare and contrast the Doer's performance with the criteria for correct performance,
4. Conclude whether the performance was correct or where it was incorrect,
5. Communicate the results with the Doer,
6. Initiate communication with the teacher, if necessary.

In Reciprocal, the student pairs of Doer and Observer are working in two sets at the same time. The Doer is practicing the task and making decisions in the Impact Set while the Observer is in observing and making decisions concerning performance of the Doer, criteria, and feedback in the Post-Impact Set. You circulate throughout the studio to initiate feedback with the Observers.

Style D: Self-Check

> *Self-Check is the first time that students provide their own feedback, using criteria provided by the teacher.*

Essence

The essence of Self-Check is that learners perform the task individually and privately and provide feedback to themselves using criteria which you provide. The purpose of Self-Check is for students to develop an awareness of their own performance, enhancing kinesthetic awareness and becoming better able to accurately assess performance based on set criteria. The role of the learner is to make decisions in the Impact Set, perform the task and make decisions in the Post-Impact Set by providing self-feedback according to criteria prepared by the teacher. Your role as teacher is to make decisions in the Pre-Impact Set and be available for questions from learners as needed. This is a further shift of decisions from teacher to learner.

The main objective of Self-Check is for each student to develop an awareness of personal performance. This kinesthetic awareness is developed when a student learns to observe his or her own performance and make assessments based on criteria. Enhanced kinesthetic awareness and objective self-observation mean that the learner is becoming weaned from total dependence on outside sources of feedback (the teacher or a peer) and is better able to rely on self-feedback.

<u>Decisions</u>
This Style continues the individualizing process by shifting decisions in the Impact and Post-Impact Sets to the learner. The dancer thus learns to apply criteria for self-improvement, learns how to maintain honesty and objectivity about performance, and learns how to accept discrepancies and one's own limitations.

The carryover of skills learned in the previous Styles enables this Style to follow in a smooth progression. In Style B, students learn to practice the task on their own using a task sheet; in Style C, they learn to use a criteria sheet to give feedback to a peer. Engaging in Self-Check requires each dancer to apply the decisions learned in Reciprocal Style to him/herself: using a criteria sheet, comparing, contrasting, and drawing conclusions about performance.

Planning and Implementation
<u>Pre-Impact</u>
You still make all the decisions in the Pre-Impact Set including deciding which tasks are appropriate, and develop the criteria sheet for the class.

<u>Impact</u>
Explain the purpose and expectations of this new Style and the roles of the learner and teacher. Then present, describe or demonstrate the task, explaining any logistics or parameters needed. Students disperse to begin. Each dancer decides where to start, and continues making decisions as in Styles B and C, and adds the new decision of self- feedback.

<u>Post-Impact</u>
As the students follow the criteria sheets, observe their performance and how they implement the criteria sheet, communicating with each student about the proficiency and accuracy in the self-check process.

Style E: Inclusion

The purpose of Inclusion is for students to select a point of entry for which they can accomplish the task.

<u>Essence</u>
The essence of Inclusion is that a task or activity is designed to provide different degrees of difficulty. The purpose of Inclusion is for students to select a level at which they can accomplish the task. Your role as teacher is to make decisions in the Pre-Impact Set and design a task with varying degrees of difficulty for the same task. The role of the learner is to make decisions in the Impact and Post-Impact Sets. In the previous four Styles, every

task designed by the teacher represent a single standard decided upon by the teacher, with each learner working to perform at that level. Inclusion Style introduces a different concept: multiple levels of performance within the same task or activity.

<u>Decisions</u>

The major decision shifted from teacher to learner is what level of difficulty to choose. In the previous Styles, every task is based on a single model or standard for correct performance. Style E represents a new conception of task design: multiple levels of performance, with students choosing the level of performance. Style E is an excellent Style to start with in children's technique and adult beginner classes, because it gives all students, regardless of ability, an entry point into dance that allows them to participate and succeed.

The "slanted-rope" example developed by Mosston illustrates inclusion beautifully and can be demonstrated in a dance class for children. If you were to have two people, one holding each end of a rope about few inches off the floor, and ask students to run and leap over it, chances are that all of them would be able to clear it, thus all are successful. Raise the rope a few inches and most would be successful again. But if you were to continue to raise the height of the rope, at each subsequent height a few students would fail to clear the rope, and would be excluded from the experience. If you were to continue to raise the rope, eventually the number of students experiencing success would be only one, and eventually none.

The horizontal rope represents a single standard of task design. At a certain height, some students can't make it over—if the objective of the episode is to have a winner and exclude other students, this single standard is appropriate, but it is not much fun and certainly does not offer much of a developmental learning experience for the students who are excluded early in the activity.

> *As the smallest (and usually weakest) member of my elementary school classes, I remember the feeling of not being chosen for activities, which may explain why I always dreaded PE classes. I also remember well the exhilarating, "yippee!" feeling when I "found" dance—and lovely teachers--in my teens: here was something that didn't exclude me!*

However, if the objective of the episode is to *include* all participants, a different paradigm is needed. If you hold one end of the rope at floor level and the other end at shoulder level, and ask students to run and leap over the slanted rope, the class will spread along the rope and students will leap over it at varying heights. Everyone will be included; everyone will be successful. The slanted rope arrangement enables students to *choose their own degree of difficulty at which they can succeed* within the same task.

<u>The objectives of Inclusion Style are:</u>
1. Inclusion of **all learners** and the opportunity for continued participation,
2. Accommodation of **individual differences,**
3. The opportunity to enter the activity at **one's chosen ability** level,
4. The opportunity **to step backward to succeed** in the activity,
5. The opportunity to **step backward to re-explore** the basics of a complex activity,
6. Enabling learners to **see the relationship between one's aspirations and the reality** of one's performance,

7. Individualization is greater than in previous Styles, because **choices** exist among alternative levels within each task.

Planning and Implementation

Pre-Impact

As in the previous Styles, you as teacher make all the decisions in the Pre-Impact set. You also prepare the dance phrase for the Inclusion episode with the various options for students to select for the degree of difficulty. Introduce the class to this Style for the first time by preparing a demonstration of the concept of inclusion (the slanted rope).

Impact

Tell students or ask questions that guide students to discover the concept of the slanted rope so they will understand the new expectations and the main objective of this Style: the inclusion of all learners by providing different degrees of difficulty within the same dance phrase.

Give students the following expectations. The role of the student is to:
1. Survey the choices
2. Select an initial level of performance
3. Perform the phrase
4. Assess personal performance against criteria provided by the teacher
5. Decide whether the same level or another level is desired or appropriate.

Your role as teacher is to:
1. Answer questions by the learner
2. Initiate communication with the learner.

Present the dance phrase, discuss the factor or factors that determine the degree of difficulty and explain logistics and the necessary parameters. The class then disperses and begins to engage in individual roles, working on the phrase as in Styles B or D.

Post-Impact

During the Post-Impact Set, learners assess their individual performances using a criteria sheet. Observe the class for moment, and then circulate making individual contact with each learner, offering feedback about the learner's participation in the role in terms of choosing the appropriate level. This will work as in Styles B and D with the added dimension of giving feedback to the learner *verifying, not approving*, the appropriateness of the selected level (The difference between *verifying* and *approving*, and the importance of this distinction, will be discussed more in the Chapter 7).

The Discovery Threshold

The Discovery Threshold represents a transition from cognitive conditions conducive to reproduction to cognitive conditions conducive to production.

When the objective of the dance class is to copy or reproduce existing or codified movement phrases, the learner is asked to engage primarily the cognitive operations that comprise memory and recall. Ballet, modern, jazz, and tap technique;

international folk dance; national or character dance and ballroom dance are examples of codified movement styles that have set criteria for correct performance. The first cluster, Styles A-E, involves replication of known material and a specific set of developmental opportunities.

When the class episode involves discovering new material, the objective of teaching episodes will shift to the cognitive process that involves the teacher and learners participating in the second cluster of Styles F-K, the production Styles. With these Styles, you seek to engage the learner in cognitive operations other than memory and recall. The objective of this cluster is for the learner to discover or create new movements or ideas. Learners are thus engaged in problem solving, inventing, creating, comparing and contrasting, hypothesizing, and synthesizing. Improvisation, choreography or composition, artistic process in performance, and independent research in dance theory are some of the classes that involve the discovery process.

Creating a classroom atmosphere conducive to engaging in discovery requires a different atmosphere from that needed for reproducing technique. This involves a new relationship between you and your students, one that you must weave deliberately with carefully chosen teaching behaviors. The Discovery Threshold represents a cognitive transition from one set of conditions to another.

> *In Discovery, learners are engaged in problem solving, inventing, creating, comparing and contrasting, hypothesizing, and synthesizing.*

The Production Cluster
Experimenting, Discovering, Creating

> *The Production Cluster represents exploring terra incognito.*

In Styles A-E, students are engaged in replication: learning established dance vocabulary, committing actions and movements to muscle memory. This vocabulary is defined by one set of knowledge in dance, the cognitive operations of memory or recall. By moving through Cued Response, Practice, Reciprocal, Self-Check, and Inclusion, dancers learn what is established in dance, where it has come from and how it is typically used; they also learn who they are within the discipline of dance and within the sphere of the medium of motion. Furthermore, each of these Styles is also about exposing learners to development of human attributes; you want your students to have opportunities to develop in both subject matter and behavior.

But another aspect of the medium of dance is also waiting to be explored: exploring the terra incognito in motion, engaging in discovering new ideas, new movements, and new ways of working. The Production Cluster takes the dancer to this new sphere beginning with Style F: Guided Discovery, in which you guide your students step by step along a path where they discover, rather than receive, the answers. In Style G: Convergent Discovery students use logic, trial and error and reasoning to reach the solution or answer. In Style H: Divergent Discovery, dancers seek to explore and generate many answers, options, or possibilities. Styles I, J, and K complete the journey from a student who relies on the teacher for guidance to a self-guiding individual.

Style F: Guided Discovery

Guided Discovery is the first Style that invites the learner to engage in discovery, along a path to a single correct answer.

Essence
The essence of Guided Discovery is that students are guided along a path of discovery to a single correct answer. The purpose of Guided Discovery is for students to discover a predetermined target, concept, or principle by following a sequenced set of questions designed by the teacher.

Decisions
Your role as teacher is to select the concept and design the sequence of questions which will guide the students to the target answer. The role of the learner is to answer the questions and discover the single correct concept. Guided Discovery crosses the Discovery Threshold; it is the first Style that invites the learner to engage in the discovery process. In Guided Discovery, the Impact and Post-Impact Sets are interwoven in a dialog, alternating questions and answers (Impact) with feedback (Post-Impact)

Planning and Implementation
Pre-Impact
The first Pre-Impact decision concerns the specific subject matter, such as a principle, law, rule, or concept—what do you want students to discover in this episode? After you determine this, develop the sequence of steps, the questions or clues that will bring students to discover the desired target answer.

Impact
The Impact Set involves actually implementing the question sequence. It is a dialog, a physical experience or a question-and-answer sequence that involves an unveiling of subject matter supported by a deliberate cognitive structure and emotional relationship between teacher and student. Each question leads the student closer to discovering the desired target: a previously unknown answer.

Post-Impact
In this Style, by virtue of discovering the correct answer, feedback is built into every step of the process. You will provide positive feedback or reinforcing behavior with each question's response. If responses are incorrect, adjustments in the question need to be made. Continuous motivation is provided by the immediate, positive reinforcement, which spurs the student on to seek the next step and the final solution.

Style G: Convergent Discovery

In Convergent Discovery, the learner is autonomous during the search for the solution and in the development of the solution itself.

Essence
The essence of Convergent Discovery is that students learn to apply logic and reasoning to discover ideas and concepts. The purpose of Convergent Discovery is for learners, now independent of the guiding comments by the teacher, to discover the solution to a problem using logic, intuition, and trial and error reasoning.

Decisions

Your role as teacher is to select or design a task that is new to the learners and that has a single correct response that can be discovered. The role of the learner is to learn to clarify an issue by identifying logical questions that lead to the answer and choose an answer or conclusion by engaging in reasoning, using logic or "trial and error." This Style calls for greater cognitive independence by the learners as they work to discover the one discovered correct answer, move, response or solution.

Planning and Implementation

Pre-Impact
You still make all the decisions in the Pre-Impact Set, as with the previous Styles: you design the problem or challenges for the episode.

Impact
The shift of decisions comes in the Impact Set. The learner makes the decision about engaging in the cognitive operations that will lead to the discovery of the solution. In this process, the learner asks (usually on a non-verbal level) himself or herself questions concerning the presented problem. It is on this point that Convergent Discovery differs from Guided Discovery. In Guided Discovery, you as teacher made the decision about each question or step along the path toward discovery of the single solution. In Style G, the learner is much more autonomous during the search for the solution and in the development of the solution itself.

Post-Impact
Your role as teacher in the Post-Impact Set is to verify the learner's solution by asking questions, if needed, about the process and the answer. The role of the learner at this point is to verify the solution by rechecking the reasoning process and often simply by seeing that the answer does solve the problem.

Style H: Divergent Discovery

In Divergent Discovery learners are engaged in producing multiple discovered responses to a problem or task.

Essence
Style H: Divergent Discovery is very important to dance, particularly for improvisation and choreography but for performance as well. The essence of Divergent Discovery is that learners are engaged in producing multiple discovered responses to a single question, problem, or task. The purpose of this Style is to engage in discovering divergent responses to a common question, situation or activity. Your role as teacher is to design suitable tasks, questions, or problems that appropriately provide for possible multiple responses. The role of the learner is to create diversity and go beyond the known. In the previous Styles, the learner has been involved in hitting a specific target or solution. For the first time the learner engages not only discovering but in producing multiple options.

The role of the learner is to create diversity and go beyond the known. In the previous Styles, the learner has been involved in working to discover a single, specific, predetermined target or solution. In this Style, the learner engages in producing multiple answers to a single question.

Verbal behavior for delivery of subject matter in Divergent Discovery includes,
- "Find four different elevations…."
- "Generate six ways to…."
- "Create three endings for …."
- "Write down five possible approaches to…." (The reason for this very directed verbal behavior will be discussed in Chapter 8, Style H: Divergent Discovery).

Planning and Implementation

Pre-Impact
In this set, you as teacher make the following decisions:
1. The general *subject matter f*or the episode, such as ballet, modern, tap, notation, choreography, history.
2. The specific *topic* that will be the focus of the episode, such as time, space, relationships, etc.
3. The *design of the specific problem* or series of problems that will enable learners to generate divergent solutions.

Impact
In this set the learner decides which divergent solutions are appropriate to the problem. The solutions generated by the student in the process of experimentation become the content of the episode.

Post-Impact
In this set the learners assess their discovered solutions by comparing the teacher-provided criteria to their performance and asking if each particular solution answers the question. If the answer is yes, then the learner knows that it is one possible option to keep and continues to generate other possible options. If the answer does not solve the problem, question or task, it can be discarded or re-worked.

When the learner can see the solution, external verification is not needed. However, given the subjective and aesthetic nature of dance, the learner may not be able to see certain aspects of the solutions. Therefore, feedback by videotape, teacher, and/or peers is valuable.

> *Noelle Martin Zygorski says when she was learning divergent and convergent, she had difficulty remembering which was which, and used > for convergent (coming down to one answer) and < for diverent (creating multiple answers).*

Style I: Learner-Designed Individual Program (LDIP)

In LDIP, the learner initiates the Style, discovers and designs the question, task or problem within the subject matter area and seeks the solutions.

Essence
Learner-Designed Individual Program is the first Style in which the learner designs, develops and performs an organized personal program, such as an independent study program in college. The learner discovers and designs the question, task or problem and seeks the solutions. LDIP is not just "do whatever you want." it is a highly disciplined approach to evoke and develop the creative capacities of an individual who is motivated and disciplined, one who takes the initiative for generating ideas and who can follow projects through to completion.

The purpose of this Style is to provide the individual student with the opportunity to develop a program based on his or her cognitive and physical capacities in the specific topic. Knowledge of one's capabilities and the process of divergent discovery, provided by the cumulative experiences in the previous Styles A-H, are required for participating in this Style. Without this background, students may have difficulties organizing the topic into suitable questions

> *LDIP provides individual students with the opportunity to practice the skills from all the previous Styles and interrelate them over a longer period of time.*

and answers, and developing a workable structure for the project. This Style requires a series of episodes rather than a single episode, as it provides the individual dancer the opportunity to practice the skills from all the previous Styles and inter-relate them over a longer period of time. In a lesson plan, allot an extended time period for this experience.

Planning & Implementation

Pre-Impact
You as teacher decide about the general subject matter area from which the learner will select the topic.

Impact
The shift of decisions occurs in this set. First the learner selects the topic that will be the focus of the study, from within the general subject matter area decided by the teacher. Next the learner identifies the questions, concepts and/or issues appropriate for the chosen topic, organizes the tasks involved and designs the program. The student collects information about the topic, answers the questions, and organizes them into a suitable framework. The student develops an answer to the question, "What will constitute a completed program?" This answer provides guidelines to develop criteria for the Post- Impact Set. During the Impact Set, you are available when the student initiates questions. You initiate contact with the student to observe the work-in-progress by listening to or watching the student's periodic presentations or questions and answers.

Post-Impact
In the Post-Impact Set, the learner verifies procedures, examines the solutions and validates them in relation to the problems. You discuss with individual learners their questions, how they think they are progressing in the program, criteria, seek conversation concerning how well they are accomplishing the criteria and if they are aware of any discrepancies.

Style J: Learner-Initiated

> *Learner-Initiated is the first time that the learner makes all the decisions in the Pre-Impact Set.*

Essence
The essence of Learner-Initiated is that it is the first time that the individual learner initiates the Style or Styles for the episode or series of episodes. This is the first time that the learner makes all decisions in the Pre-Impact Set, deciding the what, why, and how that is to be experienced. The purpose of this Style is for the learner to initiate a learning experience, design it, perform it, and assess it, based on agreed-upon criteria. The role of the learner is to create a total learning experience from idea to completion. An entire class cannot be ready for this Style at the same time; LI is not for all learners. The learner comes to you

with a willingness to conduct a series of learning episodes, having recognized their readiness to move forward, inquire, discover, and examine solutions.

Planning and Implementation
Pre-Impact
Because the content arises from the learner, it is the learner who makes all the decisions in the Pre-Impact Set, including selecting the general subject matter, the specific topic, methods and tools for dealing with the issues, and the rest of the Pre-Impact decisions including how to evaluate the process in the Post-Impact Set.

Impact
In the Impact Set, just as in the previous Style, the learner makes all decisions according to the problem or task designed in the Pre-Impact Set by experimenting, examining, and discovering the actions that will solve the problems. As in the previous Style, this process may require several weeks or more for the student to become immersed in the process of discovery and organization of the established problem over a series of episodes.

Post-Impact
Decisions in this set are made every time the learner verifies a response, checking against his or her established criteria as a valid solution to the problem. The culmination for the program can include a performance, poster presentation, written paper or oral presentation to the teacher, peers, or an audience.

Style K: Self-Teaching

> *This Style does not exist in the physical space of the classroom, but exists as a metaphysical construct in the mind any time an individual is engaged in teaching themself.*

Essence
The essence of Self-Teaching is that the learner initiates a learning experience, designs it, performs it, and evaluates it. This Style does not exist in the physical space of the classroom, but exists as a metaphysical construct in the mind any time an individual is engaged in teaching her- or himself. It is the mark of a mature learner. The purpose of this Style is to provide the learner the opportunity to make maximum decisions about the learning experience without any direct involvement from the teacher. The learner decides how much external feedback, if any, to seek. One example of this Style is when the dancer decides to choreograph a dance, works with movement material and/or background information, and may ask a colleague to provide feedback during the development process.

Summary
The individual Styles and clusters of Styles can be applied in different ways to different subjects in the dance curriculum. All subjects can employ the entire range of the Spectrum, depending on when you want students to acquire information and principles, when you want them to discover single correct concepts, when you want them to discover and invent new concepts. The versatile dance teacher can develop mobility along the Spectrum, applying teaching strategies appropriate to the task at hand.

Styles A-E are designed for the efficient acquisition of fixed or codified information, such as in classes in dance technique, folk & square, aerobics, ballroom, and dance notation. Styles F-G are options that foster discovery of single correct concepts, and could be used in technique, folk & square dance, ballroom, and notation as well as other courses such as dance kinesiology and dance history; in any course to deliver concepts and principles. Styles H-K are designed for discovery of alternatives, new concepts, and to foster creativity, and can be applied to the previously mentioned courses plus choreography, composition, and improvisation. Styles F-K especially not only engage the student in discovery but also convergent and divergent processes: reasoning, inventing, problem solving activities, and invites the learner produce information rather than replicating or receiving information.

The following are a few examples of how the Spectrum can be utilized to solve teaching problems in the dance studio and enhance learning and retention.

Problem:
With a large class, it can be difficult to give adequate individual feedback to each student.
Solution:
Using Reciprocal (Style C) enables each dancer, even in a large class, to receive immediate feedback and learn assessment skills by applying criteria and giving feedback to a peer. In Style D learners practice these assessment skills to personal performance. For both these Styles, the teacher provides a list of criteria for correct performance or a checklist; students work either in pairs to provide feedback for each other (Reciprocal) or alone (Self-Check).

Problem:
Students do not understand the many factors that are combined to make their grade and may question the teacher's grading method.
Solution:
Use of checklists will enable the teacher to sit down with individual students, review progress and identify areas that need work.

Problem:
Students at any age or level of ability can become frustrated or disinterested if the level of the class doesn't match their abilities.
Solution:
Inclusion (Style E) can accommodate individual differences, for it allows all students to enter the activity at their ability level by making choices among alternative levels within the task, whether the class consists of children learning to leap or advanced students working on complex combinations.

Problem:
Students are having trouble completing a full pirouette, or increasing the number of turns in a pirouette.
Solution:
Guided Discovery (F) can be used often in theory and technique classes by asking a series of questions that will lead the student to discover the anticipated answer. In this case, the teacher can guide students to discover the necessary principles and skills needed.

Chapter Summary

The Spectrum of Teaching Styles is a non-versus paradigm for teaching which explains a variety of teaching- learning possibilities. It brings an integrated, comprehensive approach to teaching that can be used for any subject including theory or lecture classes as well as technique or activity classes. It can be applied to classes for any age, subject, or level.

The structure of the Spectrum is based on three key premises: teaching is governed by decision-making; it is possible for both the teacher and the learner to make decisions, and teachers and learners can demonstrate mobility among a variety of teaching Styles. The teacher determines which choices are appropriate to be shifted to students. The student *moves from simple to more complex decision-making.* The Spectrum covers the range of decision-making in the teaching-learning relationship.

Both the Reproduction and Production clusters of the Spectrum offer excitement and reward for teachers and learners. Both are necessary for dance as an art form, because any art form depends on the two opposing and interdependent factors of conservation and change. No single teaching strategy or method is more important than any other; no single Style is necessarily better than any other. All Styles are available to you at any point, depending on what you and your students need to accomplish.

Questions for Reflection and Discussion

1. What is the **overall structure** of the Spectrum—what **shifts** from one Style to the next?

2. Discuss how this shift can benefit the teacher and the student.

3. Discuss transparent teaching, when you have experienced it, what it brings to the student and teacher.

4. Discuss the interplay of conservation and change in dance, when and why each is important.

5. Identify the **essence** of each Style.

6. Discuss the difference between the nature of the Reproduction cluster of Styles and the Production cluster of Styles.

7. Discuss the Discovery Threshold.

8. Discuss advantages for students' learning by receiving and by providing **feedback** to a peer.

9. Identify differences between **Practice and Self-Check**.

10. Identify important elements to keep in mind for an episode in **Inclusion.**

11. Identify differences between **Guided Discovery and Convergent Discovery**.

12. Identify differences between **Convergent Discovery and Divergent Discovery**.

13. This week as you teach, take, or observe class, identify a problem or "challenge" and consider which Style might be an appropriate **pedagogical tool**.

<u>Ahead</u>
Now that you're familiar with the overall structure of the Spectrum and the essence of each Style, let's look at the nature of teaching dance: what is content knowledge, pedagogical knowledge, how do these overlap for dance pedagogical knowledge, how the Spectrum forms a new paradigm for teaching dance.

3 The Concept of Dance Pedagogy

Coffee.
Choreograph.
Teach.
Repeat.

Dance Pedagogical Content Knowledge

Theory and information about teaching is known as *Pedagogical Knowledge*. This includes information such as learning styles, teaching strategies, domains. Theory, skills and information about a particular discipline is known as *Content Knowledge*. In dance, this includes knowing how to dance: the vocabulary, skills, and other aspects of the discipline of dance. *Pedagogical Content Knowledge* is where these two areas overlap; it concerns the application of pedagogical theory to the particular discipline at hand: how to teach dance.

Unfortunately, many dancers find themselves teaching before they can really study *how* to teach, before they gain pedagogical or pedagogical content knowledge. Thus, often beginning dance teachers practice *inadvertent teaching*; that is, teaching as one was taught without studying and questioning method and content.

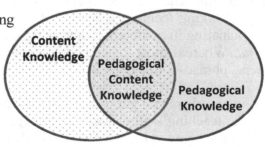

The Concept of Signature Pedagogy

Lee S. Shulman, professor emeritus at the Stanford Graduate School of Education, was the first to define and write about pedagogical content knowledge. Shulman, a significant figure in the field of education, has also further developed this idea, that of the "signature pedagogy" of a discipline: each discipline has developed a body of pedagogical practice which reflects its values, goals, and history. The way teachers approach teaching is discipline-specific; teachers in biology, English composition, and art develop different modes of instruction. For example, in literary studies, the

> *Inadvertent teaching means teaching as one was taught without questioning method and/or content.*

signature pedagogy often involves professors presenting their interpretation of a literary text to students. In medical school, novice doctors follow senior physicians on clinical rounds, implying that real learning happens by following real patients, in a way that no amount of reading books can accomplish (Gooblar, 2015).

In dance technique, the signature pedagogy tends to involve the dance teacher leading students through short movement studies or exercises which reflect the history, values and goals of the dance genre (i.e., ballet, modern, tap, ballroom), so that students learn not only the movements as such but also, in both direct and indirect ways, what is important in that genre and what makes it distinct. For example, the codified vocabulary of ballet, the emphasis on rhythmic clarity in tap, the upward sense of lift in ballroom dance, the grounded strength of modern, the relaxed weightedness of hip-hop. Choreography, improvisation, and pedagogy, as well, each have their respective accepted signature pedagogy.

Accepting a given signature pedagogy can be efficient, but can also hamper innovation. While there has been a blossoming in research and writing on teaching and learning dance, it is ironic that dance artists have little time to devote to reading about teaching. If you are teaching several hours every day, and choreographing, and possibly also performing, it is difficult to find the time to read, much less to reflect, question, and innovate!

However, it is useful to consider the common teaching practices that you fall back on. What do they reflect in terms of history and values? Is this congruent with what you want to accomplish, with what you want to pass on to your students? Are you making decisions about content and delivery inadvertently, following prior practice, or have you developed your pedagogy in reflective response to your specific goals?

Many teachers develop a personal idiosyncratic style of teaching based on methods that they have seen before, but without exploring other teaching styles. Even some dance teacher preparation programs include scant pedagogical theory aside from content knowledge. For the dance teacher, knowing how to *dance* is important; but knowing how to *teach* dance is equally important. The teacher's own dance background and continuing education—reading books, taking technique classes, attending workshops in improvisation and choreography, participating in conferences and other dance events—generally give the teacher most of the *what*. Whereas most dance pedagogy texts and courses focus on *what* to teach—exercises, steps, phrases—this book brings together the *what* and the *how* of teaching.

Dance teachers can get caught up with teaching dance *steps* rather than teaching *students*. Dance teaching skills have been "weighted heavily in favor of teaching how to do dances, rather than how to understand them" (Ross, 2000a, p. 50). However, teaching dance involves more than steps, and it is unfortunate that dance is often taught as doing *steps to music*. Students who think of dance as doing steps to music may eventually see it as a pointless, superficial activity. Many young students, as well as their parents, see dance as a rather limited career choice. When students come to college, many want to continue dancing on the level of involvement they had in high school, because it was fun, but feel the need to major in business or elementary education because those are "real" career choices.

> *Often students are surprised to learn that I have a Ph.D. in dance. I ask them if they are surprised to hear that one can get a doctorate in mathematics. "No? But there are only ten numbers! Now consider the richness of the discipline that deals with the myriad ways of moving, the many reasons why people express themselves through movement, the factors that affect how people in different cultures and different times have viewed the human body, what is acceptable in movement, psychosexual aspects of human movement...."*

This concern for *steps* may mean that teachers focus primarily on the reproduction rather than production aspects of dance: *reproduction* refers to knowledge of existing information or steps; *production* refers to creating new movements, phrases, or ideas. All aspects of dance—from performance to improvisation to choreography, from ballet to modern to ethnic dance–involve, to greater and lesser degrees, the range from reproduction to production. In the typical "recital" format of many dance studios, the reproduction aspect of dance often becomes overly emphasized to the detriment of the production or creative aspect, resulting in students who can *do the steps* but are unable to improvise or create, two very important aspects of any performing art.

> *One of my favorite cartoons in the New Yorker, by Pete Steiner, shows two dogs walking down a tree-lined suburban street. One dog, with an annoyed look on its face, says to the other, "It's always, 'Sit.' 'Stay.' 'Heel'—never 'Think.' 'Innovate' 'Be yourself.'"*

Pedagogical concerns for dance have lagged behind artistic concerns, and the study of dance pedagogy lags behind pedagogy in the other arts, such as visual art and music, which, unlike dance, have more often been included in public education in America. According to Janice Ross (2000b), although dance has not been included in the educational agenda of America's K-12 schools, progress is being made as our society becomes more comfortable with the body in issues of fitness, health, and sexuality. Whereas dance may make its appearance in schools under the aegis of physical education, new theoretical models and methods must address dance as an art form.

Pedagogical Agility

The Spectrum can help with the many challenges inherent in teaching dance. These challenges include teaching students with diverse learning styles, teaching students at a variety of ability levels in the same class, teaching a wide variety of subjects, and dealing with the multiple objectives which exist in all dance classes.

Every teacher has experienced frustration when a student is not able to pick up a movement, step or concept, when the teaching style or strategy that the teacher is accustomed to using simply isn't working at that moment, with that information, or for that student. The problem does not lie with the teacher or the student, but *between* them in a teaching style that doesn't yet allow them to connect teacher, learner, and information.

The non-versus concept of deliberate mobility along the Spectrum enables the teacher to achieve a variety of pedagogical goals.

The Spectrum represents "non-versus" education. Many philosophical conflicts concerning teaching methods occur because an individual or institution is wedded to one style, method or strategy. The philosophy of the Spectrum is a non-versus reality in which *deliberate mobility along the Spectrum* is the way to achieve a variety of pedagogical goals. It does not dictate teaching method; rather, it liberates the teacher by providing more options for presenting the subject matter. It gives teacher and students many pathways to knowledge. The Spectrum uses a series of teaching strategies as a bridge between reproduction and production learning, which can be used for all ages, all types of dance and all aspects of dance education.

The Spectrum enables the teacher to choose from several Styles for the strategy that is most appropriate. "Skillful teaching is the ability to move deliberately from Style to Style as the objectives change from one teaching episode to another" (Mosston & Ashworth 1994 p. 3). Just as agility is the ability to change directions quickly, pedagogical agility is the ability to move along the Spectrum as needs and/or objectives change in the dance classroom. Authors of books on children's dance often remind us that, when teaching children's dance classes, we must often be willing to change directions. The give and take in the interaction between teacher and children often requires pedagogical agility; it is often necessary to change the teaching Style in order to achieve the planned objective.

> *Mobility along the Spectrum is the way to achieve a variety of pedagogical goals.*

What Does the Spectrum Have to Offer Dance?

Professional dancers-turned-teachers often lack a background in motor learning or pedagogical theory, and purposeful and thoughtful attention to the cognitive and affective domains can get lost if the instructor gets overly involved in the "nuts and bolts" of "training the dancer's instrument." A dancer is not an instrument; a dancer is a person, an artist who can contribute to the artistic and creative processes. The Spectrum encompasses several domains including psychomotor, cognitive, and affective–the mind/body/spirit aspects of learning.

When teaching students how to choreograph, sometimes teachers are puzzled or frustrated when students who are superb and enthusiastic technicians are inhibited in improvisation or choreography class. The Spectrum offers many fertile opportunities for application to technique, choreography, and improvisation classes, providing a cohesive framework that can take students easily from reproduction (knowledge of existing information or steps) to production (creating new movements, phrases, or ideas).

Some teachers who have no previous knowledge of the Spectrum may employ methods similar to the Styles of the Spectrum. This varying of teaching styles is commendable. However, being aware of the *entire* Spectrum and applying it with thoughtful planning will equip the teacher with a variety of pedagogical strategies. *Gestalt* refers to a thing or event in which the whole is more than the sum of the parts. So it is with the Spectrum: using the entire Spectrum in an organized fashion will bring both teacher and students to a deeper understanding of the nature and power of decision-making, reaching a variety of objectives, offering effective feedback, connecting with diverse populations and needs.

The individual Styles and clusters of Styles can be applied in different ways to many subjects in the dance curriculum. All subjects can employ the entire range of the Spectrum, depending on when the teacher wants students to acquire information and principles, discover single correct concepts, or discover and invent new ideas. Dance teachers who are just getting started as well as very experienced teachers will find that application of the Spectrum benefits those on "both sides of the mirror." The versatile dance teacher can develop mobility along the Spectrum, applying teaching strategies appropriate to the task at hand.

> *Five reasons for using the Spectrum:*
> 1. *Personal;*
> 2. *Diversity of student population;*
> 3. *Multiple objectives of education;*
> 4. *The need for an integrated framework for teaching;*
> 5. *Active learners make for future artists.*

Five Compelling Reasons to Use the Spectrum

Muska Mosston (1992) wrote of four important reasons for developing and using the Spectrum of Teaching Styles. These reasons are: personal; diversity of the student population; multiple objectives of education; and the need for a coherent, comprehensive, and an integrated framework for teaching. An additional reason is added here: active learners can become future dance artists.

Personal

Teachers tend to develop a personal style that reflects a unique combination of past practices, aesthetic outlook, relationship to students, and personality. Though this personal style might yield failures as well as successes, the teacher will generally stay within its boundaries. This presents teaching as a reflection of personal worldview. However, the teacher must be fully invested in the concept of lifelong learning and be willing to learn new teaching methods.

When teachers benefit from expanding beyond a single, personal idiosyncratic style, teaching becomes a refreshing and renewing experience, and it will enable teachers to reach more students more effectively. A versatile teacher is comfortable with a variety of teaching approaches and is able to use them appropriately for the students and concepts being taught.

> *We must be willing to change who we are in order to become what we want to be.*

Diversity of student population

> *Sensitivity to the many different emotional, cognitive, and physical needs of students may drive your pursuit of facility with the Spectrum.*

Students come from diverse cultural backgrounds, have diverse needs and goals, and learn in different ways. Some students prefer to work individually, others in peer pairs, and some prefer to work as part of a large group. Some students prefer to receive feedback from a peer and some prefer to receive feedback directly from the teacher. Using a variety of teaching Styles will enable the teacher to reach each student's learning preferences at least once.

One way of looking at how learners gather information is in the following modes of communication:

Visual - This type of student receives information best through their eyes, what they see and read. Visual learners often prefer color illustrations, materials that have charts and graphs.

Auditory - This type of student learns best by hearing things – either recorded or in a discussion.

Kinesthetic - This type of student learns best by making physical contact with things that they are learning about. Most children are primarily kinesthetic learners to about age eight.

In any class you will likely to have students who prefer visual, auditory, and kinesthetic modes of communication. Varying your methods of presentation of subject material will enable you to reach each learner's preferred mode at least once in every class. You can also use different modes of communication simultaneously: say the vocabulary while you demonstrate and have students physically follow the movement (more on modes of communication in Chapter 6).

For example, the nature of learning dance technique involves students learning how to move in a particular way, which includes a vocabulary of steps, a vocabulary of motional qualities (such as the Limón use of weight in modern dance or the smoothness of the foxtrot in ballroom dance) and a way of conceiving how actions are motivated or initiated. While the goal of the dance technique class may be for all students to learn the specific aesthetics and movement patterns associated with a certain style, the teacher may utilize several different teaching approaches to accomplish this goal. Using a variety of approaches will greatly enrich the experience of the students in the dance studio.

Learning, like life, is a journey. Imagine several travelers meeting at a single starting point to travel to a particular far away destination. They may choose different modes of transportation and different routes to get there. These travelers may take a plane, train, car, bicycle, or even go on foot, depending on what they want to experience during their journey. The traveler who takes the Concorde will get there very quickly and will have new experiences on arrival.

> *Learning, like life, is a journey: the experiences along the journey will determine how the traveler feels and thinks once the destination is reached.*

However, the traveler who takes a bicycle will get to see the countryside, meet and talk with people along the way, perhaps get invited for dinner and eat the local cuisine. The experiences along the journey will determine how the traveler feels and thinks once the destination is reached. In addition, many different pathways may be taken to the same destination. Yes, the highway is faster, but sometimes a roadblock necessitates a serendipitous detour which enables the traveler to have new, unusual, unexpected experiences; and sometimes it is refreshing just to stop for a picnic.

Students also have many different emotional, cognitive and physical needs that affect learning. The impact of the dance class on students is more profound than just the learning of steps. Years after taking a particular class, students may remember the experience and associate it with feelings of joy, empowerment, or dread. Thus, sensitivity to learner needs may drive the teacher's pursuit of facility with the Spectrum.

Multiple objectives of education

> *Educational objectives are multifaceted.*

Objectives in the dance curriculum may be determined by the teacher, by college program requirements, by the owner of a private studio, by a school board, or by standards set on a state or national level. These objectives may be multifaceted and include skill acquisition, aesthetic sensitivity, artistic process or creativity, and cognitive reasoning, all of which can be addressed when a variety of teaching Styles are employed. Furthermore, dance education has the capacity to address emotional and social domains as well. According to Janice Ross (2000b), in order for teachers to fashion themselves into responsive physical medium, they must become attuned to the nuances of motion, emotion, and the pathways between outward form and emotional awareness and expression. It can be humanizing and humbling to see a friend or even an enemy struggle with the same challenges and limitations when learning complex dance moves. "Patience, and sometimes even compassion, can be social by-products of this aesthetic engagement and new regard for the human body that dance can introduce" (p. 27).

The need for an integrated framework for teaching

> *The Spectrum's integrated framework can be utilized for all ages and all facets of dance.*

Dance pedagogy is often seen as fragmented; there is one way to teach children's creative dance, there is another way to teach folk dance, another way to teach ballet. The studio teacher who uses a different teaching method each for an adult yoga class, a creative dance class for four-year-olds, a beginning ballet class for teens, an adults aerobics class, and a choreography seminar may feel pedagogically fragmented. University dance professors who teach classes in elementary through advanced technique in a variety of genres as well as classes in choreography, history and notation may feel fragmented. Rather than applying discrete, unrelated teaching approaches for different types of dance or different subjects in the field of dance education, the Spectrum is an integrated framework which includes teaching approaches that can be applied to all types and aspects of dance, for all ages. The Spectrum provides an integrated, comprehensive framework that can benefit educators in any subject including theory or lecture classes as well as technique or activity classes. It is a multi-purpose tool belt that you can take anywhere.

The following is a description by Muska of how he came to develop the Spectrum, from the preface of Mosston & Ashworth's The Spectrum of Teaching Styles:

"The Spectrum of Teaching Styles was conceived in 1964, when I was teaching at Rutgers University. I was struck by the tug-of-war that existed in education. It became clear to me that the hallmark of education (and of teaching) was fragmentation. Individualized instruction vs. group experiences, cognitive vs. affective education, creativity vs. conformity, the teacher's idiosyncratic preferences vs. teaching models of all sorts....This fragmentation posed a dilemma that prompted me to search for a conceptualization of teaching that would show and emphasize the relationships and connections among such aspects, rather than the isolation and disparity among them. The result of the search was the formulation of the Spectrum of Teaching Styles, an integrated structure for teaching that provides the contextual framework for the various movements that have contributed to the improvement of teaching" (Mosston & Ashworth 1990).

The nature of the tug-of-war changes, but it still exists in education, in dance, in dance education. This description is as apt now as it was then; the Spectrum continues to be that integrated structure for teaching.

Active learners, future artists

When dance is approached from the standpoint of educating the reflective, intentive individual, active learners can become future artists.

Finally, it is the hope of every teacher that students become active learners who take the initiative to analyze, question, develop alternatives, and learn how to learn on their own. According to Selma Jeanne Cohen (1972), Doris Humphrey would tell her students, "Don't just sit there like little birds with your mouths open waiting to be fed" (p. 197). She wanted her students to accept her tested and proven principles, but also to apply these principles in new ways, to think for themselves. All people possess the ability to reproduce existing ideas or movements as well as produce new ideas or movements, and every subject contains aspects that can be taught by methods inviting replication, discovery, and creativity. Dance is an art form. When it is approached with artistic process in mind, with the viewpoint of educating the intentive individual, active learners can become future artists.

Toward a New Paradigm for Dance Pedagogy

In order to shape a new paradigm, tradition and status quo must be acknowledged and honored, while remaining open to new possibilities. The study of dance is a multi-faceted endeavor, which comprises many aspects of knowledge. Two different aspects of knowledge are reflected in the words, *erlebnis* and *erkenntnis*. *Erlebnis* is knowledge attained in the presence of, or contact with, an object or event. It is the ordered, intelligible symbolic process through which the producer gives and receives information about the process itself and the meaning of its symbols. *Erkenntnis* is knowledge about something, a description and interpretation of an object or event based on observation and reasoning processes such as association, comparison, appeal to prior knowledge, and judgment.

> **Erlebnis:** *Knowledge by direct contact or doing, such as technique, choreography, improvisation.*
> **Erkenntnis:** *Knowledge by description or interpretation, such as theory, history, criticism, and analysis.*

In dance, *erlebnis* is the act of dancing: choreography, performance, improvisation; *erkenntnis* is theory, history, criticism, analysis. These two aspects of knowledge of dance are intertwined and both are essential in the study of dance, and both are addressed by the Spectrum. Learning technique, observing and discussing dances, performing, analyzing studies, choreographing, studying dance history as well as the many other facets of dance study, are all essential to coming to know the discipline of dance and oneself within dance.

Several aspects of dance make the study of dance and teaching unique. First, dance is ephemeral; dance exists only as it is performed (though this performance may be in a video, in a private setting, or in a large theatre). Second, dance depends on the intentive human body for its realization; two different dancers will understand and perform the same dance in a different way. Third, dance as a performance art tends to be a group art, typically involving several artists including the choreographer and the dancers who are often partners in the choreographic act.

> 1. *Dance is ephemeral;*
> 2. *Dance depends on the intentive human performer;*
> 3. *Dance tends to be a group art.*

Dance performers are not only responsible for knowing the steps of the choreography; they are responsible for bringing the dance to the audience; it is through the work of the dancers that an audience is able to see the dance. Thus dancers must be trained not as technicians or laborers but as *artists*. The dancer must understand and project the inherent qualities of the choreography, the energy and expressive qualities that translate the choreographer's ideas from movement into dance, and meaning to the steps.

Telesis is an excellent word to illustrate and explain the application of the Spectrum to dance pedagogy. Telesis refers to *progress that is intelligently planned and directed*. Progress is sometimes more haphazard than we would like to think; we hit upon something that works and we stick with that method, making slight adjustments along the way which seem to produce results. However, sometimes it is necessary to stand back and take a good look at the nature of the endeavor and a system for improvement. Some excellent systems might seem unusual at first but could provide a fresh or even revolutionary perspective. The emphasis must be on deliberate, not inadvertent, teaching and learning.

Progress can be hindered by unquestioned adherence to a model. Examples are numerous in the sciences, when a solution to a problem was found only after investigators abandoned a model that had always been assumed to be "true." This can also be the case in the arts and in pedagogy. Progress is often achieved when old models or methods are exchanged for new ways of thinking and a paradigm shift occurs. If a new

> *Most dance teaching is based on a model in which:*
> 1. *The teacher is the sole source of information;*
> 2. *Communication is primarily from the top down;*
> 3. *Dance pedagogy is often a dichotomy between reproduction and production.*

paradigm for dance pedagogy is to be undertaken, it is necessary to examine the status quo and some of the assumptions that might hold us back.

First, most dance teaching is based on the "bank" model which presents the teacher as being the repository for knowledge that is then imparted or passed on to students. The teacher is the sole source of information; the teacher "gives" and the learner "receives." Teaching dance technique is primarily based on models developed from the courts of Europe: the ballet master directed the action and the students obeyed. Anything else is often seen as anarchy or chaos: if students do not receive the information from the teacher, where do they get it?

> *I often tell my students that I am not the only source of information in the dance studio. Our students can be a wonderful source of information if we allow ourselves to see it. Working with children, you will realize that they have an incredible amount of information that primarily needs to be organized and shaped. Children also have an enormous capacity for self-teaching: look at all they learn in the first two years of life with little formal education.*

Second, perhaps because dance is such an intimate and personal art form, it seems as if some teachers want or need a certain distance as possible between themselves and students. Tales of teachers who stood only in one spot in the room and thumped a cane (sometimes on students!) abound in dance. Some teachers do not allow any talking or questions at all during class.

> *I remember taking a daily ballet class during a six-week summer workshop in which the teacher never gave students the opportunity to speak directly with him during class. At the end of the workshop, after almost 50 hours of contact, some students had never been given a single instance of feedback, and the teacher didn't know the names of many of the students.*

Third, dance pedagogy is often presented as a dichotomy: reproduction vs. production, following or reproducing established patterns of movements in contrast to discovering or creating new movements or phrases. Teachers may recognize only these two extremes without understanding the array of Styles in between. For example, a controversy exists concerning the teaching of dance to young children. Many educators believe that very young children should not be taught dance technique traditionally, but rather taught to explore movement concepts, and many young children (if they are fortunate to have versatile teachers) are taught creative movement using some kind of production method. However, older children and adults are usually taught technique using some type of "Follow the leader" or "Do as I do" method, and rarely taught using any type of discovery method.

This dichotomy holds back pedagogy in several ways. First, it creates a gap: educators must decide at what age it is appropriate to stop teaching dance one way and start teaching it another way. In addition, at some point children get the message that the kind of dance they're doing when they're young is a different kind of dance than what "the older kids" do—and what the older kids do is "the real thing."

Second, this dichotomy leaves a gap between technique and choreography, and often produces dancers who are *either* technicians *or* choreographers. However, all types of dance and all ages have aspects that can be effectively taught with reproduction and production teaching methods, providing a connection across ages and between technique and choreography.

> *When international folk dances are taught in an exclusively reproduction manner, students may get the impression that dance is fixed and immutable, unchanging through the centuries. However, consider the use of a production Style in class: after students are familiar with several dances from a country or region, the teacher guides them in a discussion in which they discover and identify common characteristics, qualities or features. Students identify criteria for appropriate stylistic features in order to create a dance that would be characteristic of that region, then work individually, in pairs or groups to create such a dance. By processing the qualitative features rather than simply the steps, students come to more fully know dance and the people who create and articulate it. They also realize that folk dances are created by living human beings and are subject to change, just like styles in clothing and colloquialisms in speech.*

The Spectrum addresses this gap and provides a bridge across it. Some creative dance teachers believe that production methods are the only way to teach dance to young children, and that children's creative potential for dance will be stifled by *any* use of reproduction. However, following the example of an adult in certain learning situations can be desirable—by using pencil on paper, children learn to reproduce the established symbols of letters and numbers but also learn to produce their own lines and shapes. Teachers of choreography and improvisation classes often avoid any "see and do" or "follow the leader," but episodes using reproduction can be very beneficial in such classes.

Learning dance can be an odyssey of discovery.

For example, students who have been accustomed to choreographing solos and duets eventually venture into group choreography, and sometimes have trouble articulating their movement ideas to a group of dancers. Brief episodes involving teaching a phrase to the class will help students to bridge the gap between producing their new and unique movement phrases, and having to clearly reproduce a phrase in order to teach it to other dancers in rehearsals. Also, learning movement phrases from peers in improvisation and choreography classes will provide a wider movement vocabulary for all dance students, as well as helping them identify and articulate the salient features of a new phrase.

The word "technique" implies that there is only one correct way to do a movement. Even the early modern dance, which rebelled against the methods and movements of classical ballet, assumed that the teacher presented "the way" of moving. However, learning technique can be an odyssey of discovery. By learning a specific technique, students gain insights on many levels: insights into the teacher, the genre (such as ballet, modern, jazz, tap), the sub-genre (Vaganova or Cecchetti ballet, Graham or Hawkins modern), and the field of dance in general, as well as insight into themselves as individuals and how they articulate movement.

Chapter Summary

For dance teachers, *pedagogical content knowledge* refers to a knowledge base that must include not only a thorough background in dance but also pedagogical theory. While artistic concerns drive dance education, a focus primarily on technique or "steps" may mean emphasis on reproduction to the exclusion of production aspects of dance.

The Spectrum brings an integrated, comprehensive approach to teaching that can be used for any subject and for all ages. As a non-versus paradigm for teaching, it emphasizes pedagogical agility, or the teacher's ability to shift teaching Styles in order to achieve planned objectives. Based on three key premises, the Spectrum enables the teacher to understand that every deliberate act of teaching is governed by a previously and consciously made decision, that it is possible for teacher and student to make decisions, and that teachers and learners can demonstrate mobility among a variety of teaching Styles.

This mobility or pedagogical agility enables a viewpoint that teaching is transformative for the teacher as well as for the student, helps address diversity of students and multiple objectives of education, and promotes an approach to dance education which recognizes that future dance artists grow from active learners.

Questions for Reflection and Discussion

1) Define, in your own words, **pedagogical knowledge, content knowledge, and pedagogical content knowledge**. How do these come together in teaching dance?

2) Identify the **reproduction** and **production** aspects of learning dance.

3) Discuss reasons why dance has not been typically included in public education.

4) Define "**non-versus**" and how the Spectrum represents a non-versus approach to teaching.

5) Define **pedagogical agility** and give an example.

6) Identify reasons to use the Spectrum, and give examples of how application of the Spectrum addresses each of these reasons.

7) Define **erlebnis** and **erkenntnis**, give some examples of each of these in the field of dance.

8) What is **telesis**? How does this apply to the teaching and learning of dance?

9) Discuss the "**bank**" model of education.

10) How can a **dichotomy** in an approach to dance education present problems in the teaching and learning of dance?

> ***To Do***: *Read over the essence and purpose for each of the Styles from the diagram in the beginning of the book. These will be discussed in detail in both the Theory and Application sections of the text. Notice the following words, the Style in which they are mentioned, and the context: Decisions, feedback, criteria, discovery, problems/solutions.*

Ahead

Pedagogical content knowledge begins with the basics of dance, which include a vocabulary that organizes and describes the medium in terms of time, space, and qualities of movement; understanding the parts of class and their function; and safety concerns in an art form that uses the active human body as its medium.

4 Dance Basics

> "Share your knowledge.
> It is a way to achieve
> immortality."
> ~ Dalai Lama XIV

The word "dance" covers a wide range of activities, including children's creative movement; recreational social dance; cardio and aerobics; competitive ballroom dance; international folk dance; ballet, modern, contemporary, lyrical, jazz, and tap technique for the professional; improvisation and choreography, history and theory. Its purposes include exercise, personal expression, social interaction, artistic training, and cultural tradition.

However, all dance is concerned with certain basic elements, and whether you have studied only one form of dance or many, whether you are teaching one form of dance or many, it is useful to understand ways to organize, categorize, analyze and discuss the medium of motion.

Vocabulary

In addition to being able to articulate movement physically, dance teachers must also be able to analyze and articulate movement verbally, in both artistic (qualitative) and physical (anatomical/kinesiological) terms. Having a clear and consistent vocabulary to communicate movement to students is essential. The more ways that the dance teacher can explain motion, the more likely it is that the students will go beyond superficially "doing the steps" to understanding the underlying meaning, purpose, and artistic content. Dancer Misty Copeland describes the importance of learning a verbal dance vocabulary: "I felt exhilarated, as if I was cracking the code that would lead me to a wonderful treasure. I listened and watched, learned and echoed." (Copeland p. 107).

Many vocabularies are available to the dance teacher. Each dance genre has its own particular "dictionary" of steps which range from the codified French terminology of ballet terms (such as "tendu" and "battement") to terms in jazz and modern dance (such as "pencil turn" and "twilt") to those specific to a particular choreographer or sub-genre (such as Graham falls and Humphrey spiral extensions). In addition, terms may overlap or be used slightly differently: for example, battement pointe tendu may be called just "tendu" or "brush" in modern dance. Contemporary dance classes may use an eclectic mix of terms, and teachers and choreographers may create their own specific vocabularies.

As a student, the dancer is generally involved with producing the actions the teacher describes, rather than mentally categorizing and storing, in memory, a vocabulary. The dancer as *teacher*, however, needs to attend to developing a vocabulary.

> *Watch out for confusing terms, such as a directive I heard in a studio once, "Let's go back and come back to the front," which really meant, "Let's start from the beginning of the phrase by returning to the front of the room."*

In dance, we need to be able to describe motion temporally, spatially, and qualitatively: time, space, and quality or dynamic. Being able to give an effective, accurate verbal description of movement is important for several reasons. First, having accurate verbal descriptions leads to greater student understanding of the movement task at hand and to the underlying concepts which form the basic building blocks for more complex sequences as well. Understanding what factors contribute to a correct plié at the barre in ballet class (say, having the weight centered, leg outwardly rotated, pelvis and torso aligned, foot contacting the floor properly) is a good start; understanding how these factors then relate to more advanced actions such as pirouettes and elevations is even better.

Second, having a clear vocabulary enables you to provide cue words to students, enhancing proprioception, kinesthetic recall or "muscle memory." Dr. Ruth Day, at Duke University, presented research at the American Dance Festival on what she called Memory for Movement, and her research indicates that dancers are better able to retrieve a dance phrase from memory when a single word or short phrase is associated with steps or phrases. The ballet dancers' "Chassé pas couru grand jeté," the term "fat gnomes" used by the modern dance group Pilobolus, the "cross, kick, two-step back" of the Cotton Eyed Joe are all examples of such task cue words.

> *Proprioception refers to awareness of sensations or stimuli arising from within the body, and is how dancers know how a certain position or action feels. Kinesthetic comes from the Greek, kinein (to move) and aisthesis (perception), and refers to the sensation of movement. These two terms, while subtly different, are often used interchangeably.*

Third, this vocabulary of cue words will enable you to conduct classes without constantly demonstrating. The students of a teacher who is adept at using clear verbal descriptions will be able to develop and use muscle memory, and the teacher will not be exhausted after teaching a day's worth of classes. If you've taught your students the planes of space using either the kinesiology or dance terms, you can correct a student by saying, "The sweep of the arms should remain in the table plane" or "Keep your forward pathway in the sagittal plane rather than zigzagging." Using terminology will also give students analytical tools and a vocabulary to ask questions, such as, "Is that sweep of the arms on the frontal plane?"

Fourth, using descriptive words will enable you to impart important qualities of a movement sequence to students: is the action to be done with strength or lightness, hesitantly or boldly? Is that piqué to be approached as a perch, a stab, a suspension?

> *Qualities of movement, also called Efforts, will be discussed later. For more detailed information on Efforts and Laban Movement Analysis, see books such as Effort: Economy in Body Movement, Principles of Dance and Movement Notation, and Mastery of Movement by Rudolf Laban.*

In addition, these cue or vocabulary words enable you to create task sheets and criteria sheets, and test student knowledge with written tests. And finally, having a vocabulary enables you to create lesson plans that can be used from year to year, reducing the amount of time you spend preparing for classes and enhancing the consistency of your classes.

Let's look at some ways of categorizing verbal information. Some of these concepts overlap; for example, the qualities or Efforts of sudden/sustained time are related to, yet different from, "clock time" or the beats-per-minute setting of a metronome. The Efforts of direct and flexible (indirect) space are qualities as well as being part of the aspect of space. While this list is not comprehensive, it is a way to get you started thinking of descriptive movement terms.

Qualities

Dynamics give an important and distinctive quality or texture to the movemet, like color in a painting. The work of the early 20th century movement theorist and choreographer Rudolf Laban offers a comprehensive systematization of quality in movement. Qualities, called Efforts, are divided into four basic components: space, time, weight, and flow. Each of these comprises two opposite dimensions—sustained and sudden for time, fine and firm (or light and strong) for weight, free and bound for flow, direct and flexible (or indirect) for space. Movement may gradually move from one opposite to another; the dancer may start an action with light weight, and gradually make it stronger. According to Laban, all human movement exhibits constellations of these factors that form certain identifiable textures of movement.

Efforts: Dynamic Qualities	
Time Sudden vs. Sustained	**Weight** Strong vs. Light
Space Direct vs. Flexible	**Flow** Bound vs. Free

Don't confuse "Effort" with the amount of effort or strength that we put into actions. For this reason, the word Effort as used in this context will always be capitalized.

Flow has to do with whether the movement is fluid or restrained (bound vs. free). Free flow is an action with easy fluidity and perhaps difficult to stop, like a skater gliding across the rink. Bound flow is an action that is cautious and held which can easily be stopped, lilke stepping carefully to keep from slipping on the ice.

Space is concerned with how we relate to the space around us. Direct space means pinpointing something, like pointing to a specific item in a shop's display case. Indirect or flexible space means referring to general space, like sweeping an arm from side to side to say, "I want all of them!" Flexible may also be a sense of all-around awareness (see "States of Gaze: Solid, Liquid, Gas" Chapter 6).

Weight is about an approach to weight rather than how much something actually weighs in pounds and ounces. Strong or firm weight shows that there is resistance to an action, as when an actor needs to show that the empty suitcase used as a stage prop is packed full. Light or fine weight is used to show that there is no resistance, as if the ballerina's arms are floating upward buoyed by nothing more than a spring breeze.

Time is similarly about an approach to time rather than about the actual length of time in seconds or minutes. It is typically seen as the difference between having "only five minutes" or having "five whole minutes". Sudden time is the panic of having only 5 minutes to leave the house when you can't find your keys and are still in your pajamas. Sustained time is the luxurious feeling of having five whole minutes to yourself to just breathe and be calm after a hectic day.

Movement may also be described using words such as gentle, vibratory, delicate, swinging, buoyant, percussive, suspended, collapsed.

Steps

These include the codified ballet vocabulary[6], the terms used for specific phrases such as Humphrey spiral extension and Graham fall, and general terms such as triplet and pencil turn.[7] They also include character or folk dance steps such as schottische, two-step, polka; and ballroom dance sequences such as the tango fan step and the waltz box step.[8] Every genre of dance, from ballet, modern, jazz and tap to international folk dance to the bronze, silver and gold-level steps of competition ballroom dance, has a specific vocabulary of steps with which students must become familiar. See "Dance Basics" at the end of the chapter for some basic dance steps and terms.

Time

Time may be expressed in many different ways, from the number of seconds something takes to a specific tempo or metronome beats-per-minute to a perception, quality or expression such as sudden or sustained Effort. "Rhythm" refers to the regular pattern of movements/sounds; a relationship between time and force. "Even rhythm" is when the beats in a rhythmic pattern are all the same length; "uneven rhythm" is when the beats are not all the same length, or a combination of different note values. See "Dance Basics" at the end of the chapter for more information and definitions.

Space

Space refers to organizing the shape of the dancer and the world around the dancer in different ways and includes the following:

- Size such as big or small;
- Levels such as low (on the ground), middle, and high (jumps and other elevations);
- Shapes such as bent, rounded, straight or twisted; ball, pin, wall, screw;
- Kinesiological terms such as flexion, extension, rotation. These may be used similarly to or conflict with dance terms; whereas in dance class we say, "Point your feet," this action would be described in kinesiological terms as plantar flexion at the ankle.[9]
- Positions such as the five basic foot positions, attitudes and arabesques in ballet;[10] promenade position or closed social dance position in ballroom dance, the asanas in yoga;
- Relationships include distance such as near/far, above/below, in front/in back, transverse/peripheral;
- Directions such as body directions (forward/backward), en dedans/en dehors, downstage/upstage, en croix, towards or away from the center of the circle, clockwise/ counterclockwise;
- Group formations such as double circle, square, contra lines, right-hand star (see Formations diagram at the end of this chapter);
- Planes of space such as sagittal or wheel, horizontal or table, and frontal or door (see Planes of Space diagram at the end of this chapter);
- Pathways such as central, transverse, and peripheral;
- Efforts of direct vs. flexible (indirect).

44

Cueing

Cueing refers to using words to represent actions, and is used in several ways. The teacher generally first uses cues as a way to introduce students to the specific vocabulary for a movement style. Then the teacher can use cues to "remind" students what happens next, providing mnemonics to remember phrases. Cueing can also be used to teach new phrases using existing vocabulary.

Cueing is an example of "chunking"—each cue word represents a more complex set of physical responses. For example, look at cueing for the Greek folk dance Miserlou as made up of chunks and sub-chunks of movement:

Misirlou	Circle	Step	In place, step or shift weight onto the right foot, with the left just free of the floor.
		Hold	Hold: no movement or change
		Touch	Point left toe in front of right
		Circle	Circle left toe counterclockwise around right foot
	Grapevine	Back	Step left foot behind right foot.
		Side	Step right foot to right side
		Front	Step left foot across in front of right foot, turning to face LOD (Line of Direction)
		Turn	On left foot, pivot counterclockwise a half-turn to face RLOD (reverse LOD)
	Two-step	Step	Step right foot forward in RLOD
		Together	Step left foot beside right foot
		Step	Step right foot forward in RLOD
		Hold	Hold, no change of weight
	Grapevine	Back	Step left foot behind right foot.
		Side	Step right foot to right side, turning to face center of circle
		Front	Step left foot across in front of right foot,
		Hold	Hold, no change of weight.

In this example, students must first understand the difference between a step (change of weight) and a touch or hold (no change of weight). Then they can start to group or "chunk" actions in their psychomotor memory (also called muscle memory), then combine these into larger and larger chunks, until the entire dance is one meta-chunk which, hopefully, will come back to them the moment you put on the music.

The words used for cueing may involve the direction (i.e., forward, side, back, up, down), the foot (i.e., right or left), beat or count (i.e., 5, 6 & 7 & 8), rhythm (slow, quick-quick), or other words. For more examples of different types of cueing, see the Dance Basics worksheets at the end of the chapter.

Trigger Cueing

The timing for cueing is important, especially when used as the "trigger" for the start of action in Cued Response. Trigger cueing can be auditory, visual, or kinesthetic. Auditory cues include the vocal, "5, 6, 7, 8" before a jazz combination (jazz dancer and teacher Luigi was the first to start combinations with the now-iconic "a 5, 6, 7, 8!"), "DUM dee dee, ready and ah" for a waltz, or clapping for the 5-8 counts before a tap combo. Visual cueing can be pumping a fist into the air on the rhythm to start a hip-hop phrase or twirling an index finger in the air to start a series of turns in modern class. Kinesthetic cueing can include gently tapping a student's hand to establish rhythm and trigger the start for a foxtrot, or, for a waltz, tapping a student's left shoulder on counts 1, 2, and 3, then the right on 4, 5, and a gentle push of the shoulder on count 6.

The effective trigger cue has the following qualities:
- Establishes the tempo and rhythm of the music or movement.
- Reminds students of the movemets to start a phrase or combination.
  For example, to start a country/western line dance or cardio sequence (numbers correspond to music beats or counts),
  5. "Grape"
  6. "Vine"
  7. "To the"
  8. "Right"

  Or, to start a frappé sequence,
  5. "Right foot"
  6. "Flexed"
  7. "Ready to"
  8. "Strike!"

  Or, for a waltz,
  1. "Six"
  2. "Five"
  3. "Four"
  4. "Ready"
  5. "And"
  6. "Go!"

- Gives information that students need to get started.
  For example, for a foxtrot box step,
  5. "Left"
  6. "Foot"
  7. "Forward"
  8. "And"

  Or, for a ballet/modern waltz,
  1. "Right
  2. "Arm"
  3. "Front"
  4. "Look"
  5. "To the"
  6. "Corner"

Good cueing is the kind of thing that, when done well, is invisible. Students don't notice it, they just start when they should, in the proper rhythm, on the correct foot, at the right time. However, it is more difficult than it looks, and, like dancing, takes practice. Practice cueing with different words (see the "foot", "beat", "direction" and "rhythm" cues on the "Dance Basics" teacher sheet at the end of this chapter). Rehearse cueing a variety of different ways, with different rhythms such as 3/4 or 6/8, and unusual meters in music such as Dave Brubeck's *Take 5 (5/4), Blue Rondo a la Turk (9/8), Unsquare Dance (7/4).*

Why is it not appropriate to use "5, 6, 7, 8" as a trigger cue for a waltz?

To do:
Rehearse cueing a variety of different ways, with different rhythms such as 3/4 or 6/8, and unusual meters in music such as Dave Brubeck's Take 5 (5/4), Blue Rondo a la Turk (9/8), Unsquare Dance (7/4).

Parts of the Dance Class

Warm-up

Generally we refer to the preparatory part of any dance class as a warm-up, which may be from five minutes to an hour depending on the activity and overall length of class. Warm-ups include floor exercises in modern, barre exercises in ballet, easy walks or side-steps in aerobics, a mixer in folk and social dance, a "name game" in a circle for children's creative dance.

A warm-up functions in several important ways in a dance class; each is critical to a particular aspect of dance as it functions in the many domains in the learning process. How you plan, structure, and implement a warm-up will depend on the type of dance, the ability level and age, and what you, as a teacher, choose to emphasize.

A warm-up includes the following functions:

1. <u>Physically prepares the body</u> for activity: increases the temperature of the muscles, increases the flow of synovial fluid as a lubricant in joints, elevates the heart rate. Gentle, repetitive actions raise the temperature of muscles, increase blood flow, and increase the flow of lubricating synovial fluid to the joint capsules. A warm-up prepares muscles and joints for harder action and reduces chances of injury.

Functions of a Warm-up:
1. *Warms muscles and lubricates joints;*
2. *Stretches and strengthens;*
3. *Enhances kinesthetic and spatial awareness;*
4. *Sets neuromuscular pathways;*
5. *Focuses the dancer;*
6. *Establishes vocabulary, qualities, and style of the genre.*

2. <u>Stretches and strengthens muscles</u>. Identify and focus on the muscle groups which need to be strengthened (e.g.., abdominals, quadriceps, hamstrings, hip flexors, spinal flexors and extensors) and which need to be stretched (e.g., inner thigh, hamstrings, calves). Increasing strength is accomplished by repeated flexing of the muscle against resistance (such as gravity or the weight of the body). Increasing flexibility is accomplished by slow, sustained stretches.

3. <u>Improves kinesthetic and spatial awareness</u>. A mindful and focused warm-up will increase the students' awareness of alignment or posture, movement qualities, projection, spatial awareness and overall concentration.

4. <u>Establishes neuromuscular pathways</u>, "muscle memory," or positive transfer for more complex skills; it "sets" movement patterns which are used throughout dance.

5. Some examples: characteristic use of feet and legs (such as tendus at the barre leading to temps lié and glissades across the floor), the lift in the torso that creates the "dance frame" in ballroom dance, typical steps and figures used in square dance. With practice, these movement patterns become automatic or "second nature."

Transfer

Transfer is the degree to which the learning of one skill influences the learning of another skill. Positive transfer means that learning one skill will help the learning of another skill; negative transfer means that learning one skill will hinder the learning of another skill (one example of negative transfer is poor previous training or when students have practiced something incorrectly).

Different kinds of positive transfer exist when learning movement skills. For example, simple barre exercises such as tendu (extend) and plié (bend) provide positive transfer to more complex movements and steps, such as sautés which start with a bend of the knees, a strong extension of hip, knee, ankle, and metatarsal joints, and finish with bending these joints again. Practicing the many aspects of a plié such as outward rotation of the thighs, verticality of the torso, lengthened spine, and port de bras or arm movement, will have a positive transfer to sautés or jumps.

Transfer includes right-left transfer and hand-foot transfer. For example, doing a combination on the right will help students learn it on the left. Practicing a dance phrase on the non-dominant side will provide better transfer than doing it first on the dominant side; for most students this means learning it first on the left, then the right. Transfer can also be from hands to feet: Practicing a combination using the hands will provide a transfer to the feet, as when dancers "mark" or walk through a sequence using their hands.

---

6. Focuses the dancer and helps to improve concentration. In addition to the psychomotor domain, the warm-up also addresses the cognitive and emotional domains, by helping students to eliminate the tensions and problems of the day, and devote full attention to the joy of motion. Ritual-like sequences such as a set plié series in a ballet class, the yoga "salute to the sun", a Pilates sequence, a group jog around the room, a "Name Game" for children sitting in a circle, are all ways to get the class mentally focused on the experience of dance. Also, remember that the warm-up is not just a series of exercises; it "sets the stage" for how students perceive dance.

7. Increases the dancer's understanding of vocabulary (dance terminology), time, space, and qualities of motion, and establishes a style for the class. Each genre of dance (such as ballet, modern, jazz, tap, ethnic, ballroom, creative movement) has a different overall quality or style, and each teacher may emphasize a different aspect of it. Is the overall quality lightness or muscularity? Are the movements initiated from the breath, or the joint action of the center of the body, or the upper torso? A good warm-up will "tell" your students about the style of the dance genre of the class. Give your students information about stylistic qualities and use images to help achieve the "look" for that particular dance style.

A warm-up also functions to enable the student to adjust to the surroundings. Even if you've spent most of your life in a dance studio, it is an important shift to make. The dance studio is a place in which it is acceptable and even encouraged to sit and roll on the floor. It should be a safe place to express yourself, in close proximity to, and often intimate physical contact with, other people. Such a space may be rare in an individual's life, or at least just different from their other learning or work spaces.

Other functions of a warm-up can include learning or reinforcing the protocols and procedures of dance class, and social interaction or cooperation. It is also a way to relax or prepare prior to performance (whether "performance" refers to moving and being seen by other people in the class or being seen in a theatrical setting). Each function is equally important, as each touches on a domain which is important to dance as it relates to the whole person. However, different styles of dance necessitate warm-ups that emphasize certain aspects over others.

An effective warm-up prepares the students to do the planned dance activity, and is fairly specific to the activity. For example, in a dance technique class, activities will move from small or fairly gentle movements, which increase the flow of synovial fluid to joints and blood flow to the muscles, to larger movements which will further prepare the dancer for center floor sequences. Exercises will be chosen which are similar to, or provide transfer, to other skills, such as tendus, pliés and relevés at the barre; actions which stretch or strengthen muscles, such as floor or barre stretches and developés or other actions requiring strength, balance and control; and introduce new vocabulary or motional concepts such as planes of space, elevations, turns or specific steps. Throughout the warm- up, the teacher's instructional cues to the student can reinforce and develop kinesthetic awareness, such as the sensation of keeping abdominals engaged or how it feels to transfer weight rolling from the toe to the ball of the foot to the heel; in a tap class it might focus attention on different parts of the foot and ankle.

For a class such as social or folk dance, the affective or social domain may come to the fore during the warm-up with mixer activities that help students connect with each other. In addition, awareness of social/spatial concepts such as changing relationships among participants such as moving from partner to neighbor or corner in a contra or square dance, one's relationship to a partner such as the shifts in close embrace in Argentine tango, or "floorcraft" (the ability for a couple to maneuver throughout the room in ballroom dance).

In an improvisation class, the warm-up may be done as an individual student-directed process, such as, "Stand tall on both feet. Explore how shifts of weight feel in your feet….your pelvis…. your shoulders…."

Center Floor Axial
Many dance technique classes use center floor axial ("in place") sequences such as pliés, tendus, leg swings, adagio (slow) movements for control and balance, and other standing phrases which get the dancer moving more than the preliminary warm-ups. These phrases are generally greater in length than the warm-ups, and may include elements of the locomotor ("across the floor") phrases in "lead-ups" (short phrases that contain aspects of longer phrases). This starts to set longer, more complex neuromuscular patterns in manageable chunks which will then be "plugged in" to the longer locomotor phrases. In folk dance and social dance classes, this part of class may include reviewing previous steps or dances, or working individually. In an aerobic dance class, the teacher might use this as a time to introduce new steps in a slower-tempo, low- impact style, which will later be done at a faster tempo in combinations.

Traveling, Across-the-Floor, or Locomotor Combinations
This is often the most "fun" part of the class, the part that most dancers think of as really dancing. In order to make it enjoyable for yourself and your students, be sure you have

prepared them through the warm-up, center-floor and lead-up activities. Choose actions which are of an appropriate level to your students and present the phrases in manageable chunks. Watch your students carefully to gauge how well they are picking up and what help they need.

Some things to incorporate into your center-floor combinations include:
1. Turns and changes of facing, direction and level,
2. Changes in rhythm or tempo,
3. Changes in quality or "Efforts."

Gradually move from the known to the unknown: begin with familiar exercises, adding new experiences to this foundation. The familiar allows the students to gain confidence in their abilities; the new enables them to grow.

Do not try to teach too much too fast. Learning should be like sipping from a water fountain, not trying to drink from a fire hydrant. Basic movements are the foundation upon which all other movement knowledge are built. Allow your students time to develop the ability to perform fundamental movements well, and provide sufficient time for repetition and practice. This may take the form of incorporating basic steps into various phrases, enchaînements, or folk dances. In dance technique well-done pliés and tendus are the basis for well-performed dance sequences; in ballroom dance, being able to lead confidently into basic forward, backward and turning figures is the basis for leading into all other moves.

Spatial Organization

Use of formal or informal spatial organization will set an atmosphere for the class. Ballet tends to use formal lines & rows whereas modern, jazz and hip-hop tend to use informal spacing. For informal spacings, encourage students to "Find your personal space, a place on the floor where you will be able to stretch your arms in all directions without bumping anyone else." Don't be afraid to move students if needed.

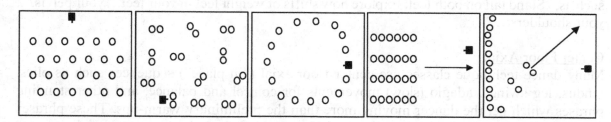

In beginning classes, you may need to direct students to respect the space of others as well as their own space. Students may not be aware of large open spaces into which they could move. Rotate spaces regularly during class; "Front line (or, "people in the front of the room") move to the back; everyone else move forward." This makes sure you can pay attention to everyone equally, and that no one gets "stuck" in the back of the room. Encourage those who "hide" in the back to come forward; all one ever learns from the back of the room is that they can't see or hear what you're teaching. Sometimes a shy student will need a gentle "invitation" to step forward. Be patient, understanding and encouraging.

Encourage, don't force. See Chapter 6 for suggestions on depolarizing the room.

Practice locomotor activities in several possible directions: down the floor from back to front, cross the room from one side of the room to the other, around the room clockwise or counterclockwise, on the diagonals. The diagonal is the longest pathway possible in the room, usually used for large movements and leaps. Moving in large groups will help unsure students to feel confidence as part of the group and enable them to watch others if necessary; moving diagonally across the studio in twos and threes gives students a "break" and helps avoid fatigue, allows them to observe each other and allows you to focus attention more individually. It also gets students away from the mirror and makes them use their brains more to remember sequences.

Locomotor groups may be random and informal or arranged in lines or formations. Informal groups allow the students to quickly group themselves; formations introduce the idea of moving in a particular spatial arrangement.

Designate a definite starting cue for each group and the interval between groups as they begin. "Start every 8 counts" or "Let the group ahead of you do it to the right, left, right, left." This lets beginners know what is expected, empowers them while keeping them attentive, maintains even spacing and prevents something that looks like a herd of wild animals wandering across the floor! The class will feel more comfortable when specific directives are established.

> *Changing the direction and/or formation of locomotor activities from time to time keeps things fresh. Several weeks after the start of a semester I like to get everyone out of their "comfort spot" at the barre by calling out "Mix it up! Find a new spot at the barre (or on the floor) in 10 seconds....9....8...7..." etc. In modern class after students are comfortable with the standing center-floor exercises, I have them all face different directions, and change facing (and/or location) between exercises.*

More complex pathways add challenge and excitement to the class. Having groups which must overlap or cross paths makes the students aware of personal and shared space, requires them to watch for subtle cues from other dancers who cross their pathway, and keeps them alert. Watch for overcrowding, which can frustrate students and increase risk of collision.

Choosing Safe Material

Why are certain actions, exercises, or sequences traditionally practiced in class? The origins of a movement style may date back hundreds of years or more, and aesthetic tradition, in most movement styles, typically pre-dates safety concerns. The actions and movements used in dance may arise from years of tradition and may be culturally specified (such as ballet, yoga, folk dance); they may arise from an individual choreographer's personal artistic vision (Graham modern and Luigi jazz styles), or be determined by a certifying organization (aerobics, competition ballroom dance).

Dance is a physical activity; it has been called a contact sport, and dancers have been called the athletes of the gods. Training can be rigorous; repetition is needed to build the strength, stamina and flexibility; and to develop the kinesthetic awareness and efficient neuromuscular pathways needed for participants to dance well. However, in addition to the artistic, expressive purposes of dance, as teachers we need to be aware of the physical capabilities and limitations of the human body. Keeping our students dancing is one important aspect of teaching.

However, we also need to keep in mind that not everyone who enters our classes has the intention or the potential to be a professional. Children's dance classes will often have a focus on expression, creativity, and individuality, while adult recreational classes in ballet, Middle-Eastern dance, ballroom dance, and other dance styles will have a different focus and will include different exercises than professional training classes.

Any action taken to an extreme has the potential for injury: even the seemingly innocuous and inert action of sitting in front of a computer keyboard typing all day can cause repetitive motion syndrome (RMS). A single grand plié may not be a problem for a young dancer with healthy knees; a long series of them done daily over many years may contribute to overuse injuries for an older dancer.

Several aspects should be taken into account when choosing material for class:
1. The purpose for the class (such as recreational or for professional training);
2. The ability level of students: their level of muscular strength and endurance, their flexibility, and spatial and kinesthetic awareness;
3. The age or developmental level of students: the cognitive level, physical maturation and psychomotor abilities that accompany each age;
4. Where the class fits in with other aspects of a student's life.

Let's look at each of these aspects.

First, consider the purpose of the class and movement style: A recreational class of folk dance should probably not include the extreme squats and kicks characteristic of certain Russian dances, but a professional who is training to perform and keep alive traditional dances must know how to do them accurately and safely. A once-a-week class in jazz dance for adult beginners has a different purpose than a daily technique class for pre- professionals. The level of kinesthetic awareness needed to do ballet well is different from that needed for aerobics or recreational social dance.

> When choosing material for class, consider:
> 1. The purpose for the class;
> 2. The ability level of students;
> 3. The age or developmental level of students;
> 4. Where the class fits in with other aspects of students' lives.

Second, consider the age or developmental level of the class: What pre-school children can understand and do safely is very different from what adults can do, both in terms of what they can understand, what they can execute mindfully, and the stresses that their still- developing bodies can weather: a child's bones sometimes don't fully ossify or harden until age 18. Until then, damage to the bone growth plate can result in stunted growth of the affected bone. Also, a class for older adults such as a "Golden Oldies' Tap" class should consider the fact that older adults will tend to be less flexible but will benefit from exercises for balance and strength.

Third, consider the students in the class in general. Some actions or exercises may be safe *if they can be done correctly,* but it may be that performing certain exercises correctly can only be done by an individual who is already strong, flexible, and kinesthetically aware, and getting to that point may require some intermediary steps. For example, double leg lifts, in different variations from lying flat on the floor to a "V-sit" or pike are often taught, purportedly to strengthen the abdominals. Someone who already has strong abdominals, a flexible lower back, and very good kinesthetic awareness will probably be able to do a certain number of these without danger. However, the nature of the beginner in a dance class is someone who has not yet developed the kinesthetic awareness to know when they are doing something incorrectly or putting themselves at risk for injury, and it is your responsibility to help them. Some instructors keep with very conservative guidelines which prohibit such exercises; others use these only for intermediate/advanced classes.

Your considerations might also include understanding where the class fits in with other aspects of a student's life. Is this a once-a-week recreational class, a fitness training class, or one of several daily professional training classes? Other factors to be considered include the issue of how many repetitions are optimal to produce the desired results. More is not always better; repetition can produce both good and bad results. Among the good things that happen when sit-ups, stretches or tendus are repeated include greater blood supply to a muscle, enhanced strength and increased flexibility. However, problems can occur as a result of mind/body fatigue. First, as the target muscle becomes overloaded or fatigued, students inadvertently and subconsciously shift the action slightly to take the stress off the target muscle, which can result in an exercise or action being done incorrectly. Second, rather than continuing to do the exercise mindfully and with awareness, students may start to divert their attention away from the action at hand. Both these situations result in an exercise not being performed with the necessary care and mindful intent.

As teachers, we have a responsibility to our students to safely prepare them to engage in dance. This means evaluating the demands of certain actions and movement styles, and considering these in relation to the individuals in the class. It also means doing a lot of decision-making, informing, and adapting.

Consider the following:
1. You've been teaching cardio dance classes, and your typical population has been 18-24 year olds. On the first day of a new session, you notice that one student is older, and, looking through the information sheets that you require students to fill out, you see that this non-traditional student is 50 years old and has a relatively sedentary lifestyle. How does this change what you plan to do in class?
2. You've included a certain abdominal exercise in your classes because you remember doing it as a student and feel that it "really works the abs." Looking over the class one day, you notice that several students are doing it incorrectly and their backs are arching off the floor. What do you do?
3. Reading through a new dance exercise instructor's manual, you notice that several of the stretches you've always done in jazz class are counter-indicated (not recommended). What should you do?

Dance is not "one size fits all." Not everyone is able to perform certain exercises correctly and safely. Some books and instructors solve this problem by simply banning certain exercises outright. Some teachers start every student at the safest, most basic level; then, through cautious and measured training and careful assessment and observation, give permission for certain students to move to the next level towards the "ideal."

Situation #1 above is a "Reality Check": this time you were able to *see* that one student was different from the rest, but how many times did you have a young, seemingly healthy student in class who had been very sedentary, perhaps harboring an undetected health risk? Don't assume that all fit-looking students will be able to do an exercise properly or safely; neither should you assume an older adult will be unable to keep up.

Situation #2 above is a "Wake-Up Call": just because *you* can do it correctly doesn't mean that it is safe for your class (or perhaps even for you). Many exercises, especially those for the abdominal or "core" muscles, need a certain level of kinesthetic awareness and strength to be performed safely.

Situation #3 above is a "Stop Sign": Stop and think about where you are and where you are going. Consider the purpose of the class, the purpose of the exercise, and your personal philosophy for teaching. Some exercises aren't necessary for an aerobics class but are essential for the study of dance technique. In addition, consider the level and function of kinesthetic awareness mentioned above: dance technique will tend to focus on acquiring a higher degree of awareness of proprioception than aerobic dance.

When considering an exercise as part of a warm-up, keep in mind the functions of a warm-up discussed earlier, and decide whether the exercise fulfills any or all of those functions. Always have a purpose for an exercise, either for safety or because a student inevitably *will* ask you why it is included!

> **To do**: *Consider the role of each of the functions of warm-up above and how you would address it in the following classes:*
> * *A college cardio dance class*
> * *An advanced hip-hop class in a dance conservatory*
> * *An improvisation class for 7th graders in a public school*
> * *A "Dance for Parkinson's" class for residents of a retirement home*
> * *A social dance class in a community dance program*
> * *A creative dance class for 4-5 yr. old children*

Chapter Summary

Every teacher will create a personal method of describing and organizing the materials to use. As your proficiency with dance and teaching continues to evolve, you will find new material and new ways of categorizing and applying material. Regardless of which way you organize your information, understanding the underlying concepts of dance will enable you to teach with purpose and clarity.

> **To do**:
> *Choose a basic phrase in a specific dance genre: a ballet enchainement, a short folk dance such as La Raspa, a jazz or hip-hop sequence, a ballroom dance sequence such as the Magic Left Turn. Find three different ways to express or cue the phrase, as clearly and succinctly as possible.*

Questions for Reflection and Discussion

1. Identify and discuss reasons for developing a **vocabulary** for dance.

2. Identify and discuss the **aspects of dance described by a vocabulary**.

3. Define **proprioception**.

4. Identify and give examples of some ways to describe **time**.

5. Identify and give examples of some ways to describe **space**.

6. Define **cueing** and discuss how it functions in a dance class.

7. What are the **six functions of a warm-up** in a dance class? Are there others that you would include?

8. Define **transfer**, and give examples of what you can do as a teacher to use and enhance transfer.

9. Discuss the factors involved in **choosing safe material** for various classes.

Ahead

Now let's take a look at some of the basics of dance pedagogy, which include basic definitions, decision sets, information on how to select a Style and plan lessons, and a close look at the factors involved in a teaching episode.

Each of the eleven Styles and how they relate to every other Style within the Spectrum will be discussed in detail in Chapter 5. Therefore, Chapter 4 will define and discuss basic terms and concepts which will be used in their description and application:
1. The *pedagogical unit* and the *Ob-T-L-Ou* relationship;
2. *Behaviors* and *roles*;
3. The three *decision sets* and the *decision categories;*
4. *Observation strategies* for the dance teacher;
5. *Feedback*, and different functions, types and modes of feedback.

The following are hand-outs for students which you may wish to adapt for use in various classes that you teach. The "Dance Basics" worksheet is to help students define vocabulary and different verbal cues for basic steps; the "Planes of Space" worksheet is to help students understand the dance and kinesiological terms for the three planes of physical space. The first of each pair of hand-outs is for the student to fill in, the second is the teacher's answer key (also on the website teachingdancespectrum.com).

World Dance: Dance Basics
(Students)

Beat or Count:_____

Accent:_____

Rhythm:

- <u>Even Rhythm</u>_____
- <u>Uneven Rhythm</u>_____

Step:_____

Tap or touch:_____

Measure:_____

Elevations:_____

- Jump:_____
- Hop:_____
- Leap:_____
- Sissonne:_____
- Assemblé:_____

Line of Direction or Line of Dance (LOD) :_____

Position:_____

Formation:_____

Basic steps:

<u>Two-step</u>

- Direction:_____
- Foot:_____
- Rhythm:_____
- Beat:_____

<u>Schottische</u>

- Direction:_____
- Foot:_____
- Rhythm:_____
- Beat:_____

<u>Polka</u>

- Direction:_____
- Foot:_____
- Rhythm:_____
- Beat:_____

<u>Waltz</u>

- Direction:_____
- Foot:_____
- Rhythm:_____
- Beat:_____

<u>Grapevine</u>

- Direction:_____
- Foot:_____
- Rhythm:_____
- Beat:_____

Foxtrot: Westchester Half-Box Progressive
- Direction:
  - (Lead) _____
  - (Follow) _____
- Foot:
  - (Lead) _____
  - (Follow) _____
- Rhythm:_____
- Beat:_____

Salsa
- Direction:
  - (Lead) _____
  - (Follow) _____
- Foot:
  - (Lead) _____
  - (Follow) _____
- Rhythm:_____
- Beat:_____

Lindy (Single)
- Direction:
  - (Lead) _____
  - (Follow) _____
- Foot:
  - (Lead) _____
  - (Follow) _____
- Rhythm:
- Beat:_____

_____
- Direction:
  - (Lead) _____
  - (Follow) _____
- Foot:
  - (Lead) _____
  - (Follow) _____
- Rhythm:_____
- Beat:_____

World Dance: Dance Basics
(Teacher)

Beat or Count: _The basic unit that measures time_

Accent: _Stress placed on a beat to make it stronger or louder_

Rhythm: _the regular pattern of movements or sounds; a relationship between time and force_
- Even Rhythm _Beats in rhythmic pattern are all the same_
- Uneven Rhythm _Beats in rhythmic pattern are not all same: combination of quick/slow beats._

Measure: _A group of beats or counts; usually 2, 3, or 4 beats or counts._

Step: _Transfer of weight from one foot to the other_

Tap: _A touch of part of the foot to the floor; no change of weight. AKA point or touch._

Elevations: _Often called jumps. Classified by feet that push off the floor and feet that land on the floor._
- Jump: _2 feet to 2 feet_
- Hop: _1 foot to the same foot_
- Leap: _1 foot to the other foot_
- Sissonne: _2 feet to 1 foot_
- Assemblé: _1 foot to 2 feet_

Line of Direction or Line of Dance (LOD) : _Counterclockwise(ccw) around floor_

Position: _Body shape. Every dance genre has a vocabulary of specific positions_

Formation: _Spatial design of a group (i.e., single circle, double circle, square, etc.)_

Cues for Basic steps:

Two-step
- Direction: _Step together step; step together step_
- Foot: _Left right left hold; Right, left, right hold._
- Rhythm: _Quick quick slow; Quick, quick, slow. Uneven rhythm_
- Beat: _2/4 or 4/4 meter; 1 and 2, 1 and 2; OR 1 and 2, 3 and 4_

Schottische
- Direction: _Step, step, step hop; step step step hop_
- Foot: _Right, left, right (hop R); Left, right, left (hop L)_
- Rhythm: _Quick, quick, quick, quick; quick, quick, quick, quick. Even rhythm._
- Beat: _4/4 meter: 1,2,3,4_

Polka
- Direction: _Hop step together step; hop step together step._
- Foot: _(hop right) Left right left. (hop L) Right left Right._
- Rhythm: _Ah Quick, quick, slow; Ah quick, quick, slow. Uneven rhythm_
- Beat: _2/4 meter: Ah 1 and 2, ah 1 and 2_

Waltz
- Direction: _Down up up, down up up_
- Foot: _Right, left, right; Left, right, left_
- Rhythm: _Even rhythm in 3 or 6 counts._
- Beat: _1, 2, 3; 1, 2, 3; OR 1, 2, 3, 4, 5, 6_   Even rhythm of 3 or 6

Grapevine
- Direction: _Side, cross bk, side, touch OR Cross bk, sd, cross ft, touch_
- Foot: _Right, left, right (touch L); Left right left (touch L)_
- Rhythm: _Quick, quick, slow; quick, quick, slow_
- Beat: _Uneven, 4./4 meter: 1,2,3-4; 1,2,3-4_

Foxtrot: Westchester (Progressive Box Step (or Half Box Progressive)

- Direction:
  - (L) *Forward, hold, side, together; Forward, hold, side together*
  - (F) *Back, hold, side, together; Back, hold, side together*
- Foot:
  - (L) *Left, hold, right left; right, left right.*
  - (WF *Right, hold, left right; left, hold, right left*
- Rhythm: *Slow, quick quick; Slow, quick quick*
- Beat: *4/4 meter: 1-2, 3, 4*

Salsa

- Direction:
  - (Lead)Forward, back, together; Back, forward, together
  - (Follow) Back, forward, together; Forward, back, together
- Foot:
  - (Lead) Left, right, Left, shift; Right, Left, Right, shift
  - (Follow) Right, Left, Right, shift; Left, Right, shift
- Rhythm: Quick, Quick, Slow; Quick, Quick, Slow
- Beat: 1, 2, 3-4; 1, 2, 3-4

Lindy (jitterbug, swing) (Single)

- Direction:
  - (M) *Sd, Sd, bk fd, OR: Side, side, Rock step OR Side, side, ball change*
  - (W) *Same as above but starting on Right rather than left*
- Foot:
  - (M) *Left, right, left right*
  - (W) *Right, left, right left*
- Rhythm: *Slow, slow, quick quick*
- Beat: *4/4 meter: 1-2, 2-4, 1,2*

TBA, depending on what you decide to cover

- Direction:
  - (Lead)
  - (Follow)
- Foot:
  - (Lead)
  - (Follow)
- Rhythm:
- Beat:

Formations

Circle

△	Male
▢	Female
◯	Non-gender specific

Line

File O–O–O–O–O–O–

Square

Broken Circle, Serpentine

Double Circle

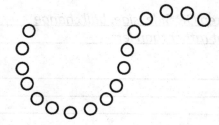

Double Line, Contra

▢◁
▢◁
▢◁
▢◁
▢◁

Planes of Space
Student Hand-Out

The three planes of space describe the height, depth and width along which actions take place. They may be referred to using dance or kinesiology terminology.

A
Dance: _____
Kinesiology: _____

B
Dance: _____
Kinesiology: _____

C
Dance: _____
Kinesiology: _____

PLANES OF SPACE
Teacher Key

The three planes of space describe the height, depth and width along which actions take place. They may be referred to using dance or kinesiology terminology.

A
Dance: Door
Kinesiology: Frontal

Actions which lie along the door or frontal plane are those which move sideways. Reaching the arms out to the sides, doing a tendu á la second, doing a cartwheel or dancing a grapevine step are all actions on the door or frontal plane.

B
Dance: Wheel
Kinesiology: Sagittal

Actions which lie along the wheel or sagittal plane are those which move forward/backward. Bending forward, doing an arabesque, doing a forward roll or leaping forward are all actions on the wheel or sagittal plane.

C
Dance: Table
Kinesiology: Horizontal

Actions which lie along the table or horizontal plane are those which sweep parallel to the ground. Bringing the arms from á la second to au milieu devant in a pirouette, swinging a baseball bat, or swiveling the head from side to side are all actions on the table or horizontal plane.

(This plane is also called the transverse plane, but that term can be confusing if you also use Laban's terminology, for pathways, of peripheral, central, and transversal.)

5 Dance Pedagogy Basics

I'm a Dance Teacher:
I Turn Coffee into
Choreography.

What are the building blocks of dance education? What is a course, a class, a unit, a lesson, an episode? What is the process for planning and deciding what to teach? Let's look at each of these in more detail.

Definitions: Course, Unit, Lesson, Episode

Course

A full dance course is generally 6-15 weeks or more. Each individual lesson may be from 30 minutes to over 3 hours in length. A course is usually composed of units; a unit is composed of individual lessons; a lesson is composed of episodes.

Unit

A unit is a series of lessons on a certain topic. A course may comprise several units; for example, a fifteen-week semester course in international folk dance might include separate units on Eastern Europe, the British Isles, and Western Europe; a dance notation course might include units on supports, turns, and elevations. The 9-month course entitled Jazz Journey at a private studio (below) includes several units on different historical styles of jazz dance.

Jazz Journey: length of course: 9 months.
Unit 1: 6 weeks. Review of general jazz technique.
Unit 2: 2 weeks. Popular music and dance of the 20s.
Unit 3: 2 weeks. Jazz music and dance of the 30s
Unit 4: 2 weeks. Jazz music and dance of the 40s
Unit 5: 2 weeks. Jazz music and dance of the 50s
Unit 6: 2 weeks. Jazz music and dance of the 60s
Unit 7: 2 weeks. Jazz music and dance of the 70s
Unit 8: 4 weeks. Jazz music and dance of the 80s
Unit 9: 4 weeks. Hip hop music and dance of the 90s
Unit 10: 4 weeks. Techno music and jazz dance of the millennium
(Thanks to Maria Triano of PA Dance Network for this example)

Lesson

A lesson is composed of one or more episodes, each one planned in terms of the activity, the Style, and any other logistical arrangements (see sample lesson plans later in this chapter). Lessons may also vary in length; most children's dance lessons are 30-60 minutes in length; most adult technique lessons are 60-120 minutes in length.

The term "class" can be confusing; does it refer to a multi-week course or a single lesson? Rather than use this confusing term, "course" will be used to refer to a multi-unit dance experience, "lesson" will be used to refer to a single meeting time.

Episode[11]

An episode is a unit of time during which the teacher and learner are in the same Style with the same objectives; it may vary in length from a minute to an hour or more. A teaching episode begins when you engage the learner and finishes when you move to another Style.

Episodic Teaching

A well-planned dance class may include several episodes in different Styles (see lesson plan examples later in this chapter). For example, the teacher may start a technique class with a barre or warm-up in Style A: Cued Response, have a brief episode in Style F: Guided Discovery for explanation and clarification of a concept, introduce a center-floor sequence in Style A, have students work on their own in Style B: Practice or Style C: Reciprocal, then finish with Style E: Inclusion. "Episodic teaching" is the key to effective teaching: when you feel that one teaching Style is not working at any particular moment, you may switch to an episode in another Style.

Tip: *The Quick Episode Sandwich. Sometimes while you and the class are engaged in an episode, you'll sense an existing or potential problem which can be clarified, solved or averted by "sandwiching" one episode within another or switching to an episode in another Style for just a moment.*

"Golly, I can do that??" Sure! There are no Spectrum Police. Insert an "episode sandwich" in which you briefly switch into a different episode, then return and continue with your planned episode. You can do this for the whole class or just for a few students, to give them the assistance they need without stopping the action for the whole class. Watch for more Quick Episode Sandwich tips later in the book.

Roles, Behaviors and the Pedagogical Unit

Let's look in detail at the two most important aspects of teaching: the teacher and the learner. Specifically, looking at the roles and behaviors of the teacher, the learner, the material the teacher plans (objectives), and what actually happens (outcomes).

> *Far from attempting to separate personality from action in a behaviorist or stimulus-response manner (which may disturb teachers who have a humanist approach), these concepts can help us to understand why we do the things we do. Early childhood educators often caution against identifying the quality or personality of the child with his or her actions or behavior. "Good girl, you cleaned your plate" or "Good boy, you waited quietly" may imply to the child that she is good or worthy of love only when she eats everything in sight or when he doesn't say anything. Praising the appropriateness of a certain behavior in a given situation or in a specific role provides a greater awareness of our abilities to select actions to meet certain criteria in given situations, and helps students learn to choose actions in terms of their appropriateness for a situation.*
>
> *Consider the behaviors of moving quickly in time to the music, contacting other people, and changing direction rapidly, as opposed to sitting quietly and listening intently. Which behavior is appropriate for attending a classical music performance? Which is appropriate for participating in square dances?*

Roles and Behaviors

The concept of roles and behaviors needs clarification here. Teaching involves not only introducing students to new ideas and concepts, but also helping them understand when to apply certain actions and strategies.

> *The word "etiquette" is derived from the French for ticket, tag, or label. In good manners or etiquette, we follow the clearly defined labels for behavior for our roles.*

Teaching sometimes seems to be a paradox: it is very personal, yet it is concerned with a body of knowledge and abilities that are acquired through study and practice. Like dance, teaching is both a learned activity and a reflection of ourselves. In our everyday lives, we have many roles. Spouses who work together deal with their dual roles as business partners and marriage partners. Parents who coach Little League, who are den leaders for Boy or Girl Scouts, who home-school or perform a myriad of other activities, find themselves in changing role situations. You may find yourself in fluid roles throughout the day: Conducting a dance pedagogy seminar, teaching a ballet class, rehearsing a modern dance work, advising a student dance organization, talking with the student who also teaches your child, asking for advice from a student who happens to know more than you do about computers, all mean different interactions and different roles between yourself and your students.

In many classes, the teacher does not appreciate students correcting each other or allow it; it is not the role of one student to correct another during class, and it may appear that one of the students is trying to assume the teacher's role. In the Spectrum, Style C: Reciprocal involves students in the roles of Doer and Observer, but neither takes the role of Teacher.

Dance students benefit from understanding that life involves constantly-changing roles. For example, Christina and Lauren are friends in the college dance program. When Lauren is a dancer in Christina's rehearsal, Lauren takes on the role of dancer, whose task is to perform the choreography set by Christina. When Christina is a dancer in Lauren's dance, the roles are reversed. Unless a choreographer asks dancers for assistance, input or feedback, it would be a breach of the unspoken etiquette of rehearsal, regardless of the length or depth of their friendship, for one to act in role of the other.

> *I attended a conference at which a former student of mine was presenting a lecture-demonstration. Prior to the presentation, I approached her with some students in tow and introduced her as "my colleague," which seemed to surprise her. She gave an excellent presentation that contained intriguing information new to me, and during the period for dialog I asked several questions. When we met for lunch later I told her that I enjoyed learning from her presentation. We talked about how our roles change throughout life. She seemed to enjoy the realization that we learned from each other.*

> *I will always cherish the fact that when I was doing my doctoral work in dance, my father, Richard Goodling, enjoyed hearing about my studies and research. A Ph.D. himself, he was pleased that his five children grew up to be adults in a variety of successful careers that were different from his own. He learned new things from each of us, and we each felt honored by this. The concept of lifelong learning, and understanding that it can come from your students and your children, is extremely valuable and rewarding.*
>
> *I would like to credit Betsy Blair, teacher, performer, choreographer, poet, artist, and good friend in Durham, North Carolina, who first enabled me to make the transition from student to colleague.*

The Pedagogical Unit[12]

In planning a lesson, the teacher must consider the relationship that includes the teacher (T), the learner (L), objectives (Ob) which the teacher *anticipates* accomplishing, and outcomes (Ou), the objectives that were *actually* accomplished. The objectives, the teacher, the learner, and the outcomes for the dance class form a relationship. The relationship is the interaction among you, your students, what you would like to have happen, and what actually happens. This interaction is the <u>pedagogical unit</u>, and it involves certain teaching behaviors, certain learning behaviors, specific objectives to be reached, and results in specific outcomes. Each Style in the Spectrum is defined by the behavior of the teacher (the decisions made by the teacher), the behavior of the learner (the decisions made by the learner), the objectives intended for this relationship, and the outcome. The Ob-T-L-Ou is unique for each Style.

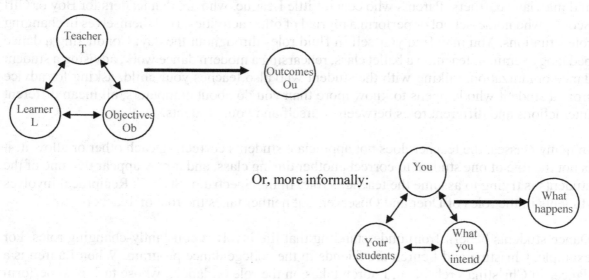

Objectives are concerned with both subject and behavior. Subject objectives (Obs) pertain to the content of the class, for example, a time step in tap, pencil turns in jazz class, the waltz box step in ballroom dance, the dance Ve David in an international folk dance class, the exploration of time in an improvisation or choreography class. Behavior objectives (Obb) refer to human behavior, such as accuracy of performance (for example, ballet footwork), self-assessment (for example, assessing use of the spine a modern dance class), initiative (for example, in choreography class).[13] Both subject objectives and behavior objectives always exist in teaching. The subject and behavior objectives that you choose to reach will guide you in selecting a teaching Style.

The objectives are an *expectation*: what you *expect* to achieve. A teaching episode always results in an outcome, which may or may not match your intended objective! Outcomes include behavior outcomes (Oub) and subject outcomes (Ous). The subject matter objectives, behavior objectives, teacher behavior and learner behaviors all interact to produce subject matter outcomes and behavior outcomes. Every dance lesson involves an interaction of objectives, teaching behavior, and learning behavior that produces outcomes. This interaction is diagrammed below.

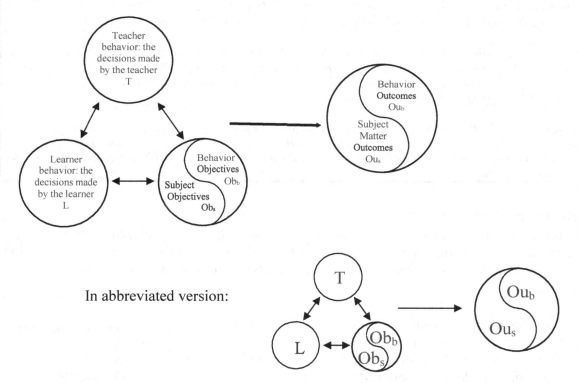

Objectives affect teaching behavior, which in turn influences learning behavior, and helps determine which Style of the Spectrum the teacher chooses. This interaction results in an outcome in subject matter and behavior. Thus, when planning the teaching episode, it is essential for you to decide not only *what* to teach but also *how* to teach it, depending on your objectives. In a successful class, the *outcomes* agree with the *objectives*: *intent is congruent with action.*

> *Congruity between intent and action is just one way to measure success. Remember, though, that we're teaching human beings to engage in an art form, and success can happen when something entirely different and wonderful occurs! Yes, being open and flexible are essential in teaching dance; you may have a perfectly delightful outcome which was entirely unplanned.*

Sometimes you'll decide which Style to apply for a particular learning episode based on your objectives for that event. At other times, you'll select a teaching Style based on the learning style of your dancers. Congruency among the teacher, the learner, and objectives aids success.

Decisions[14]

The Spectrum of Teaching Styles is based on the premise that teaching is a chain of decision-making: every deliberate act of teaching is a result of a decision that affects the thinking, feeling, and behavior of both the teachers and students. Whereas most decisions are made deliberately and thoughtfully, none should be made inadvertently or overlooked entirely. It is helpful to identify decisions that may be taken for granted or may appear self-evident, to think through each of these decisions and how they apply to each lesson.

> *The following are examples of decisions that are often made inadvertently. Consider each decision and the effect on the class, an intermediate/advanced level classes in a studio which includes drop-ins.*
>
> *Teacher A enters the studio at precisely 9:00 a.m., stands at the front of the room, and gives the terminology for the combination in an even voice once, then gives a nod to the accompanist and watches from the front of the room as the class does the combination. Corrections are given to the class as a whole as the teacher stands at the front of the room.*
>
> *Teacher B enters the studio and greets familiar students by name, then seeks out new students and asks their names. The teacher greets the accompanist by name, then addresses the class and asks, "Is anyone working with an injury today?" After giving the combination, the teacher moves throughout the room to give individual corrections.*

The Three Decision Sets[15]

Decisions that are made in the teacher-learner relationship are categorized in three sets: the Pre-Impact Set, the Impact Set, and the Post-Impact Set. We touched on these earlier; now we'll look at them in more detail. These decision sets occur for every episode during a dance class.

1. The Pre-Impact Set includes all decisions that are made during planning and defines *intent*.
2. The Impact Set includes decisions related to the implementation of the plan in class and defines the *action*.

> **The Three Decision Sets:**
> Pre-Impact: Intent
> Impact: Action
> Post-Impact: Assessment

3. The Post Impact Set includes assessment and evaluation decisions; the *congruity* between Pre-Impact and Impact Sets: the *congruity between intent* and *actions*. It includes assessing a student's performance during class as well as evaluating your own ability to make your intentions for the lesson actually work in practice.

The following chart presents the three decision sets and the decision categories associated with each.

The Three Decision Sets
Decisions that are made in the teacher-learner relationship are categorized in three sets.

The Pre-Impact Set: Intent	The Impact Set: Action	The Post-Impact Set: Congruity between Intent and Action
Includes all decisions that are made during planning.	Includes all decisions related to the class itself and performance in class.	Includes decisions in evaluation of in-class performance and the congruity between Pre-Impact and Impact Sets.

Decision Sets	Decision Categories

Pre-Impact: Planning *Intent*	1. Objective of the episode
	2. Selection of a teaching Style
	3. Anticipated learning style
	4. Whom to teach
	5. Subject matter
	6. Time:
	   • When to start
	   • Pace and rhythm
	   • Duration
	   • When to stop
	   • Interval
	   • Termination of lesson
	7. Modes of communication
	8. Treatment of questions
	9. Organizational arrangements
	10. Location
	11. Posture
	12. Attire and appearance
	13. Parameters
	14. Class climate
	15. Evaluation procedures and materials
	16. Other

Impact Execution or Performance *Action*	1. Implementing the Pre-Impact decisions 2. Adjustment decisions 3. Other
Post-Impact Evaluation *Analysis, Assessment*	1. Gathering information concerning performance in the Impact Set (i. e., observing, listening) 2. Assessing this information against criteria 3. Providing feedback to the learner 4. Treatment of questions 5. Assessing selected teaching style 6. Assessing anticipated learning style 7. Adjustment decisions 8. Other

The Pre-Impact Set

The Pre-Impact Set of decisions deals with planning the interaction between teacher and learner: you plan the interaction between you and your students, usually in a lesson plan that may or may not be written down. In most Styles the teacher makes all decisions in the Pre-Impact Set. Some decisions in the Pre-Impact Set are made when planning the night before a lesson, sometimes in planning months in advance, and sometimes in an adjustment decision the moment before the episode.

Beginning teachers will probably want to consider and write down every aspect, and even advanced teachers benefit from re- considering each part of a lesson plan. These decisions include all details of the lesson; some tend to be taken for granted, many will appear self-evident, but from time to time it is helpful to review the details of every lesson. The following are the decisions in the Pre-Impact Set.

> *The Pre-Impact Set involves planning the interaction between you and your students.*

1. Objectives. This answers the question, "Why?" What are the specific expectations of class? What are the goals? For a ballet class, it might be, "Introduce grand jeté en tournant" or "Discover principles of static and dynamic balance." An objective for an improvisation class might be, "Explore shared weight with a partner." An objective for a ballroom class might be "Improve leading and following skills," or "Have the entire class learn everyone else's name."

2. Selection of a teaching Style. This answers the question, "How?" The answer will enable you to identify the teaching behavior that will bring the learning behavior that will bring the learner to the objective of the episode. Consider your students and objectives when selecting a teaching Style.

3. Anticipated learning style. This decision can be driven by the needs of your students or by selection of a teaching Style.

4. Whom to teach. This decision concerns the participants in a class: the teacher can choose to address the entire class, part of it, or individuals.

> *Have you ever taken a class in which it seemed that the teacher was teaching only the best students, or only the worst students, or only the students that she or he already knew? This is another example of an inadvertent decision—one would hope that such exclusion was not a conscious decision!*

5. Subject matter.
    *   Type of subject matter. This answers the question, "What?"
    *   Quantity of tasks: This answers the question, "How much?" or "How many?"
    *   Quality of performance. This refers to the question, "How well? What are the criteria?" The criteria for quality for a beginning-level children's ballet class are obviously different from the criteria for quality for an advanced class.
    *   Order of performance. This refers to the question: "In what order—sequential or random—will tasks be performed?" In a modern technique class, a dance phrase will usually be done in a particular sequence. However, a directive from the instructor to the students may be, "You may choose to re-order the phrase, repeat certain sections, or leave certain movements out entirely."

> *I remember being exhilarated, empowered and sometimes terrified when Ann Deloria, teaching at the University of North Carolina at Greensboro, would use this in her modern dance technique classes.*

6. <u>When to teach.</u> Time decisions are made about the specific starting time of each task. In technique class, you or your accompanist generally cues the dancers when to start, the pace and rhythm, etc. However, in an improvisation, you may shift this decision to the students, telling them that "Within the next ten minutes, you may start dancing at any time, dance for as long as you wish, 'finish' when you want, then sit along the edges of the studio and observe." In a notation class, students may be working from scores while you are available as a resource, and thus students may be starting at different times, working through sections of a dance at their own pace.

7. <u>Modes of communication.</u> In a class, for example, you may give the directive that, for the next ten minutes, students are to communicate only non-verbally, or that students must create vocalizations without words to communicate. In a ballroom class, the students might be directed to communicate only through the signals of leading and following for one dance, then to stop and verbally give each other feedback as to the effectiveness of a lead.

8. <u>Treatment of questions.</u> In any class, participants may ask many different kinds of questions that may be dealt with in various ways. Some technique teachers do not allow questions until all students have attempted the phrase at least once, while others invite immediate questions. Teachers may wish all questions to be addressed to themselves, or allow students to ask and answer questions among themselves. Whatever your choice, it is useful to state your expectations concerning communication and questions so that students know when and how they can direct questions.

9. <u>Organizational arrangements.</u> These are decisions about logistical needs, such as equipment, and classroom management.

10. <u>Where to teach.</u> This identifies the spatial relationship among you and your students. In many technique classes, the students are formally arranged in rows facing the teacher who stands in front of the mirror. In other classes the teacher might be standing in the center of a circle of students, or sitting as part of a circle.

11. <u>Posture.</u> This refers to alignment and shape of the body during the task. In most dance classes this is inherent in the movement phrase and genre. Ballet, modern, jazz, tap, ballroom and folk dance styles all have distinctive features for alignment and carriage. Except for improvisation or choreography classes, decisions concerning posture are generally not given to students. However, certain decisions concerning posture may be given to students in episodes in certain Styles. This will be addressed later in the presentation of each Style.

> *A teacher who studies and revises teaching methods continues to grow and learn from every lesson.*

12. <u>Attire and appearance.</u> This includes decisions about clothing, hair, jewelry and footwear. In a yoga or aerobics class this might be as simple as "Wear comfortable non-restrictive clothing." In an advanced ballet class in a conservatory it might refer to color of leotard and tights, arrangement of hair and prohibition of all jewelry. Again, some decisions concerning attire and appearance may be shifted to students in certain Styles, and this will be addressed later in the presentation of each Style.

13. <u>Parameters.</u> This refers to limits, particularly of location, time, posture, and attire. What are the acceptable limits? For example, what is acceptable footwear? If a student is more than two minutes late, are they allowed to enter class?

14. <u>Class climate.</u> This refers to the affective and social conditions that evolve in any class, resulting from the sum total of all the previous decisions. Some classrooms have an air of formality, others are more informal and laid-back. This involves a constellation of qualities including dress code, parameters, and the overall manner of the instructor.

15. <u>Evaluation procedures and materials</u>. This refers to evaluation that will take place in the Post-Impact Set. What kind of evaluation, what materials and criteria will be employed, how do they relate to the objectives, what is the quality of the performance—these are issues of evaluation.
16. <u>Other</u>. This is open-ended; other categories can be defined and included here.

These decisions don't occur in a set order. All of this information goes into the general mix of things from which you develop your plan.

Questions, Anyone?

Let's look at how to initiate or invite students' questions. Asking, "Does anyone have any questions?" is almost guaranteed to cut off questions from all but the most intrepid students. Why? First, not allowing questions is often the norm in many dance studios, so speaking in class may feel unusual or strange to students. Second, confessing to having a question may be seen as "bad" in dance class, and nobody wants to look as if they don't know exactly what they're doing. Third, students may have so many questions, they won't even know where to start!

A more fruitful way to open the door to student/teacher exchange is to ask, "What questions for clarification do you have?" This approach establishes the expectation that students do have questions and that you value and will address their questions. It is a simple change in verbal behavior but makes an enormous difference.

Observation of your class will inform you whether your students are really ready to go on or if they need more information. However, rather than just giving them very detailed instructions from the beginning and risking "information overload", remember that it is useful for students to identify their own problem areas and initiate interaction with you. But they may need a gentle little nudge. For example, if you see that they aren't quite getting the footwork, you could prompt them by asking, "What questions do you have about the footwork?" This directed verbal behavior will also reduce the possibility of off-task or inappropriate questions.

Also, be patient with questions; research literature in several studies shows that most teachers are unable to wait more than two seconds for a response. It always seems that the questions come just after I say, "OK, let's go on...."! Also, reward questions with a smile and positive manner, as in, "Great question! I'm so glad you asked, Aston," even if you'd rather move on, so that students realize that you really do want them to ask questions.

The Impact Set

The purpose of the Impact Set is to implement and follow the decisions made in the Pre- Impact Set. This is when the learners are engaged in active participation, following through with the Pre-Impact decisions: they are performing, practicing, observing, doing, giving feedback. The Impact Set in every episode includes the following:

1. Expectations
   a) Behaviors, or roles of teacher and learners
   b) Subject matter delivery or demonstration
   c) Logistics
2. Action

> *The Impact Set in every episode includes:*
>
> 1. *Expectations*
>   a) *Behaviors of teacher and learners (roles)*
>   b) *Subject matter delivery (demonstration)*
>   c) *Logistics*
> 2. *Action*

Expectations: Behaviors or roles

It is imperative that your students know and understand your expectations for a given episode. Certain behavior is tacitly understood in many classes. Most students in intermediate and advanced classes understand how they are expected to respond to given cues. However, in beginning or elementary classes you cannot assume that students intrinsically know what to do, and need to make these behavioral expectations clear. Take the time to explain expected behaviors, regardless of level or subject, when facing new students—in a master class, on the first day of a session or with "drop-in" or one-time students—or when using a new Style with a class for the first time.

> **_Tip_**: *If you've ever taught a class and wondered, "Why are they acting this way?!" then you've probably experienced an expectation gap, a dissonance between student expectations and your expectations. Let's face it, students do space out, are inattentive, or seem to be following a different set of rules, but if you have a class or students who do this consistently and it bothers you, you probably have an expectation gap. Consider making certain expectations very clear, either by addressing the class as a whole or talking privately with those certain students. Remember that teaching and learning involve an interaction or relationship, and if that interaction or relationship is frustrating to one or both of you, you have it within your power to change it.*

When using a variety of Spectrum Styles, the explanation of expectations makes it clear that the particular relationship between teacher and student will vary from Style to Style, and that in the Style for the current episode, certain behaviors are expected. As students become familiar with the expectations for a particular Style, the teacher can simply announce the name of the Style and move on to delivery of the subject matter. This is often made easier by use of the Classroom Charts, listed at the end of the book, which may be posted in the classroom.

> **_Tip_**: *Download the classroom charts, enlarge, print and laminate them as posters. Display or keep rolled up until you're ready to use for a particular Style in class.*

The initial introduction or explanation for a given Style is very important, because it shapes not only how students will approach the task, but how they will relate to the teacher, to each other, and to dance. Consider the following examples:

- "We'll do this as Cued Response: I will stand at the front of the room to demonstrate the sequence. Watch closely during the demonstration and listen for descriptions of steps. Then you may ask questions. When questions have been answered, we'll all do it together. (Demonstrates and deals with questions.) Now please start in first position, arms en bas, port de bras á la second during the 8-count introduction of the music, then begin."
- "Let's practice this in Reciprocal. The purpose of this Style is to work with a partner and learn to offer feedback to that partner. Each partner will have the opportunity to do both roles. To clarify the role of each person in the Doer-Observer-Teacher Triad...."

> **_To Do_**: *To illustrate the importance of defining expectations, consider the two following situations.*
>
> *Teacher One stands at the piano and gives a quick verbal description of the phrase in dance terminology, then cues the pianist to begin. In another class, Teacher Two stands at the barre and performs a full demonstration while giving counts, repeats the demonstration on the other side, then asks if students have any questions. Students who are accustomed to the expectations of one teacher and then take class with the other will likely be frustrated due to dissonance between the expectations of teacher and students.*
>
> *1. Identify some of the problems that might arise for the students of Teacher One who then take a class with Teacher Two.*
> *2. Identify some of the problems that might arise for students of Teacher Two who then take a class with Teacher One.*
> *3. Reflect on your expectations for a class from your perspective as teacher. Consider the problems that students might encounter, and identify how you will explain your expectations to students.*

Expectations: Subject matter delivery or demonstration

When the objective of the class is to copy, reproduce or approximate a movement or phrase, as in most technique, international folk dance, ballroom and aerobics classes, a demonstration is provided as part of the Impact Set. For tasks that have a model for performance, the whole task, its parts, and terminology are demonstrated. This establishes *criteria* for students to follow. The demonstration may be by you, a student you have chosen, a videotape, or pictures.

You then explain any details necessary for understanding the task. The amount of time for delivery or demonstration and explanation will vary. For some tasks only a demonstration is needed, for others a detailed verbal description may be necessary; an explanation without a demonstration is used for episodes that use Styles in the Production cluster of the Spectrum.

Expectations: Logistics

Logistical concerns in dance typically fall into three main categories:

A. Spatial organization. Learners may be organized into lines, circles, or randomly, to allow efficient participation in the activity and interaction with the teacher.
   - "Spread out and find a place where you're not touching anyone or anything, and can see me."
   - "Get a partner and form a double circle, holding hands in promenade position."
   - "Escort your partner to a clear space on the ballroom floor and face a counter-clockwise line of direction in closed social dance position."
   - "Please sit in your assigned seat."
   - "Two by two across the floor from corner number three."
B. Equipment. In the dance class, equipment is often minimal, but probably includes a musical accompaniment (such as piano, drum, compact disk or cassette player), a chalkboard, whiteboard, or smartboard, and sometimes a projector. Equipment can be used effectively when organized to facilitate maximum learning for each student with minimal waiting. For example,
   - During a special episode in a technique class, the following stations may be set up: a video taken during last week's class so that students can observe and critique themselves, a computer with the video demonstrating and describing specific steps, a poster with criteria sheet and a space for students to work at the barre, mats for students to lie in constructive rest position and practice mental rehearsal, and music for students to work with on the diagonal across the floor.
   - In a dance notation class, stations may be set up for students to practice dictation from a video demonstration, work on the computer using notation software, and practice sight-reading scores.
C. Task sheets. A task sheet may be in the form of a single-sheet handout for each student or pair of students, a poster, or a transparency projected on the wall. Most students benefit from having a written reminder of key points, so task sheets can contribute tremendously to the learning experience.

The three "expectations" may be delivered in any order depending on the objectives and needs of the lesson. Deliver the three expectations separately, however, rather than together, to avoid confusing or distracting learners.

Logistics typically request learners to move, so deliver these as the last of the expectations to avoid interfering with observing and listening. An example of a confusing or distracting delivery of expectations is the following:

Teacher: "OK, everyone, get a partner and we'll work in pairs in Reciprocal Style. Sarah is passing out criteria sheets, so please get one from her. Decide who will be the Doer and Follower first, spread out and find a good spot to work. Now watch as I demonstrate...."

You've lost the students' attention to the logistics of deciding who goes first and where they're going to relocate, getting criteria sheets, general talking, and other distractions.

_To Do_:
Determine a more effective order and strategy to deliver expectations in the example above.

Action

This is when the learners are engaged in active participation: they are performing, practicing, observing, dancing. Keep necessary explanations concise and clear, and remember that the primary purpose of explanations is to clarify the "doing-ness" of the class: that time when students are actively engaged in the subject matter of the class, whether it is observing, writing, choreographing, improvising, performing an eight- measure jazz sequence or dancing an exuberant jitterbug.

The Post-Impact Set

The purpose of the Post-Impact Set is to assess the performance of tasks done during the Impact Set and give appropriate feedback to the learner. This set of decisions gives information to the learner about the performance of the task, and also about the learner's role in following the teacher's decisions. The Post-Impact Set also deals with decisions about evaluating the congruence between intent in the Pre-Impact Set and action in the Impact Set, which determines if you need to make changes in the next episode. As with any evaluative procedure, these decisions are made in the following sequence:

1. Gather information concerning the learner's performance in the Impact Set. In the dance class, this typically involves observing, sometimes listening and/or touching.
2. Assess the information against criteria. By comparing and contrasting the information about the learner's performance with your set criteria or model, you can make decisions concerning performance and thus feedback.
3. Provide feedback to the learner. These decisions involve *how* to provide feedback and *what kind* of feedback to offer the learner. Feedback can be given immediately or delayed until a certain time, and may be verbal, gestural, or written (more on feedback in the next chapter).
4. Answer or deal with questions. After you provide feedback, you'll decide how to treat questions.
5. Assess the chosen teaching Style. Analyze and decide about the effectiveness of the chosen teaching Style and its impact on your students.
6. Assess anticipated learning style. Categories 5 and 6 are concerned with *congruity between intent and action*. In connection with the previous decisions, decide whether your students reached the objectives of this episode.

> *The Post-Impact Set:*
> 1. *Gather and assess information*
> 2. *Provide feedback*
> 3. *Answer questions*
> 4. *Assess congruity between intent and action*
> 5. *Adjustments*

7. <u>Adjustments</u>. What, if any, adjustments will you need to make for subsequent episodes in order to provide more congruity between intent and action?
8. <u>Other</u>.

The Post-Impact Set of decisions offers feedback to students about the performance of the task, and about their role in following your decisions. Information or corrections on posture can be done through the various modes of communication: verbally, kinesthetically through hands-on correction, with a visual demonstration, using a videotape, with wall posters or charts, with assigned readings. Delivery of feedback may be different depending on the Style for the teaching episode; for example, feedback may be delivered by you to individual students or to the class as a whole, by students to each other, or by students to themselves.

<u>Adjustment decisions</u> are concerned with how to deal with the gap between the ideal and the real. Respect failure, because it enables success. Life is not perfect; neither is a plan, and when mistakes or mishaps occur, what is important is how you deal with them. When this occurs, you will make adjustment decisions in one of three ways:
1. You can choose to ignore the problem, which may result in frustration.
2. You can identify the decision that caused the problem, correct it, and continue with the teaching episode.
3. If the problem is severe, you may decide to terminate the episode and move on to another activity.

As one teacher put it, teaching is messy, no teaching is perfect, and there is no such thing as a perfect class. Remember that your goal is not to attempt to teach the perfect class, but to reflect on your students and the subject matter, and choose a teaching Style that will bring these together to accomplish your chosen objectives.

> *Life is not perfect; mistakes or mishaps occur. Respect failure; it enables success.*

For example, you may demonstrate a phrase and, after the music begins and students attempt it, you see that many students are struggling. Or, when using a checklist, you might discover that the checklist is incorrect, or upon reflection you discern that it is not adequately detailed. Identify the problem and decide whether intervention and information will rectify the problem, or if it is time to switch to another teaching Style or move on to another task.

> *Problems such as the ones mentioned above will arise. Don't give up by saying, "I tried it and it didn't work." Benjamin Franklin's statement, "Nothing ventured, nothing gained," urges us to try out new ideas. If you were following directions to arrive at a friend's house for a special dinner invitation and you got lost, you wouldn't just give up and go home. Figure out where you took an incorrect turn and get back on track— arriving at your goal is worth the effort.*

Decisions in the Pre-Impact Set may occur prior to the face-to-face interaction between teacher and learners, as when the teacher does the pre-class planning. However, these Sets can be somewhat fluid and overlapping. It is possible for adjustment decisions to occur during Impact or Post-Impact Sets during

> *When one teaching Style is not working at any particular moment, switch to an episode in another Style.*

one episode which form the Pre-Impact Set for a subsequent episode. For example, as you observe your class during the warm-up, you realize that you need to make a change in what you had planned for later in the class. Often you're evaluating, making adjustments, and re-structuring a lesson as students are doing a phrase. For example, you have planned (Pre-Impact Set) to cover certain material using a specific Style, but as students are doing the phrase (Impact Set) you evaluate their performance (Post-Impact Set) and make a mental change in the second part of the phrase (Pre-Impact Set). In other words, you deliberately switch gears on the fly.

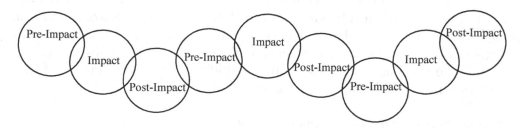

Planning

"'Would you tell me, please, which way I ought to walk from here?'
'That depends a good deal on where you want to get to,' said the Cat.
'I don't much care where—' said Alice.
'Then it doesn't matter which way you walk,' said the Cat.
'—so long as I get *somewhere*,' Alice added as an explanation.
'Oh, you're sure to do that,' said the Cat, 'if you only walk long enough.'"[16]

The "Alice in Wonderland" approach to curricular design: just go for a while and you'll end up *somewhere*. While sometimes desirable to allow the material or students to take you along an unknown path, generally when you embark on a journey, you have at least a vague idea of where you want to arrive. If you're in New York and want to get to France, you've got to point your ship east and keep your hand on the helm.

Remember "telesis?" Plan and direct the progress of your class. Teaching involves planning; planning involves deciding where you want to go and the steps you will take to arrive at your destination. Teachers often think of "lesson planning", but it is essential to look beyond the singular lesson to how that lesson fits into the larger picture. Plan for the semester, session, year, whatever the structure of your studio or school. Planning involves a cyclical process of reviewing your goals for the entire course, each lesson within the course, and reflecting on how each episode within the lesson contributes to your goals.

Why, What, How?

In order to get to plan your progress and arrive at your destination, three big questions to ask are *Why?*, *What?*, and *How?* Don't just charge in and include things in class just because it's always been done that way. Question, reflect, prioritize, select. Knowing **why** will help you to choose **what**, and will guide you in **how** to present it. The answers to the questions below will enable you to make decisions concerning subject matter, Style, and other choices.

1. **Why** are you teaching this class? Identifying the *purpose*, your *philosophy*, and the *needs of the students* will help you to select material.

2. **What** do you want to include? The priorities, philosophy and purpose you identify will enable you to prioritize: select or create actions, sequences, phrases, and steps to carry out your goals.
3. **How** will you approach this material? Choose the Style that will be most effective.

As a teacher, you not only choose what material to cover, you also choose how to organize and present it. Following are just two (of many) different ways to organize a course in world or international folk and ethnic dance. The first focuses on dance as a reflection of culture with units for dances from various countries or regions. The second focuses on relationships (partner, group), formations and the psychomotor skills of dance with units for learning the basics steps, working with a partner, and working with a group.

Example: International Folk Dance (a socio-cultural approach)
Unit 1: Introduction to the basics
- World dance as a reflection of culture
- Diversity and cultural awareness
- Roles of men and women
- Dance as individual expression; dance as cultural tradition
- Watch and discuss video, "Sex and Social Dance" from *Dancing* series Unit 2: Dances of North America
- Reading and discussion of origins and influences of dances of Canada and the United States
- Cowboy Boogie, Cotton-eyed Joe, Virginia Reel, La Bastringe, etc.
Unit 3: Dances of the British Isles
- Reading and discussion of influences and origins of dances of Ireland, Great Britain, Scotland
Unit 4: Eastern Europe…and so forth

Example: International Folk Dance (a psychomotor approach)
Unit 1: Introduction to the basics
- Definitions:
  o Time: Tempo, meter, beat, accent, measure
  o Space: Formations and positions
  o Basic Actions: Step vs. touch; elevations (jump, hop, leap, etc.)
- Basic steps and their application
  o Two-step: Cotton-eyed Joe, Gie Gordons
  o Schottische: Bummel Schottische, Korobushka
  o Polka: Heel & Toe Polka, Doudlebska Polka,
  o Grapevine: Cowboy Boogie
  o And so forth
Unit 2: Formations: Working as an individual (C&W line dances such as Cowboy Boogie), as a member of the group, as a couple, etc.
- Closed circle, non-gender specific dances: Alunelul
- Broken circle, non-gender specific dances: Hora, Hasapikos, Misirlou
Unit 3: Your relationship to a partner: Working as a couple, gender roles, etc.
- Contra: Virginia Reel
- Couple dances: Gie Gordons, Road to the Isles, Cowboy Cha-cha
- Double circle couple dances: Klumpkojis, Korobushka
Unit 4: Your relationship to each member of the group
- Square dances: definitions and relationships: partner, corner, opposite, right-hand lady, etc; head couple (or head & foot), side couples. Texas Star, Arkansas Traveller…and so forth.

Structuring the Lesson
Structuring the lesson gives direction and purpose to your teaching. Lessons should follow a planned order. The simplest plan is to start with an introductory activity, such as a warm- up

(dance technique), mixer (ballroom dance), reading, story, or video (folk dance or creative dance) or explanation (improvisation or choreography). Then review previous material, especially if new material builds on it. Next is activity for synthesis, practice, or creation, depending on the nature of the class. Finally, a wrap-up, conclusion or closing action. In general, move from the old to the new; from introduction to synthesis or creation, from small to large; from personal to shared space.

Even though classes in folk dance or social dance don't need the same type of warm-up as for dance technique, some kind of introductory activity is needed: remember that warm-ups function in the affective and social domains as well as the psychomotor domain. The order and content of the lesson will vary with the material selected for the class. Some other examples include:

Modern dance
1. Warm-up
2. Movement combinations:
    a. Axial (turns, elevations)
    b. Locomotor
3. Creative problem-solving
    a. Presentation of a problem
    b. Student experimentation with the problem
    c. Presentation of problem solutions and evaluation
4. Warm-down and/or wrap-up

Ballet
1. Barre: move from small to large: Tendus, plies, ronds de jambe, etc.
2. Center floor adagio
3. Petit allegro
4. Center floor turns
5. Grand allegro
6. Reverence

Creative dance for children (theme: tight and loose qualities of movement)[17]
1. Name game
2. Warm-up sequence
3. Exploration of elements with cross-overs: for example, explore tightness with shapes, steps, moves, etc, then explore looseness with shapes, steps, moves, etc.
4. "The dance of the Spaghetti Monsters"
5. Goodbye dance

Social or Ballroom dance
1. Greeting: Ask students how they are, who danced since last week, etc.
2. Have pairs review dance steps and figures that they remember from last class.
3. Introduce a new step or move and allow them to practice for 2-3 songs
4. Have men and women trade roles. After the song, let them share their experiences with each other/ the group; discuss what it means to lead and to follow, what skills these roles have in common, what skills are specific to each.

International folk dance
1. Start with an easy mixer.
2. Ask students which previous dances they'd like to dance today.
3. Introduce new dances

4. Divide students into groups and have them create a new dance, or a variation for a step in an existing dance.
5. Show the variations or dances.

The "Introduce, Review, Build" Cycle

In general, every class will involve a cycle of activity and information: basic material will be *introduced*, then *reviewed*, then *built upon* in subsequent episodes or lessons. This is "episode building."

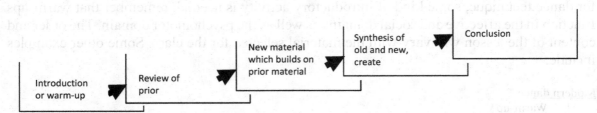

The following is one way to organize a modern dance course which meets for two hours three times a week. Notice that basic material is *introduced*, then *reviewed*, then *built upon* in subsequent lessons, and the content includes time to experience the movement theme, idea or concept improvisationally and in group compositions. Each week is a separate unit which builds on previous units.

Modern Dance

Week 1: Introduction to the basics such as expectations, vocabulary, parts of class, protocols.
- Day 1:
  - o Go over syllabus: expectations and requirements of attire, attendance, written assignments, quizzes, final movement exam and final written exam.
  - o Discuss aspects of dance study including the kinesiological/anatomical, historical/theoretical, and aesthetic.
  - o Through interactive and experiential activities, individually and with partners, **introduce** students to terms including axial/locomotor; levels (high, middle, low), directions (forward, backward, sideways), qualities (just strong and light today), beat, rhythm, body design, group design.
  - o **Introduce** vocabulary of improvisation and composition.
- Day 2:
  - o Discuss functions of a warm-up (for more detail, see "Warm-up" below.
  - o **Introduce** core warm-up lying on floor: pelvic tilts, hip flexion, curl-up sequences.
  - o **Introduce** stretching sequences: First and second position sitting.
  - o **Introduce** standing axial sequence: Pliés in first with port de bras and "roll-down" port de corps, brushes (tendus) from first position.
  - o **Introduce** "traveling across the diagonal":
    - Walking with a partner.
    - With music, attending to beat and tempo, pairs entering every 8 counts.
    - With music, attending to which foot (right or left) initiates first step.
    - With a run.
- Day 3:
  - o **Review** previous warm-up material lying on floor. **Add** leg extension.
  - o **Review** previous sitting stretches. **Add** fourth position circle stretch (quads).
  - o **Review** plié sequence. **Add** second position with lateral tilt port de corps.
  - o **Review** brushes (tendus). **Add** dégagés.
  - o **Review** traveling across the diagonal. **Add** walks with quarter notes vs. half notes ("quick, quick, quick, quick, slow, slow").
  - o **Discuss** further the concept of note value: whole notes; half, quarter, and eighth notes.

- o **Experiential**: Divide class into four groups; each group moves as a specific note value.
- o Rotate so that each group experiences moving with each note value.
- o Have each group create a brief phrase that includes at least three of the four note values. Discuss having a beginning, middle and end. Have each group show their study; discuss (this is an opportunity to re-inforce concepts such as levels, directions, body design, group design). Suggest that they do stretches in first and second positions over the weekend, and wish the class a great weekend.

Week 2: Note Values
- • Day 1:
  - o Warm-up: **Review** previous material. **Add** "boomerang" (envelope) leg to core sequence, spiral extensions, third position pliés, grand battements.
  - o Across-the-floor: Note Values phrase
  - o Experiential: Introduce Motif Writing hand-out (Units of Action), go through each symbol/ concept with movement.
- • Day 2:
  - o Warm-up: **Review** previous material.
  - o Across-the-floor: **Review** Note Values phrase
  - o Experiential: **Introduce** Laban direction symbols; have students experience and experiment with using different body parts, locomotor & axial, small and large, etc.
- • Day 3:
  - o Warm-up: **Introduce:** student-centered warm-up: flex/extend/rotate/circle at each joint, with focus on kinesthetic awareness and choice of speed/direction for every action.
  - o Experiential: Have students work in groups or pairs to review Note Values phrase and use Motif Writing to score the phrase. Have groups exchange scores to reinforce underlying concepts, compare and contrast choices and strategies. Suggest that they listen to and "count out" music this weekend, and wish the class a wonderful weekend.

Week 3: Directions
- • Day 1: **Review** warm-ups; **Add** next level. **Introduce** Directions phrase
- • Day 2: **Review** and **add**. **Review** Directions phrase
- • Day 3: Student-centered warm-up, this time focusing on spatial concepts of direction, level, body
- • parts. Use motif writing and Laban symbols to score Directions Phrase. Share and discuss; answer questions.
- • Week 4: Pathways
- • Week 5: Falls
- • Week 6: Turns
- • Week 7: Elevations…and so forth

Lead-Ups and Break-Downs

Lead-ups and break-downs enable you to use a conceptual approach to dance technique, to create comprehensive understanding by relating one skill to others which share certain characteristics. A lead-up is a planned series of class phrases or sequences, each of which contains part of the longer main sequence being presented, which is presented and performed prior to the longer main sequence. A break-down involves dissecting one aspect of a skill, after presenting the main sequence. Let's take a look at each of these.

Lead-ups are activities that lead students on the path to generalized knowledge and ability; to enable them to link skills with understanding. For example, students can learn that certain principles govern rotations like ronds de jambe en dehors, and these are related to turns such as pirouettes en dehors; or that ronds de jambe en dedans relate to piqué turns en dedans. Students will then be better equipped to analyze the directions of turns in a complex combination and how to stabilize the core and provide more torque or rotational force for the type of turn. Lead-ups such as brushes or degagés across the floor in jazz class will enable students to have better leaps. Using proper terminology for the 5 basic elevations (i.e., jump, hop, leap, sissonne, assemblé), and teaching students how to analyze and differentiate among them, will enable students to recognize these elevations. This will, in turn, enable students to pick up combinations more quickly and effectively.

Rather than teach an across-the-floor combination as a whole from start to finish, analyze its component parts so students can practice each concept as part of a shorter phrase, to enable students to focus on and embody each concept or section individually, and to understand it better and more deeply, before putting it into the longer overall combination.

For example, a locomotor combination may include slides or chassés, a turn, jump, fall, rise, and leap. Identify each essential skills and put it into a shorter repeated phrase so that students first practice the slides or chassés across the floor with the arms and/or focus needed for this particular sequence. Because this part of the combination is short and simple, students can really focus on doing it completely; for example, using the 3 "F's" of feet, focus, and fingers.

Then practice the turn, which might be, "step, step, turn, pause", again with the arms, spotting, and other skills specific to the combination. Again, because the sequence is short, remembering what comes next is less of an issue, and students can focus attention on doing the turn well. Do the same with the "fall and rise" part of the combination as a short across-the-floor combination, and then do the same with the leap.

Now start to assemble it with the linking steps, or shifts of weight, or whatever transitions are needed to bring it all together. While it may take longer to get through to the end of the combination or the dance, you are equipping your students with the necessary understanding and analytical skills to be better and more intelligent dancers.

Break-Downs are when you and the students are working through a sequence or combination and stop to dissect one aspect of a skill within it: break it down into its smaller component parts. For example: students are learning a new combination but are having trouble with one part of it. Experience will tell you where you will typically need to break something down. Welcome opportunities to break something down; it gives the class the opportunity to explore a skill or concept in more depth. To solicit questions and encourage critical thinking, ask students what they would like to break down or detail in a combination or phrase, and use Style F: Guided Discovery. This helps take dance beyond "just doing the movement" to greater understanding.

Lead-ups and break-downs are essential to effective teaching in several ways. First, they enable you and the students to introduce and/or go over class material in smaller, more manageable bites. For students, being faced with a long and complex chain of movement can be like trying to drink from a fire hydrant—too much, too fast. Most importantly, lead-ups and break-downs enable students to really understand, rather than just superficially copying, aspects of dance material as concepts: for example, use of feet in elevations and turns, characteristic use or shapes of arm, how the torso initiates or reacts to changes of weight in the feet.

Selecting a Style for Your Objectives

The Spectrum ranges from one extreme, in which you make all the decisions, to the opposite extreme in which the learner makes all the decisions, and the many Styles in between. In planning a class, first consider the objectives of the class. This has long been standard pedagogical practice. However, your approach and delivery of the subject matter will produce a particular set of outcomes that may or may not match your intended objectives.

> Every deliberate act of teaching is a result of a decision that affects the thinking, feeling, and behavior of both the teachers and students.

Not only is it important to consider the objective for an episode and select a Style which will facilitate students' achieving that as an outcome, but it is also important to consider overall long-term objectives for the unit or course.

- If one of your objectives is for students to learn to accurately access their own performance, give themselves feedback, to understand what needs improvement and how to go about improving, a series of episodes in Styles B-E will have a greater chance of success than episodes exclusively in Style A: Cued Response.
- If your objective is for all students to learn phrases, a dance or dances quickly, accurately, and uniformly, Style A: Cued Response will be a more appropriate choice than the discovery and production Styles.
- If your objective is for students to experiment, explore, and create new movements and phrases, the production Styles G and H will be more appropriate than reproduction Styles.

Writing Unit and Lesson Plans

Planning classes is similar to learning to dance or drive: At first, you think of every detail ("point the foot, turn out the thigh and engage the abdominals"; "put your foot on the brake, turn on the engine, put the car in gear"), and at first, your planning will probably be very detailed and explicit, but eventually much of the planning will become second nature.

In planning units, lessons and episodes, consider the following[18]:

> Don't just plan a lesson. Plan the lesson as part of the whole course.

1. Subject Matter: Subject matter refers to the genre or aspect of dance and level, such as advanced jazz, beginning ballroom dance, elementary dance notation.
2. The Overall Objectives of the Lesson: Objectives state in broad terms what the learners are expected to have accomplished by the end of the unit or lesson: what you want to accomplish.
   Week or Lesson Number: This information gives the temporal location of the episode within the lesson and the lesson in relation to other lessons, such as, "Day 2, Week 3," "Tuesday, Week 4."
3. Episode Number: A lesson is typically composed of several episodes in different Styles, so listing the episodes helps you envision how the class will unfold. For example, the first episode might be a warm-up in Cued Response, the second episode working with partners on a previous dance phrase in Reciprocal, then working individually in Self-Check on another combination, and returning to Cued Response for a large locomotor phrase.
4. Specific Tasks: Identify and describe the specific tasks that the learners will engage in to accomplish the overall objectives of the episode. What are they doing: side falls in modern dance, the time step in tap class, a 32-count phrase in jazz class, performing and observing choreographed studies.
5. Objectives of the Episode: This can refer to a particular *step* such as the waltz box step or a pas de chat, or how dancers exhibit certain *qualities* such as application of Laban's

Efforts, or how learners engage and develop certain *behaviors*, such as socialization and cooperation.

6. <u>Style</u>: Identify which teaching Style will accomplish which objectives.
7. <u>Logistics</u>: Decisions concerning logistics in dance typically fall into three main categories:
   A. <u>Spatial organization</u>. Dancers may be organized into lines, circles, or randomly spaced, whichever you determine will enable your students to have efficient participation in the activity and interaction with you as the teacher.
   B. <u>Equipment</u>. In the dance class, equipment is minimal and may include a musical accompaniment (i.e., piano, drum, MP3, online link); a chalkboard, smartboard or whiteboard; and sometimes a DVD player or Youtube video. Most dance technique classes do not use much equipment, but equipment can be used effectively when organized to facilitate maximum learning for each student with minimal waiting. For example students may work at different "stations" which utilize a video from a previous class or an instructional video (such as the Video Dictionary of Classical Ballet), a wall chart listing important aspects of a movement or phrase, a computer.
   C. <u>Task sheet</u>. A task sheet may be in the form of a single-sheet handout for each student or pair of students, a poster, or a transparency projected on the wall. Most dance teachers use verbal description and visual demonstration, but task sheets can contribute tremendously to the learning experience. Most students benefit from having a written reminder of key points.
8. <u>Time</u>. Decide on a reasonable length of time for the episode to allow for most, if not all, learners to reach your objectives. The amount of time allotted depends on the complexity and length of the task or dance phrase, the objectives, and the capability of the learners. Planning a time for an episode helps you manage and balance class time, keep the class moving along, and helps prevent getting bogged down in any particular part of class. Have you ever had the experience of never getting to the "good stuff" you had planned for the end of class because certain activities at the beginning always took too long? Planning a particular length for an episode is designed to help you proactively troubleshoot.
9. <u>Comments</u>. This space on a lesson plan is for statements, questions or suggestions after the conclusion of the lesson, such as what didn't work, ideas for the next lesson, etc. Reflect on your lesson, how you delivered it, and how students reacted, to give yourself feedback. The process of reflecting on classes and thinking proactively helps you to improve your teaching.

While it is often tempting to jump into planning the first lesson, (as in, "Yikes, I'm teaching this class tomorrow!"), start by mapping out the overall course and units first. Consider the following unit and lesson plans:

1. The first one is a blank unit plan,
2. The second is an example of a unit plan for a modern dance class,
3. The third is a blank lesson plan,
4. The fourth is a lesson plan listing the episodes in one lesson in the modern dance class introducing falls in Style C: Reciprocal Style,
5. The fifth is a lesson plan for a children's dance class which focuses on elevations.

Unit Plan

Name:
Subject:
Overall Objectives:

Week No.	Subject Matter	Objectives	Style	Logistics	Music	Time	Comments
	What will you do?	*Why* are you doing it? The Learning Focus	*How* do you present it?	*What* do you need to organize?	*What* music do you need to have ready?	*How long* will it take?	*How* did it go?

SAMPLE Unit Plan

Name:

Subject:

Overall Objectives:

Week No.	Subject Matter	Objectives	Style	Logistics	Music	Time	Comments
	What will you do?	**Why** are you doing it? The Learning Focus	**How** do you present it?	**What** do you need to organize?	**What** music do you need to have ready?	**How long** will it take?	**How** did it go? And miscellaneous comments.
1	*Introduction to concepts of time (beat, note values, meter, acceleration, deceleration), space (axial/locomotor; near/far; high, middle, low levels), qualities of movement (strong/light, free/bound)*	*For students to enjoy moving freely within the dance studio, get to know each other, and become experientially familiar with the basic vocabulary of the dance medium.*	*Discovery Styles: F: Guided Discovery and G: Convergent Discovery*	*Expect initial self-consciousness, so be prepared with energetic, up-beat music; be very specific with tasks. Take time to thoroughly explore each concept.*	*Mickey Hart: At The Edge*	*Two 2-hour classes*	*On 3rd day, show video, "Power of Dance" from Dancing series, discuss.*
2	*Introduction to dance technique: Warm-up: *Core *Sitting stretches*	*To understand spatial organization in the dance class: axial/floor work, locomotor sequences on the diagonal. To learn basic dance vocabulary.*	*Reproduction Styles: A: Cued Response*	*Task sheets for warm-up; Practice chart and explain roles and expectations. Explain spatial organization and take time to organize lines & rows for floor work, to organize lines for across-the-floor sequence, pairs in diagonal work; take time to work with students on getting themselves organized spatially and temporally.*	*Brent Lewis: Mumbo Jumbo Patrick O'Hearn: Sacred Heart*	*Two 2-hr. class*	*On day 3, do self-directed warm-up and structured improvisation in mirroring, responding.*
3	*Note Values Phrase. Expand on the warm-up. Introduce Motif Writing symbols*	*For students to understand symbol systems for dance and how to use them to analyze movement, record sequences, and enable creative and individual expression.*	*C: Reciprocal*	*Criteria sheets for plies, poster of Style C: Reciprocal.*		*Three 2-hr. classes*	*On day 3, use self-directed stretching.*
4	*Directions phrase. Introduce Directions symbols. Review Motif Writing symbols*	*More application of analyzing, writing and reading skills*	*Style D: Self-Check*	*Have criteria sheets and Style D: Self-Check poster*	*Brent Lewis: Jungle Sugar*	*Three 2-hr. classes*	*On day 3, yoga and relaxation.*

Lesson Plan

Name:
Subject:
Overall Objectives:

Episode	Subject Matter	Objectives	Style	Logistics	Music	Time	Comments
	Specific Tasks	*Why* are you doing it? The Learning Focus	*How* do you present it	*What* do you need to organize?	*What* music do you need to have ready?	*How long* will it take?	*How* did it go?

Subject: Elementary modern/contemporary dance technique   Week: 5

Overall objectives: Introduce falls, Reciprocal Style, use Guided Discovery dialectic (see example Chapter 8)

Episode #	Subject Matter Specific Tasks	Objectives Learning focus	Style	Logistics	Time	Comments
1	"What is a fall? What is the one essential element of a fall?" "Temporary loss of balance!"	Understand nature of falls, physics of a fall, explore different falls.	F Guided Discovery	Students sitting informally on the floor.	5 min.	
2	Do basic floor warm-up that we've been working on for three weeks.	Have students focus on the sensation of gravity in the body during the warm-up.	A Cued Response	Students on the floor in self- selected places in lines and rows.	30 min	
3	Introduce sitting side fall	Have students organize mind/body to roll through side fall, prepare for kneeling fall.	B Practice	Students choose location, facing, etc. Have task sheets.	5 min.	
4	Kneeling side fall	Introduce Reciprocal; prepare for full standing fall.	C Reciprocal	Have students get partner nearest them. Distribute checklists.	15 min.	
5	Full standing fall	Understand and trust off-balance.	B Practice	Students on the floor in self- selected places in lines and rows.	10 min.	
6	Dance phrase with partial and full falls	Learn to incorporate falls within a dance phrase.	A Cued Response	Students spread out informally or in lines and rows to learn dance phrase.	20 min.	
Etc.						

Sample Lesson Plan

Name:

Subject: 5-6 yr. olds

Overall Objectives: Teach children about different elevations

Ep. No.	Subject Matter	Objectives	Style	Logistics	Music	Time	Comments
1	Do basic floor warm-up	Stretch the body and warm up muscles	A: Cued Response	Students on floor in circle	Sing or chant	10 min.	
2	Barre exercises: Plies in first and second position	Help students understand body alignment	A: Cued Response	Students lined up at barre	Ballet for Beginners: plies	5 min	
3	Go through different elevations: hop, jump, leap.	Inform children of differences in elevations	F: Guided Discovery	Center floor spread out (Perfect Spot)	Ballet for Beginners : Jumps	10 min	
4	Jumping from high levels, from middle and low levels	Show difference in doing elevations from different positions. Prepare for Popcorn Dance	G: Convergent Discovery	Center floor spread out	Offenbach Can-Can	5 min	
5	Popcorn Dance	Use what we learned in class to create a dance about popcorn	H: Divergent Discovery	Start together in a huddle with small hops roll out, big jumps, leaps around room, finish in big exploded shape!	Trisch-Trasch Polka	10 min.	
6	Jello (relaxing)	Relax muscles, calm down	A: Cued Response	Spread out, lying on floor, Perfect Spot	Pachelbel Canon	5 min.	
7							
8							
etc							

The Telesis of Teaching

Whether you've taught before or are about to embark on teaching as a new journey, get in the habit of keeping and organizing materials and planning carefully; it will help immensely and make your work more efficient, consistent, satisfying, and enjoyable.

Remember the self-transformative nature of teaching: teaching is also learning. Even though teaching should be personally enjoyable and satisfying, accomplish this by putting aside your own personal needs and interests and focusing on your students and subject of dance. Whether your purpose in teaching is on dance as exercise, personal expression, cultural tradition, or performance, certain aspects of organizing the material of dance remain constant.

Become thoroughly familiar with the materials of dance that you will be using in the lesson. Spend time in advance to structure lessons in detail and become completely familiar with the materials you have selected. This will give you a sense of confidence and self-assurance which will carry over to your students. Play through the music you'll be using and become familiar with it. Practice using the proper terminology for the subject. If you plan to use props, take time to explore using them yourself: manipulate the hula hoops, toss the scarves. This will not only help you troubleshoot, it will give you ideas as well.

Establish a filing or "information retrieval" system. Efficiently organized computer files and databases will allow you to find needed information quickly. Keeping lesson and unit plans in digital or e-format means that your teaching can be efficient and consistent. In addition, discovering new material (and re-discovering old material) will keep your teaching and outlook fresh.

Update your outlook. When you first start to teach, you may have trouble switching from the "student" role to the "teacher" role, but in time you will make this shift more readily. In the "teacher" mode, you are in authority, and have certain privileges and responsibilities. To make this shift, you may need to change your attitude toward:

1. Dress style. Whether your training included a strict dress code or allowed students broad ranges of acceptable attire, as a teacher your outfit speaks before you do, and sets the tone for your class. You should be the most professional-looking person in the studio, which includes everything from hair and hygiene, to clothing and footwear.

2. Authority. Realize that aspects of a teaching situation — including class schedules, studio rules and assigned duties — are not set for your convenience. You will often experience conflicts between personal and professional life in time commitments, energy commitments, space commitments. Work to understand both sides of the conflict, think through priorities and responsibilities, discuss them with others, and try to work things out equitably. Make it your goal to be the first to step down when emotions flare. And realize that you are not the center of attention, you are part of a bigger picture which includes everyone from administration to custodial staff, and especially students.

3. Criticism. While you may first feel defensive or resentful when given criticism, be willing to accept it positively, graciously and objectively. Give yourself time to think it through, constructively use criticism that is offered, and learn to grow through the guidance and feedback of others.

4. <u>Work</u>. Teaching is a job and a calling, exhausting and energizing, frustrating and rewarding, and can be more fun than seems possible. Be open and positive, plan well, and teaching dance will be enjoyable.

Finally, remember that you will always have much to learn.

Reflection and Goal-Setting

Teaching is a lot like sailing: You need to chart a course but since you can't control the wind or the tides, every voyage will be different. However, the best sailors don't just leave things to chance; they know the currents, read the weather, and are able to quickly adjusts their sails.

> *A log is a record of important events in managing, operating, and navigating a ship. The log that a captain keeps will include information such as time, date, weather, destination, and passengers. It may also include whether fuel was taken on and engine hours, if the course needed to be changed for weather, maintenance, and even observations such as wildlife such as seabirds and marine mammal sightings, fishing locations, and jokes told by the crew. These can be used to make the next trip easier. Think what information you want to include in your teaching log.*

Most of this book is about how to keep your teaching engaging, enjoyable, and constantly educational for yourself as well as for your students. The way to do that is to constantly be thinking about how to improve your teaching.

<u>Reflection</u> <u>Identify positive aspects of your teaching</u>	Always	Sometimes	Rarely/Never
1. Subject Matter			
a. I use appropriate subject matter			
b. I present subject matter in an interesting and effective way			
c. I use variety in:			
i. Body Parts			
ii. Space			
iii. Time			
iv. Energy			
2. Presenting Subject Matter			
a. I connect with students in a meaningful way.			
b. I use variety in tone and quality in my voice.			
c. The music I select and use has variety and supports my chosen subject material.			
d. I give directives and expectations with confidence.			
e. I detect non-verbal signals from students (knowing when students are off-task, disconnected, out of control, etc.), respond to them, and act on them effectively.			
3. Responding			
a. I detect indications of how students feel (confident, bored, etc.) and respond to them.			
b. I respond effectively to ideas students offer.			
c. I notice and respond to each student at some point in the session.			
d. I bring energy and excitement to the lesson.			

Goal-Setting Identify specific goals to improve your teaching.	Priority	Secondary
1. Subject Matter		
a. I want to work on choosing a greater variety of appropriate subject matter		
b. I want to improve how I present subject matter to make it more interesting and effective		
c. I want to improve using a variety of activities including:		
i. Body Parts		
ii. Space		
iii. Time		
iv. Energy		
2. Presenting Subject Matter		
a. I want to focus on connecting with students in a meaningful way		
b. I need to practice using variety in tone and quality in my voice.		
c. I want to focus on choosing a variety of music which supports my subject material.		
d. I want to practice giving directives and expectations with confidence.		
e. I need to be more conscientious in detecting non-verbal signals from students (knowing when students are off-task, disconnected, out of control, etc.), respond to them, and act on them effectively		
3. Responding		
f. I want to focus on detecting indications of how students feel (confident, bored, etc.) and respond to them.		
g. I want to focus on responding effectively to ideas students offer.		
h. I need to really notice and respond to each student at some point in the session.		
i. I want to bring more energy and excitement to the lesson.		

Chapter Summary

Thoughtful and reflective teaching starts with planning, reflecting, and deciding. Every deliberate act of teaching is a result of a decision that affects the thinking, feeling, and behavior of both the teachers and students. Decisions that are made in the teacher-learner relationship are categorized in 3 sets: the Pre-Impact Set, the Impact Set, and the Post-Impact Set. Episodic teaching enables you to switch from one Style to another in order to reach a variety of objectives. Understanding the dynamics of the pedagogical unit (Ob-T-L-Ou) will help you more fully understand objectives and outcomes, plan how to reach those objectives, and determine whether those objectives have been reached. Reflection on your teaching helps you to make positive changes.

Questions for Reflection and Discussion

1. Define an episode, a lesson, a unit. Give an example of episodic teaching.

2. Why is it useful to use the terminology of "roles" and "behaviors"? What are some of your roles throughout a typical day, week or month?

3. Define the pedagogical unit. What are objectives? What are the two kinds of objectives? What are outcomes?

4. Discuss the relationship formed by Objectives, Teacher, Learner and Outcomes. How does each affect the other?

5. Why is it important to inform students of expectations? Discuss unspoken or tacit expectations in dance classes.

6. Define the 3 decision or Impact Sets. What are some examples of these in a various classes? How do they feed into each other during a class?

7. Identify the decisions in the Pre-Impact Set, the Impact Set, and the Post-Impact Set.

8. Define adjustment decisions in the Post-Impact Set and give examples. Why are adjustment decisions necessary?

9. Why is planning important for the teacher and for the learner? Discuss the essential questions to ask and answer that will guide your planning.

10. Discuss the "review, introduce, build" cycle.

11. Identify and discuss factors to consider when selecting a Style.

12. Discuss the telesis of teaching.

13. Reflect on the quote, "The difference between a beginning teacher and an experienced one is that the beginning teacher asks, 'How am I doing?' and the experienced teacher asks, 'How are the children doing?'" (Esmé Raji Codell).

14. Reflect on the quote, "No one learns as much about a subject as one who is forced to teach it." (Peter F. Drucker).

Ahead

Teaching involves bringing together planning, reflecting, deciding, observing, and giving feedback. Feedback, or communication regarding performance ("How am I doing?") is one of the most important aspects of the teacher-learner connection. Unless students know what they are doing and how it may need to be changed, they will continue to make mistakes. Observation techniques enable teachers to clearly see what and how students are doing. The next chapter details the functions and types of feedback, how it is communicated through various senses and the complexities of using touch as feedback, as well as observation strategies and tailoring feedback for optimal learning.

6 Feedback and Observation

> Look in the mirror.
> That's your
> competition.

Introduction

Feedback refers to the information, judgment, correction, assistance or adjustment given to a student about performance, and is one of the most important factors in successful and efficient skill acquisition in dance. Performance improves faster with accurate feedback than without it. Perhaps most importantly, feedback represents the connection between teacher and student; a connection which is objective as well as deeply personal, intellectual as well as emotional, and artistic.

Feedback can involve information from teacher to student, to a single student or to an entire class. It can also be an invitation to a response, to enable information to flow from students to teacher as well. Furthermore, it can provide for a transactional relationship toward developing analytical skills and critical thinking (Akinleye and Payne, 2016). Through feedback purposefully combined with transparent teaching, students can receive thoughtful and reflective feedback from the teacher, learn how to analyze a peer's performance to give and receive different types of feedback, then how to apply these learned skills to providing feedback to themselves.

Dance is a fleeting, ephemeral activity. Once warm, muscles need to continue moving. The pace of class needs to move to keep attention and maintain interest and excitement. Complex movements flow by quickly. Observing everyone in a group and incorporating feedback while sustaining the energy and action of a class can be a challenge. Due to the rapid and complex nature of the movements in dance, students benefit from guidance in what to attend to and how to make changes.

Just think of everything that has to happen for the lovely flying leap called a grand jeté: the dancer launches into the air, pushing off powerfully with the back leg, keeping it straight, lifting it as high as possible directly behind the body, pointing the back foot into the "wing" shape which looks so beautiful in photographs. Bringing the front leg straight and horizontal to the floor, the dancer maintains as much outward rotation as possible on both legs while keeping the chest lifted and open, shoulders relaxed, with arms shaped in two outwardly and upwardly floating lines, fingers energized but without tension, head turned at exactly the right angle to show off the line of the neck, the gaze dreamily past the audience, a smile which may be mysterious or triumphant depending on the choreography. It occurs in a split second. This does not happen naturally; every micro movement has been learned, thought out, practiced, coached, explored, cultivated, experimented with, and drilled. It is the goal of the teacher to provide feedback to enable students to do it well, to explore various applications of the information, and ultimately, to continue the process on their own.

Different students, at different levels, have different feedback needs. Feedback is a multifaceted and complex phenomenon in dance. The feedback we provide to students involves not just the outcome or shape of the movement, but sensations, sounds, meaning, and motivation. The words "right" and "wrong" are value-laden and many dance teachers don't want to polarize human movement choices to imply that a particular movement should never be done. However, it's OK to tell students, "That sense of lightness is appropriate in ballet, but since the style we're working with is Limón modern dance, we need more of a sense of weight….", or to work with a bandwidth of correctness such as, "Your fourth position can be larger or smaller. For a pirouette, the larger it is the more torque you can achieve for multiple turns, but that also means it will be more difficult to maintain the squareness of the pelvis." It's OK to tell students that a particular movement is inappropriate in a certain context: "That's not what is needed for this dance, but you might remember that for another work," or "That wouldn't be appropriate for rumba, but for bachata …."

In addition, the way in which dance typically has been taught—in an authoritarian, teacher-knows-best, no-talking-allowed format—has not exactly embraced dialog and interaction for the purpose of developing critical thinking. Technique need not be approached only as a specific set of skills to be mastered, but also as a way of learning more about the individual thinking body. While feedback from a teacher is important for improvement, it must also be part of a larger picture toward enabling students to become more observant, analytical, and self-aware.

Details of Feedback
One important role for a teacher is to provide information to students concerning successes, errors, adjustments and other aspects of in-class performance. To better understand feedback, it is important to look at factors such as its origin and timing, function and purpose, and how it is communicated: the where, when, which, how, why, and what.

Intrinsic/Extrinsic
Feedback may originate from within or from outside the individual. *Intrinsic* feedback can be felt through touch or proprioception (also called kinesthesia, or the sensation of the body's movement in space). It can be heard, as sounds in tap dance, or seen by students. It may occur during movement or as

Intrinsic feedback comes from inside (feeling the movement). *Extrinsic* feedback comes from outside (seeing or hearing about the movement).

a result of movement. *Extrinsic* feedback, also called augmented feedback, is information from an outside source, supplementing a student's own sensory information or intrinsic feedback.

Timing: Concurrent/Terminal

Concurrent feedback is provided while the dancer is moving.
Terminal feedback is provided after the movement is completed.

The timing of feedback delivery is important. *Concurrent* feedback is provided while the student is moving; for example, telling students to work through the arch of the foot while they are doing a tendu sequence at the barre, or the sensations that occur during movement, such as feeling the heel maintaining contact with the floor in a demi plié. *Terminal* feedback occurs after the movement is completed; for example, after watching a student do a center-floor sequence several times, "You fall backward every time you do the twilt. Remember to engage your abs and pecs right before you hit it so your right arm doesn't get behind you."

With concurrent feedback, the teacher can usually see immediately if the student understands and applies it. With terminal feedback, what you say might just whiz past students without leaving any notable impression, especially if they aren't given time to practice it. "Uh, yeah, sure, I got it….(what did she just say?)" Be sure to give students time to repeat or practice to incorporate the feedback.

Program/Parameter

The information contained in the feedback may deal with different aspects or scope of information. *Program* feedback deals with the fundamental movement pattern; for example, "Step right, step left, step right, hop on the right foot, then step left, step right, step left, hop on the left foot" for a schottische. *Parameter* feedback is concerned with details on changeable aspects or qualities: criteria for performance such as such as keeping the legs straight, pointing the feet, qualities such as lightness or free flow.

Program feedback deals with the basic movement pattern, such as which foot goes where: the "What".
Parameter feedback is concerned with changeable aspects or qualities of the movement; the "How".

Modes of Communication

Feedback can be delivered via different modes of communication: visual, kinesthetic, or verbal/audio.

- Visual feedback may include facial expressions such as a frown or an approving smile, hand movements to indicate the direction of the hips in belly dance or a turn in jazz, and a full demonstration. Visual feedback also includes a written analysis or description, drawing or photograph. Another example of visual feedback is to video a class and have students observe themselves.

Modes of Communication for Feedback can be:
1. Visual
2. Kinesthetic
3. Verbal

- Verbal/audio feedback includes, "Super!" "Drop your elbow just a little" and "Gently, smoothly, with tenderness." Verbal behavior includes vocalizations as well as words, such as singing the rhythmic cue of a waltz, "DUM dee dee, DUM dee dee, dum DAAAH de dum". Other examples include tapping a tap dance combination or clapping a rhythm.

- Kinesthetic feedback enables the student to feel corrections, and may include moving the spine into the proper shape for a back arch or having the student in the leader's role in ballroom dance experience the follower's role. Touch may be *passive or active*.

Passive touch is when a body adjustment is physically initiated by someone else, and active when the change is generated by the mover (Brodie & Lobel, 2012; Schmidt & Wrisberg, 2008). Kinesthetic feedback can include having a student put their hands on the teacher. For example, in beginning adult classes, I demonstrate that the proper way to initiate movement of the arms isn't just a matter of pressing down the shoulders, but involves keeping the trapezius relaxed, using deltoids rather than trapezius to lift the arm: Standing in front of a student, I have the student put their hands on my shoulders and feel the soft (released) tone of the muscle. Then I tense the trapezius while initiating a lift of the arms to the side. Finally, I do the same arm movement with the trapezius released so the student feels the released quality of the muscle throughout the action.

> *In children's classes I sometimes ask, "What is wrong with this arabesque?" and demonstrate an arabesque with a bent leg, or oddly bent arms. Whoever correctly diagnoses the problem is allowed to "fix" me by straightening my leg or correctly placing the arms. This is fun to do with children's classes but be prepared for an attack of the Lilliputians as they all want to offer you kinesthetic feedback simultaneously!*

- In all levels of classes, students can learn to provide kinesthetic feedback to each other in Reciprocal learning, such as adjusting the shape of arms or making sure knees are straight. This helps both students in the reciprocal pair: the person doing the movement receives immediate feedback; the person assisting engages in analysis and active thinking which enables better performance.

Functions of Feedback

Feedback functions in several ways: as *information* to identify and correct errors, as *reinforcement* for doing movements and tasks correctly, as *motivation* to continue, as *analysis* of performance, and as a way to develop *transactional* and critical thinking skills. Understanding each of these functions will help the teacher to choose and deliver feedback to enable students to become proficient, thinking dancers.

As information to identify and correct errors ("Flex, don't point, your foot on count 4"), feedback should generally be prompt and specific for two important reasons. First, it leads to better performance. Students who understand what corrections should be made will be better equipped to learn how to make similar analyses and corrections for peers and for themselves. Second, it enables students to change a movement pattern before practicing incorrectly too many times and

Functions of Feedback:
1. Information
2. Reinforcement
3. Motivation
4. Analysis
5. Critical Thinking

developing poor movement habits: it is much easier for students to learn something correctly the first time than to have to re-learn or undo bad training. Feedback that tells a student when something is being done correctly will reinforce correct performance or behavior. Telling a student that what they're doing is not just correct but valued ("That was beautiful!") will usually mean that they will continue doing it.

Positive feedback can tell students that they are making progress ("You have come such a long way in the past three weeks!") and that they are valued, and thus can provide powerful motivation. Even feedback which is neutral ("Good morning, Pei!") can tell the student that they are recognized.

Feedback can also be used to guide students toward analysis of performance ("See what shape your arms are now? Rotate your elbows back a little more to give a rounder shape"), detecting and improving errors as well as developing a feeling for how "correct" feels ("Your leg isn't straight yet…. Keep going…. *Now* it is straight! Do you feel that?"). Using feedback to guide students' thinking about what they are doing ("Do you feel what you're doing with your hip in that turn? Yes, and what can you do to counteract that?") is an essential part of enabling students to develop an accurate internal model and kinesthetic sense of the action.

Another important function of feedback, which starts with analysis but goes further, is as opening a doorway to transactional (bi-directional) interchange with students (Akinleye and Payne, 2016). When teachers use feedback which goes beyond the "fix this, correct that" or technique-as-skill-set aspect of dance, they promote critical thinking skills ("I saw your turn on the left foot; tell me about that").

When feedback is given directly after the task, the learner can remember what was done, apply the information, and immediately practice the task again (mentally or physically), incorporating the feedback. Directing students to evaluate their performance before receiving feedback can further benefit students by enabling them to form an intrinsic plan for correcting errors.

Dance teachers usually worry about being able to provide enough feedback, struggling to get to everyone at least once in a class. However, in private lessons or individual coaching sessions, beware of the opposite problem, of offering feedback too immediately and/or too frequently. Giving feedback too frequently has a negative effect on learning (Schmidt, 1991). And continuing to give concurrent feedback, while the student is dancing, can also make students dependent on external feedback. Give students' minds time to work on what they're learning and to discover what and how they need to adjust; also give them time to formulate informed responses and initiate interaction with you.

The function of feedback as improving performance is just part of its importance. Perhaps more important is how teachers use it to encourage students to critically evaluate information. This means moving beyond thinking of feedback as one-way, primarily as correction or "fixing what is wrong," and taking students from skill acquisition to critical thinking, enabling students to understand how to build knowledge in dance. Feedback can be most effective for this purpose when it becomes a multidirectional mode of communication, to facilitate transactions that occur in the triad of the student, the information (usually movement), and the teacher.

Types of Feedback
Regardless of the mode of communication, feedback is one of four types, and each type can be communicated in a variety of ways:

- Value. Value feedback includes a word or expression that reveals judgment. Value feedback may be *specific or non-specific*. Non-specific verbal feedback includes statements such as, "Yuck!" and "Your notation assignment is well

Four types of feedback:
1. Value
2. Corrective
3. Neutral
4. Ambiguous

done." Specific value feedback includes statements such as, "Great footwork, you're really pointing your feet well now."

- Corrective. This type of feedback focuses on an error. It includes information that identifies the error and/or how to correct it. *Visual corrective* feedback might be a demonstration of what was done incorrectly and how to correct it. *Verbal corrective* feedback includes, "The leap should land on the right foot, not the left" or, "Push off the back foot more to finish the pirouette." *Kinesthetic corrective* feedback includes slightly lifting a students' hand or re-shaping a sickled foot.

- Neutral. Descriptive and factual, neutral feedback acknowledges what the learner has done by describing or offering factual statements which do not judge or correct. Neutral feedback may also include an invitation for reflection and interaction. Neutral verbal feedback includes, "Your notation assignment included four of the required elements." "You turned clockwise." "Tell me about your decision to include the compass turns." *Visual neutral* feedback includes performing a movement the way a student does it or having students watch a video of themselves performing a phrase. *Kinesthetic neutral* feedback can include allowing a student to feel correct muscle action: "Put your hands between my shoulder blades" (press scapulae together). "Feel what is happening?" (Widen or move scapulae apart). "Now what's happening?"

- Ambiguous. Ambiguous feedback does not convey to the learner precise information about the performance, can be misinterpreted, and isn't always desirable. *Ambiguous verbal* feedback includes phrases such as, "Well, I had hoped for better," and, "Is this really an advanced class?" *Ambiguous visual* feedback includes making a tortured face or shrugging shoulders. *Ambiguous kinesthetic* feedback might be randomly touching a student's shoulder or hugging that adorable but incorrigible youngster.

Tailoring Feedback for Optimal Learning

Choreographers select movements and movement qualities carefully to convey a particular effect to the audience; similarly, teachers should consider the purpose and the effect that is being conveyed to the learner when choosing and delivering feedback. How much, when, and what kind of feedback should be provided to students for an optimal learning experience will vary. Tailoring feedback for students takes thought, care, experience, and intuition.

Consider how the different *types* of feedback fulfill the different *functions* of feedback (information, motivation, reinforcement, analysis, and critical thinking):

Information. *Corrective* feedback lets students know exactly what was wrong and how to correct it, and enables quick and accurate skill acquisition. "Start with your weight on the left foot so that the right foot is released and ready to step out," and, "Plié on the upbeat to land on the beat" are examples of verbal corrective feedback for information.

Motivation. *Value* feedback is a powerful motivational tool in the classroom. Many students seek, often on a subconscious level, to know what the teacher values and will strive to win approval. Value feedback works in the affective domain and is important on an emotional level. Specific value feedback such as, "The second section of your study really held my interest with all its intricate interweaving" also gives students information; it lets students know what the teacher liked and why. Non-specific value feedback such as, "Excellent!" is especially appropriate for building esprit de corps, as when giving feedback for a group project. Positive value feedback used judiciously can build confidence, but too much of it can start to ring false, with the cloying sweetness of too much sugary candy. Neutral feedback can also be a powerful tool to motivate, by encouraging students to critically evaluate information, and to initiate opportunities to respond and interact with the teacher.

> *Watch out for the use of "first person" in your verbal behavior in feedback: "I'd like to see everyone...."* *"Tell me what the answer is...." This puts the focus on the teacher and his or her pleasure, rather than on the student, which tends to maintain a certain dependence. Also watch for delivering monotonous feedback; beginning teachers are often heard repeatedly delivering "Good job" or "Awesome" as the only feedback.*

Reinforcement. Just about any form of feedback functions as reinforcement depending on the situation and what the teacher is trying to reinforce.

Analysis. Feedback can enable students to analyze their own performance. *Neutral* statements, factual and non-committal, state what occurred, enabling the learner to draw conclusions and self-correct if necessary without being told by someone else. While at first neutral feedback may not seem very useful, it goes beyond a quick correction, and lets a student know that the teacher saw what they did and are willing to help them understand and improve their performance. Neutral feedback is the only form that allows learners to reflect on the task and form their own opinion. Use neutral feedback to guide students to analyze the situation and develop their own feedback.

Critical Thinking. Feedback, especially value and neutral, can help students to develop critical thinking skills. Crafted to create alternative models for exchange to encourage students to critically evaluate information, feedback can enable them to develop critical thinking skills.

When it is necessary for performance to improve quickly, specific value and corrective statements are more appropriate than non-specific value, neutral and ambiguous feedback. However, if students are always told exactly what was incorrect and how to fix it, they may rely on teacher feedback and not develop the internal sensing that enables self-corrective analysis. When it is desirable for students to learn to reflect, make their own assessments or analyze their own mistakes, apply neutral feedback to inform the student that an error was made but allow self-discovery of the correction. Consider the following exchange:
- Teacher: "You finish count 8 on the left foot; however, the first count of the next measure begins with a step on the left." (Neutral feedback)
- Student: "What am I doing wrong? I'm so frustrated!" (Student wants the teacher to give the answer)
- Teacher: "Do it again... (Observes).... In the turn you changed feet." (Neutral feedback) "Do you feel where that happened?" (Invites sensing and reflection)
- Student: "Oh, I need to stay on the same foot!" (Student discovers the answer)

Or,
- Teacher: "You did a double turn." (Neutral feedback which tells the student that the teacher did observe him or her)
- Student: "Yeah, but I always fall out of it." (Student aware that something was wrong)

- Teacher: "Which direction did you fall?" (Question guides student to analyze and discover)
- Student: "When I turn right, I seem to fall to the left." (Student shows ability to analyze the movement, the first step toward discovering a solution)
- Teacher: "You are able to balance in a static position, but not when you turn."
- Student: "Hmm…I wonder what I'm doing to change my posture when I turn? Let me try a few things…." (Student starts the process of critical thinking to apply exploration and experimentation to the movement problem)

Different situations, student needs, and objectives are all factors in selection of feedback. Specific corrective statements are useful for having students quickly improve their technique, or in rehearsal when it is necessary to quickly achieving consistency of timing or line. Neutral statements let students know that they are noticed, but are allowed to think things through. Value and neutral feedback is also useful to lead students to discover an answer or solution rather than telling it to them. In improvisation and choreography classes, neutral feedback tells the student that they are noticed and that their work is witnessed, but allows them to reflect and form their own opinions.

Certain students respond more positively to certain types and modes of communication of feedback. Furthermore, using a variety of feedback helps expand the students' ability to receive a variety of feedback. Apply a variety of feedback and remain open to the needs of the subject and level of the class, the changing needs of each student, and the class as a whole.

As dancers gain experience, feedback serves different purposes. Beginners who may not have much confidence need encouragement, and will benefit from positive value feedback. As their commitment becomes more secure, their focus shifts to their progress, when *specific corrective* feedback is more useful. When first learning a movement pattern, dancers generally need *program* feedback, which deals with the fundamental movement pattern; for example, "Three runs and a leap, stepping right, left, right, and leaping onto the left foot." As students become more proficient in the phrase, add *parameter* feedback, which deals with details such as Efforts or qualities of movement. Giving parameter feedback while the student is still in the "what goes where" phase will only be frustrating. As the student is able to perform the movement with greater proficiency, provide more specific feedback.

Beginners will tend to stay longer in the phase of learning which requires program feedback; it's all new to them. Give students time in Practice learning, providing program feedback either verbally or via task sheets, to enable them to become more proficient in the phrase. Once students get the overall pattern or phrase, parameter feedback will enable them to engage on a deeper level, understand that there's more than meets the eye, and start to develop the artistry involved with musicality and timing, qualities or Efforts of movement, and choices in slight variations in head and arm movements.

Keep in mind that everyone is a beginner at some point when learning a new move or new choreography. Even the most advanced dancer will typically need program feedback when learning a complex new phrase, then parameter feedback as the concept becomes clear and they can attend to qualitative features of the dance and focus on polishing performance.

Feedback which is too vague ("Stay on top of your leg" can be frustrating ("What does the teacher mean, aren't I already on top of my legs?", "What does it mean to 'pull up?'"), while feedback which is too detailed ("Keep your head upright, shoulders even, spine straight, the circle of your arms balanced, both thighs outwardly rotated, don't hike your hip, fingers reaching gently and lightly and oh yeah, remember to spot") will be overwhelming.

In addition, feedback offered too often can hinder learning by not allowing students time to develop the kinesthetic knowing which is necessary to learning to self-correct, while not receiving enough information can mean that students practice and thus reinforce incorrect movement patterns. Noncontingent feedback, or phrases like "Good job", when the student knows it wasn't well done, or "You can do better", when the student is trying their hardest and doesn't know how to do better, can discourage students.

Least helpful is to give corrective feedback that is identical to what a student already feels. For example, if a student knows that they fell to the left out of a turn, the last thing they need to hear is, "Don't fall to the left." (If the student asks *why* they always fall to the left, feedback can help them determine what's happening and how to maintain balance). A series of questions guiding them to discover the correct answer can be better feedback than telling them outright what was incorrect and how to change it.

> Be sure to choose feedback appropriate to the age as well as ability level. Children ages two to about seven years are in what Piaget termed the preoperational stage (Stinson 1985). They can copy movement, but have limitations to understanding and self-correction. Their ability to accurately imitate shapes is limited to one part of the body at a time: they may be able to copy the feet but not do a good job of adding arms. They can copy shapes or positions, but not grasp the transition from one shape to the other. During this stage, value and corrective feedback can focus on motivation. Descriptive feedback ("You arms were very round and big!") is effective. Keep it short, simple, and straightforward, using a combination of visual, auditory, and kinesthetic modes. Around ages seven to ten is the beginning of stage of concrete operations, when children can understand that the line of the arms in second position is a body line parallel to the floor. Around ages 11-12, children complete the concrete operational period and enter the formal operational period, thinking more like adults. There is an increase in production of gray matter in the brain just before puberty, with most of the changes in the frontal lobe. This area of the brain is concerned with abilities such as planning, short-term memory, selective attention skills, organizing thoughts, and problem-solving. Children at this age become able to see and evaluate themselves from the outside, are able to engage in problem-solving, and have concrete goals for improving technique.

Delivering feedback effectively is important, but making sure students are able to *use* feedback is even more important. Just as food is usually intended to be eaten for enjoyment and nourishment, feedback is intended to be used by students for enrichment, to engage students in several domains and to stimulate critical thinking so that students embody new levels of thought. All the most wonderful and insightful feedback in the world is useless if it isn't applied. After offering corrective feedback for example, pause to make sure the student incorporates the feedback into performance.

Addressing Touch as Feedback

Touch can be an extremely effective tool for teaching. It is a link between an individual's inner world and the outer world. It heightens body awareness, awakens attention and enables students to connect the cognitive, emotional, and physical. It gives the teacher the ability to reach students who are primarily kinesthetic learners and enable multi-intelligence learning. It enables confirmation of material, clarification of a body location, and reaffirmation of a dance movement pattern. Some dance forms, such as ballroom and social dance, ballet and contemporary partnering, and contact improvisation, depend on touch and would be impossible to teach or perform without it. Touch provides the most personalized attention and individualized correction possible. It enables the teacher to provide kinesthetic feedback for a single dancer while simultaneously directing the entire class verbally (Cartagena, 2015), and provides a supportive learning environment.

"Correcting" is a commonly-used term. However, it can imply that there is one right way to do something, it is the instructor's role to tell students when they are wrong, and that they are like a piece of machinery that is off and needs to be fixed. More useful terms for providing kinesthetic feedback are **assisting** and **adjusting**. "_Assisting_ captures the expression of moving or touching someone in order to deepen or support the receiver and is usually held longer than an adjustment. An _adjustment_ refers to the short and simple corrections to initiate a subtle change in position or bring awareness to a specific body area" (Loebsack, 2011).

Touch is direct, powerful, and must be addressed carefully and thoughtfully. It can enable teachers to empower students to develop more effective tactile intelligence. It provides a two-way exchange of information: we receive, as well as give, information when we touch. Explaining how and why we touch students can demystify it, enable students to know what to expect with touch, and help students become better at receiving it in ways that will help them link kinesthetic and cognitive knowing. In order to increase touch self-efficacy (Cartagena, 2015) or effectiveness when using touch, it helps to know more about the nature of touch and how it is used in the studio.

> *The human need for touch has been dramatically demonstrated. "As late as 1920, the death rate among infants in some foundling hospitals in America approached 100 percent. Then Dr. Fritz Talbot of Boston brought from Germany an unscientific-sounding concept of 'tender loving care.' While visiting the Children's Clinic in Dusseldorf, he had noticed an old woman wandering through the hospital, always balancing a sickly baby on her hip. 'That,' said his guide, 'is Old Anna. When we have done everything we can medically for a baby and it still is not doing well, we turn it over to Old Anna, and she cures it.' When Talbot proposed this idea to American institutions, administrators scoffed at the notion that something as archaic as simple touching could improve care, but statistics soon convinced them. In Bellevue Hospital in New York, following a rule that all babies must be picked up, carried around, and 'mothered' several times a day, the infant mortality rate dropped from 35 percent to less than 10 percent" (Brand and Yancey, 1987, p. 138).*

Two important qualities of touch, *cutaneous* sense and *kinesthesis,* are useful in providing feedback in dance (Outevsky, 2013). Cutaneous sense involves awareness of the outer surface of the body through touch of the skin, while kinesthesis, sometimes called proprioception, is the internal perception of the body in space. Hands-on

> *Cutaneous* sense is awareness of the outer surface of the body through touch of the skin. *Kinesthesis,* also called proprioception, is internal perception of the body in space.

feedback makes use of cutaneous sense and kinesthesis to enable students to develop a greater sense of one's own body, its shapes, and how it moves.

Types of Touch

Identifying various types of touch can enable the teacher to develop clarity in touch. Yoga teacher educator Chris Loebsack (2011) identifies the following types of touch:

- Palpation. Investigates and enables the teacher to kinesthetically gather information. For example, putting a hand on the student's thigh when sitting in first position to see if the quads are engaged or relaxed.
- Directive/energetic. Helps the student feel a line of energy. For example, standing behind the student and running hands from the shoulders gently downward on either side of the spine, to help them understand how it feels to release the trapezius and enable the feeling of "allowing the shoulder blades to release down the back".
- Awareness/adjusting. Draws the student's attention to that area with a quick, simple touch that enables a slight change in position, such as a light touch under a student's hand to raise it slightly.
- Assisting. Directs a student's body toward skeletal alignment and joint safety using a firm and full contact touch. It is a longer or deeper touch than assisting, and can involve moving part of the body or center of balance to support or deepen a movement. For example, with the student standing with one leg turned out and raised to the side, supporting the raised leg and assisting rotating it out, to gain greater height in a side leg extension or grand battement á la second.
- Stabilizing. Supports the student in balancing. For example, with the student standing on the ball of one foot with arms open to the side, stand behind the student with arms open to the side and slightly forward, so that the student has a stable base to push down against, to find how the latissimus dorsi help provide support and stabilization in balances.

- Nurturing: Emotionally comforts the student. For example, a hug, squeeze, or pat after the student has shared a personal experience. Use this type of touch with tact, intuition and discretion to avoid misplaced or confused emotion within the student.
- Random/ambiguous. Without a specific purpose, this kind of touch can be confusing to a student. For example, touching a student's shoulder while directing them to tap the right foot to the floor.
- Sensual/Sexual. Inappropriate in the teacher/student setting, avoid this kind of touch.

Additional types of touch include:
- Oppositional. Enables student to feel an oppositional action, such as gently pulling the leg away from the hip socket so that the student must pull the leg into the hip socket with more energy, or resisting the push of a leg forward in a degagé so the student has to give more "push" outward.
- Celebratory or congratulatory (Knapp & Hall, cited in Cartagena, 2015), such as a high-five, fist bump, or pat on the back.
- Repatterning (Groff & Meaden, cited in Cartagena, 2015). Moves the student through a pattern of movement. For example, guiding a student's arms through a pathway, or the leg through a fan kick.

Self-Touch As an Intrinsic Learning Tool
Dancers often handle their own bodies, in self-touch, in very loving (and perhaps seemingly sensuous) ways. The teacher can help students discover how to provide self-touch feedback to clarify body structure, to intensify an action, and promote efficient movement. For example, when explaining joint and muscle action, have students palpate bony landmarks on themselves such as the hip bones, pubic bone, collar bone, and others. This can help students develop body mapping or developing a sense of the size and shape of the body from the inside, clarify the exact location of a bone or muscle, and deepen understanding of how the body functions. It can also help with intensifying an action, such as pressing the left hand against the navel while reaching forward with the right arm, for a feeling of pulling back from the core while reaching forward. Self-touch can also facilitate release of muscular tension to promote efficient movement. For example, during a forward kick or grand battement devant with the right leg, have the student run the right hand under the gluteus, along the hamstring, back of the knee and calf, then off the foot, to facilitate the feeling of releasing the muscles in the back of the leg to allow the leg to swing more freely. Becoming comfortable with self-touch can also help students become more comfortable with touch initiated by the teacher or a peer.

However, watch that students don't become "touch junkies", craving external kinesthetic sensation. Self-touch can become a distraction and a detriment to performance. The purpose of kinesthetic feedback is for the student to develop awareness and reduce dependence on it.

Before Using Touch
Touch or kinesthetic feedback is an essential part of teaching a kinesthetic art form. In dance class, teachers often use kinesthetic feedback, using touch to adjust the line of the back, tilt of the pelvis, turnout of the thighs, or shape of the arms, and dancers become accustomed to being touched in class. However, some students, especially beginners, are not accustomed to being touched; some do not like to be touched. Some students concentrate so completely when they are dancing that they may be startled when they are touched.

In addition, touch can be perceived as particularly intimate, and may be perceived differently if the teacher is male. Barry Kerollis says, "I've struggled throughout the entirety of my career as a dance educator with the decision on whether I should be a hands-on teacher" (Kerollis, 2017). Make sure to communicate about touch before using it. Kerollis says that a waiver, explaining that touch is an essential aspect of teaching and learning dance, can be an educative as well as protective measure: it informs parents and students about how physical touch is used as kinesthetic feedback in the studio. Acknowledge the power that touch has, both in teaching dance and as a trigger or "hot spot" for an individual. An issue may arise unexpectedly; be prepared to talk about it with respect.

One option is to briefly request permission before touching a student or use humor:
- "Keep your pelvis straight, not tilted to the side. May I adjust your hips to show you how?
- "Let's look at how the hip flexors and abs work together. I need a volunteer who doesn't object to being prodded and poked a bit."

Students must be able to accept kinesthetic feedback comfortably in order to benefit from it. Especially with a class of beginning dancers, or when facing a new class of any level for the first time, prepare students for use of touch by announcing the plan to circulate throughout the class giving assistance and feedback, which often involves kinesthetic feedback and hands-on assistance or adjustment. When having students provide reciprocal kinesthetic feedback in class, preface it with a conversation about touch, and make students aware that they will be learning to provide feedback through touch. Kinesthetic communication is an important part of the learning process in dance. It is important to let students know that permission will always not be asked, and that they need to take care of themselves, be aware and always be in communication.

Information as a Two-Way Street
In order to really connect with students, it is important to *receive* feedback and information as well as give it. Don't be afraid to request information from students during class. The information received will enable giving personal feedback, make logistical decisions, and make adjustment decisions that may prevent injury and keep the entire class participating fully. Consider the following questions:
- "Is anyone working with an injury today?"
- "Some of you can do a half-turn and a catch step to start the phrase on the other side facing backward. Who wants to do that?"
- "How's your ankle today, Peng?"
- "What are some things we need to keep in mind while executing our stretch sequence today?"

Such questions seeking specific information will enable conducting class effectively by making adjustment decisions, stating expectations or dealing with logistics. Knowing that several students have knee problems means being able to say, when starting the warm-up, "Those of you who have knee limitations, do a slow demi plié instead of the grand;" or, prior to jumps, "Some of you may choose to be kind to your knees and relevé instead of jump." Asking about limitations or injuries also makes students aware that their safety and well-being is important. In addition, it makes them aware that they need to think about what they are doing, and that they can and should learn how to adapt exercises and/or movement phrases for themselves. And asking students to recall prior corrections or important aspects of movement keeps them cognitively engaged.

What's In a Name?

Learning and using students' names during class is an extremely important form of feedback in and of itself, as it acknowledges each student as an individual, not just a mass of moving bodies. Internationally-known teacher Lynn Simonson mentions being in someone's class for six months without the teacher learning her name. "It was always, 'Okay, you.' I felt invisible.... When someone validates your existence by saying, 'I notice you, you are important,' then that comes through in the dancing" (Elia, 2000, 52-54).

Watching the swimming instructor work with my daughter and another child, I kept hearing this: "Isabelle, keep your fingers together....nice, you two....straight knees, Isabelle.... good job, girls...keep going, Isabelle....." I'm sure Isabelle's mother was pleased, and I kept thinking that surely he would, at some point, use my daughter's name, too. After 20 minutes I couldn't take it anymore. I went over to the instructor and said, "My daughter's name is Emily." "Oh, sorry, what have I been calling her?" "Nothing." He looked stunned. "Was it really that obvious?" To a parent, it was quite obvious.

As a teacher, I knew the feeling of not remembering a student's name; as a parent, what I heard was a lack of connection from the teacher to my daughter. If you teach children, remember that not only is it important that the children know that you value them, but it is also important that the parents know, too. It is just as important for adult students to hear their names, too!

Using students' names lets them know that the teacher knows them. Making a point of learning and using students' names early in class reduces behavior problems and produces more focused, attentive, and respectful students. Calling a student by name means being able to reach out and touch them all the way from across the room, whether that "touch" is a pat on the back or a (gentle) kick in the seat. When a student has been trying to hang out in the back of the room, all that is necessary is to say, "Good rhythm on your two-step, Brett." Not only Brett, but the whole class knows, that they aren't invisible.

Observation Strategies For The Dance Educator

> Observation is important for safety, information, and evaluation.

Observation has several purposes. It enables the teacher to give feedback and make adjustments so students can learn effectively. It provides information on the conduct and social ambiance of the class, on learning problems or frustrations that might be occurring. It helps the teacher understand the effectiveness of the teaching method being used. Observation is also used for safety purposes, to ensure that students will not injure themselves or other students by performing a skill improperly.

Effective educators use observation to help make informed choices about structuring class content in developmentally appropriate ways using a logical progression. In order to provide usable feedback that will enable members of a class to learn and to improve, the teacher must be able to see every student in the class clearly, detect errors in performance accurately, and then determine the most appropriate type of feedback.

It is important to become fully aware of the dance studio environment as a whole, as well as to notice individual students. The ability to observe students is especially challenging due to the dynamics of the dance studio. Through careful and trained observation, the teacher can come to know what students are doing and how they are progressing. Observing students in the complex environment of a dance class requires specific strategies. Four important aspects of observation involve location, types of gaze, the intent of the observation, and what the teacher is doing during observation.

Location, Location, Location

It is common for beginning dance teachers to get stuck in the front of the room, right in front of the mirror (often near the sound system or pianist), and to rarely move out of this comfort zone. This places an invisible wall between teacher and students. It also "polarizes" the room: the front is "good" and the back is "bad". This polarization of the teaching and learning space has many hazards; it is important to be free to move throughout the classroom for several important reasons.

> *In order to provide feedback that will enable students to improve, the instructor must be able to*
> 1. *Observe every student in the class clearly,*
> 2. *Detect errors in performance accurately,*
> 3. *Determine the most appropriate type of feedback.*

First, it is difficult for the teacher standing in the front of the room to truly see every student in the class. Students in the front few lines tend to receive more feedback. Students in the back of the room tend to be seen more as moving bodies than as individuals; visual expression and facial nuances which give important information on the student's sense of frustration and success are often lost over distance.

Second, it is even more difficult for students to see from the back of the room, where the visual field is full of distractions, such as the movement of other students. Following other students is not the same as following the teacher; trying to copy an imperfect copy is not the same as seeing the real model or demonstration. Furthermore, distance tends to make students in the back feel that their participation is of less importance, and they are likely to put forth less effort. However, forcing to the front of the room those students who tend to gravitate to the back of the room may give them the sense that "everyone is looking at me," which may exacerbate the feelings of inadequacy that took them to the back of the studio in the first place.

Third, the teacher who operates solely from the front of the room can only give verbal feedback to the class in general. Hands-on, kinesthetic feedback is essential in an art form and activity that uses the human body.

Fourth, observing the class from a single angle or viewpoint is not always the best way to gather information for feedback. For observing alignment, see students from the side; to pick up on tension in the shoulders or lower back, observe students from the back. Learn to depolarize the studio by changing location within the room often. This accomplishes several things. First, it means that there is no "back of the room" in the room. All students may be facing the same direction, but all have an equal opportunity to be seen, noticed, and given feedback.

> *Don't get "stuck" in the front of the room:*
> • *Depolarize the room.*
> • *Move to where students can see you and you can see them.*
> • *Move to within arms reach.*
> • *Get a whole new view.*

Second, it enables observation of students from all angles. Third, and most importantly, it enables close proximity between teacher and students, to interact as people rather than as distant objects.

Consider the optimum location for observation of each student and each dance phrase. This location depends on the content of the activity: observing for projection and focus might best be done from the front of the room, but be prepared to move to the side of the room to observe alignment and to the back of the room to gauge tension in the shoulders and spine or certain aspects of footwork. Each viewpoint affords a different perspective of student performance.

> *To emphasize dropping the torso and head completely upside down in full body swings, students face the front of the room as I lie belly-down on the floor at the back of the studio and look toward the front of the studio. "Every time you hit the bottom of your swing, you should be able to see my face back here!" Then I call out the names of students who are dropping deeply enough—I can see their faces from here—or who isn't, or I make funny faces at them.*

Three states of gaze: solid, liquid, gas

Let's take a closer look at how we see the studio and everything in it. Our gaze, or how we attend to the world around us, takes different forms depending on the purpose of the observation. Think of these as the three states of gaze: gas, liquid, and solid.

- Gas: When we are attending to a swarming mass of children doing chassés around the room foremost to make sure no one is colliding, we are using our *gas* state of gaze: our focus is like the oxygen that fills the room. We de-focus our eyes and gather in everything at once. Improvising in a room full of people, or leading a partner in a rapidly swirling sea of waltzing couples, uses this state of gaze.
- Liquid: When we do a quick headcount in class to see if any preschoolers were left behind during the "parade to the potty" or when we check to see if everyone in folk/ethnic dance class has a partner, we are in the *liquid* state of gaze. Our eyes slide quickly over everyone in the group. We may sift for something unusual or abnormal—is the assistant standing next that challenging child who likes to climb on the piano?—but otherwise our gaze continues to flow.
- Solid: When we focus completely on one thing, whether it is a person or a place, we are using our *solid* state of gaze. Following one person leaping across the floor, watching one person in the jazz combination to make sure they shift weight with the correct timing, our focus is solidly on one thing at a time.

Specific vs. General Observation

When the teacher informs students what is being observed, they can focus on improving a specific aspect of performance.

Much teaching uses general observation: the teacher does not go into an observation with the intent to look at anything specific; "I'm just watching the class." The teacher may use *general* observation in order to gain information that will enable *specific* observation. While doing a general observation of a class, the teacher may notice something in particular that needs specific attention.

On the other hand, the teacher may start an observation knowing what specific skill or body part will be the center of attention. Being specific about what is being observed, and having a vocabulary to express it, will build more acute observation skills for the teacher. The teacher can also inform students what will be observed; when students have a clear understanding of their final goal, they can focus on improving a specific aspect of performance, and skill acquisition is more efficient and effective. Rather than saying, "I'm watching your footwork" (or saying nothing at all), specify, "As you perform the phrase this time, I will be watching for the three different ways of using the foot on the floor that I mentioned earlier: the brush, as in the tendus at the barre; the piqué or stabbing action of the ball of the foot (or full pointe); and the toe-ball-heel roll-through." Thus, in a roomful of moving bodies who may be committing a variety of technique crimes, the teacher can select certain aspects of performance, call students' attention to that aspect before they begin, and observe selectively. Students will know what, in specific, to focus on in practice and performance of the phrase.

> ***TO DO:*** *Take a moment to practice each of the three states of gaze right where you are sitting, and notice what you notice and how it feels. First focally "float" in the air of the room. Imagine you are absorbing the flavor of the air with all your skin. Next allow your gaze to flow over all the architecture of the room, as if you are gently rinsing it with your eyes. Now find one small thing on which to solidify your focus—a corner where two walls and the ceiling meet, the spot where the leg of a chair contacts the floor, a single letter on the notice on the bulletin board. Return to liquid gaze to find another spot for your solid gaze, then float your gas gaze again.*

Watch More, Dance Less

It is very difficult for the dance teacher, who is obviously in this field because they love to dance, to *not* perform in class. Too often, beginning dance teachers make the mistake of "dancing" every phrase with every group in class. It is true that students need to observe a good demonstration; however, it is the role of the students to learn and perform; it is the role of the teacher to inform, observe, and give feedback. Teaching is not dancing. The teacher who attempts to dance through the entire class is doing a disservice to students and the teaching-learning process.

First, the teacher who is dancing is not completely involved in observation and giving feedback. Second, students who become accustomed to a class of constant demonstration will use visual cueing as a crutch and will be less adept at developing the observational skills and memory needed for active and effective learning through self-feedback. You may find that when you stop demonstrating, students have no idea what to do, because their attention was focused on watching you, rather than learning the sequence. Third, the act of dancing affects observations: when the teacher is dancing, students may be perceived as performing with more precision or energy than when the teacher is standing and observing them. Activity clouds observation. Fourth, as mentioned above, certain aspects of the dance phrase may best be observed from a different point of view than the one the teacher has when performing; dancing limits the angle and field of vision. Finally, the teacher who always dances through a full day's load of classes may become too exhausted to teach well. Save the performance for a single demonstration of the phrase, for a demonstration of performance skills. Teaching will be less tiring and more effective for both teacher and students.

In spite of all this discussion of the specifics of observation, keep in mind that much observation is still intuitive rather than systematic. Trust your instincts, what you see out of the corner of your eye and with your heart.

Use of Imagery in Dance

Imagery is a powerful tool for teaching dance, especially for feedback. Using imagery can help students improve focus and concentration, learning, memory, and performance. Research shows that imagery engages the brain's circuitry the same way that actually moving does: mental rehearsal of a dance sequence can be just as effective as actually moving through it. And the more vivid that imagery, the more effective it is.

Images maybe primarily anatomical, such as telling students to allow the scapulae to glide over the ribcage in back, or rotate the greater trochanter back and drop it down as the leg raises to second which facilitates turn-out. Pictorial images include feeling effervescent bubbles floating up from underneath the arch of each foot to help students keep their arches lifted, or sensing having a long tail like a cat, lengthening downward toward the heels.

Imagery can be used before, during, and at the end of class, as well as between classes. Before class starts, imagery can enhance body awareness and remind students of the small postural shifts necessary to transition from everyday life to be ready to dance fully within their bodies. It can be used during class to facilitate efficient movement, such as imagining the arms and legs like tassels that move easily from the joints. Encourage students to use imagery when they are waiting their turn in technique class. Use it at the end of a class to review material, reinforcing the "feel" of the movements in the muscles. Suggest that students use imagery on their own as a replacement for physical practice if they are tired or injured, to prevent bad habits due to exhaustion or prevent further injury. Collect examples of anatomical and pictorial imagery and use a variety in class. Some good resources for imagery include writings by Lulu Sweigard, Eric Franklin, Irene Dowd, and Glenna Batson.

Applications of Feedback

Being transparent in delivery of feedback from teacher to student can help guide students to provide feedback to each other and to themselves. The teacher facilitates this by periodically giving students Practice, Reciprocal, Self-Check, and Inclusion, and Guided Discovery experiences.

Practice. The essence of Practice learning is that time is provided for the learners to rehearse a task or tasks individually while the teacher circulates throughout the studio to provide feedback privately to each student. This is different from when the teacher circulates during barre or warm-up: in Practice, students may choose, among other things, what direction to face, when to start and stop, and how fast or slow to do the

> *Practice:* Students individually rehearse a task.
> *Reciprocal:* Students work in pairs to give and receive feedback.
> *Self-Check:* students apply feedback to themselves
> *Inclusion:* Students choose the level of difficulty for which they can accomplish the task.
> *Guided Discovery:* Students are guided to discover a single solution or answer.

task. The task could be as short as a single jump or as long as a complex dance phrase. In addition to challenging students to remember key aspects such as the order of the phrase, an important purpose is for the teacher to be able to interact personally with students to provide feedback, answer questions, and explain an aspect in more detail.

Reciprocal. The essence of Reciprocal learning is for each student to give and receive immediate feedback from a peer. Students work in pairs with different roles: one student, the "Observer", has a checklist of criteria prepared by the teacher while the other student, the "Doer", practices the assigned task. Doer and Observer then trade roles so that each student is provided the opportunity to practice each role, giving and receiving feedback.

Three main aspects are hallmarks of this event. First is the opportunity for immediate feedback for every student. This includes the opportunity to have repeated chances to practice with a personal observer and discuss the specific aspects of the task or phrase. It also means that students can practice without the teacher necessarily knowing when mistakes were made and corrected.

> *Three main aspects of Reciprocal Learning:*
> 1. *The opportunity for immediate feedback,*
> 2. *The ability to internalize criteria and corrections,*
> 3. *The social relationship between peers.*

Second is the shift for the decision of feedback to learners, which creates a new reality with new roles for the students, in which students develop observation skills and become familiar with criteria for performance from a more advanced perspective. Through learning to observe and provide feedback to a partner, students develop an awareness of personal performance. This kinesthetic awareness is developed when a student learns to observe a peer's performance and make assessments based on criteria. Enhanced objective observation is a first step to becoming weaned from total dependence on teacher feedback.

Third is the social relationship between peers, with new psychological demands on teacher as well as learners. The socializing process is important, as students give and receive feedback with a peer. Partners engage in several steps, which include observing the peer's performance, analyzing the performance in terms of established criteria, formulating conclusions, and choosing appropriate feedback for the partner. This involves developing the patience, tolerance, caring attitude, and confidence to work with another learner. Furthermore, it involves experiencing the rewards of seeing a peer succeed and developing social bonds among students that endure beyond the task and often beyond the class.

A diagram of the interactions in a Reciprocal episode looks like this:

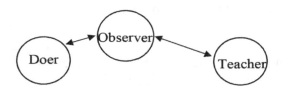

The Teacher-Observer-Doer Triad
The teacher circulates throughout the studio to initiate feedback with the Observers.

In Reciprocal learning, the focus for feedback provided by the teacher must shift. Reciprocal learning gives the Observer responsibility for providing feedback on performance directly to the Doer. So rather than focusing on the student who is doing the phrase (the Doer), the teacher will focus on providing feedback to the Observer *concerning the feedback they give to their*

Doer. The role of the teacher now is not to give corrections or suggestions to the Doer, it is to make sure the Observer knows how to use criteria to give appropriate feedback to their Doer. Make it clear that the Doer communicates only with the Observer; do not usurp the role of the person who provides feedback to the Doer.

Feedback from teacher to Observers focuses on guiding them to accurately assess performance and choose feedback which is appropriate for their partner. The "Pretty Good" syndrome can occur when the Observer doesn't attend to the specifics of the criteria, and relies instead on personal values. For example,
- Teacher: "How is your partner doing?" (Initiates conversation with Observer)
- Observer: "Pretty good."
- Teacher: "What does that mean? Specifically, how is your partner doing?"

A better way to initiate communication with the Observer:
- Teacher: "What is your partner doing well?" (This verbal behavior reduces the "pretty good" syndrome by immediately asking the Observer to focus on specific criteria).

Then the exchange may continue:
- Observer: "She is keeping her pelvis aligned and head up during the grand plié."
- Teacher: "Your observation is accurate. You know how to follow the criteria sheet. Did you tell your partner what she is doing well?"
- Observer: "Um....No."
- Teacher: "An important part of your role as Observer is to give feedback to your partner. Please use the criteria to give specific feedback to your partner."

If the Observer has missed a crucial aspect of performance or offers inaccurate feedback to the Doer, it may take all of a teacher's restraint not to jump in and make the correction to the Doer: after all, that's what teachers do! Remember that the focus now is not on providing feedback to the Doer but to guide the Observer to do so, and communicate only with the Observer and refer to the criteria sheet.
- Teacher: "Let's look at the criteria sheet again. What is the second point? How did your partner do with that?" (This makes the Observer focus on the information contained on the criteria sheet.)
- Observer: "Oh, I see! (to Doer): Let me watch you again."

Reciprocal learning is an excellent way for students to learn to engage the cognitive operations involved in comparing and contrasting performance with criteria. It is also an excellent way for students to learn how to give clear and objective feedback, which will likely translate into an enhanced ability to receive and apply feedback.

Self-Check. Engaging in Self-Check requires students to apply the decisions learned in Reciprocal learning to themselves: using a criteria sheet, comparing, contrasting, and drawing conclusions about performance. The main objective of Self-Check is for each student to develop an awareness of personal performance by providing self-feedback. This kinesthetic awareness is developed when students learn to observe their own performance and make assessments based on criteria. Like Practice, it enables students to be individually observed, given private feedback, and initiate questions and interactions. However, keep in mind the difference between Practice and Self-Check. In Practice, the students remember the basics of the task, so provide *program* feedback as needed. The objective for Self-Check, however, is for each student to develop an awareness of personal performance, so see if students can provide parameter self-feedback.

When providing feedback to students in Self-Check, it is important that the teacher's verbal behavior reflects the different nature and intent of this interaction: ascertain whether each student can compare, contrast, and draw conclusions concerning criteria and personal performance. Feedback serves to guide learners to sense (see, feel, hear) any discrepancies; for example, "How does the sound of your brush back or side compare with the sound of your brush front?", or "What do you feel happening in the plié before the turn?" Talk with students and really listen to what they say; if they are unaware of discrepancies, frame guiding feedback questions carefully to lead them to see these accurately and discover problem areas without increasing the frustration that can occur with questions that the learner cannot answer.

Another approach is to ask a general question such as, "How are you doing?" This enables the learner to decide how to respond, such as:
- "Fine!"
- "I can't get it, and I don't know why."
- "I can't get it yet, but I know how to fix it."
- "I can do it and I understand the criteria sheet."

The first response may mean that the student is able to do it, but might also mean that the student has problems but doesn't want the teacher to know. Ask questions that invite the student to focus on criteria and performance. The second statement reveals that the student is unable to identify or correct an error; so guide the student with neutral feedback. For the third and fourth statements, the student should be able to verbalize specifically what they are doing; the teacher can verify it, give encouragement, and move on. A better way to initiate communication is to refer to a specific aspect of the task such as, "What are you doing well and what are you having trouble with?" or "How are your elevations?"

Inclusion.
The essence of Inclusion is that a task or activity is designed to provide different degrees of difficulty. Students choose the level of difficulty or point of entry for which they can accomplish the task. For example, in a certain phrase, students may choose to pause in arabesque, do a relevé in arabesque, add a temps levé sauté or even add a cabriole. The nature of teacher-provided feedback focuses on verifying, not approving, the appropriateness of the selected level.

Avoid using value feedback (i.e., "Excellent" or "You can do a harder level!") for this Style. It is the students' responsibility to select a level that is appropriate, not to please the teacher. Feedback from the teacher is to guide students if/when they consistently make inappropriate level decisions. Feedback is to verify, not approve, of the level chosen by the student. It is appropriate, and sometimes very important, to ask a student why a particular level was chosen ("Tell me about your choice of this level"). For example, a fairly advanced student may choose to do a simple relevé rather than a double or triple turn in a combination. When interacting with the student, it might be discovered that the student, who is capable of a triple pirouette, has made a conscious decision to do the "no-turn" version in order to identify problems with balance, arm position, alignment, or push-off, and will use this information when doing a triple pirouette. Harder is not necessarily better, and working at a simpler level will often yield positive results for the student.

Guided Discovery

In Guided Discovery, the teacher designs a series of questions and feedback answers to guide students along a path of discovery to a single solution or answer. Rather than feedback designed to correct a student's response or performance, Guided Discovery uses neutral and/or value feedback during the question sequence, verifying the student's response to each question and guide the learner along the cognitive path that converges on a single target answer.

For Guided Discovery, by virtue of discovering each answer in the series, feedback is built into every step of the process. The teacher provides positive feedback or reinforcing behavior with each question's response. If the responses are off-track, adjustments to the questions need to be made. Continuous motivation is provided by the immediate, positive reinforcement, which spurs the student to seek the next step and on to the final solution.

An example of a Guided Discovery dialectic is for students who are working on turns and need to discover the source of torque or rotational force. This is a good one to use when students are having trouble completing a full axial turn such as a pirouette, or increasing from a single turn to multiple turns.

- Question 1: "So, you're trying to move from doing a single to a double pirouette en dehors. What do you need in order to make that change?
- Anticipated response: "Get more force" or "go faster" or "push harder," etc.

- Question 2: "What propels you in a pirouette?"
- Anticipated response: "The arms."

- Question 3: "Try doing a turn using only the force of your arms: stand in passé relevé, then use your arms to propel you in a full turn." (Students try this method and realize that actions of the arms alone do not provide adequate torque for a turn. Notice that, in this instance, *the movement itself provides intrinsic feedback).*

- Question 4: "Now try doing a turn without pushing with your arms: stand in 4th position (or 1st, or 2nd, or whichever you choose for this episode) with your arms held crossed over your chest. Now push against the floor to propel you in a full turn (students do it). So, which gives you more force, the arms or the feet?"
- Anticipated response: "The feet!"

- Question 5: "Which foot?"
- Anticipated response: (Students will try each one several times. Again, experimenting with movement provides feedback.) "The foot that comes up," etc.

- Question 6: "So, in order to get more force for turns, what do you need to do with that foot?"
- Anticipated response: "Push harder," "Push with the whole foot," "Make sure the whole foot, not just the ball of the foot, pushes against the floor," etc.

Feedback in this application can often be reinforcing with a "Yes!", a smile or nod. Feedback is also built into the task, as students try out different options; the teacher only needs to confirm it.

Summary of Application

The various applications of feedback in learning experiences bring students along a path from dependence on external teacher-provided feedback to internal self-feedback. Practice enables students to refer to a task sheet, improve muscle memory, and receive individual feedback from the teacher. Using Reciprocal enables each dancer, even in a large class, to receive immediate feedback and learn assessment skills by applying criteria and giving feedback to a peer. In Self-Check, learners apply these assessment skills to personal performance. Inclusion enables students to develop critical thinking skills, choose a level that is appropriate for their learning at that moment, and develop a realistic concept of ability. Guided Discovery applies all these skills to being able to explore and experiment with movement to make further decisions and choices. Students become better listeners, better able to understand and follow feedback and criteria. One additional important purpose of the individual feedback which the teacher can provide in Practice, Self-Check, and Inclusion is for the teacher to be able to give students brief one-on-one coaching or individually explain aspects of a phrase or task in more detail.

Chapter Summary

Thoughtful and thorough observation techniques will give you feedback on the congruity between intent and action. Being an intentive observer will inform you on the conduct and social ambiance of the class, what learning problems or frustrations are occurring, and the effectiveness of the teaching method that you are applying. From this information you can determine what type of feedback will be most appropriate to enable learners to achieve success.

The teacher-learner connection in dance is, by its very nature, very intimate. We're not working at a remove from the material: the dancer's body IS the material. Havelock Ellis' quote, "Dance is the only artform wherein we, ourselves are the stuff of which it is made" hits home especially when it comes to the relationship between ourselves and our students.

Dance is an art form. Teaching is also an art form: as teachers, what we produce is students who become individuals who can think, analyze, and synthesize (whether they become professional dancers or just wonderful humans). The material we use is the individual spirit, and the tool we apply to this material to shape it is feedback. Feedback is a connection between teacher and student, similar in many ways to the connection between performer and audience: objective and personal; intellectual, physical, and emotional. Commend, rather than condemn.

Commend, rather than condemn.

Dance is ephemeral, and the feedback we give is multi-faceted and complex, dealing with shape and sound, motivation and meaning. It can be information from teacher to student or an invitation to transaction between student and teacher or among students; to a single student or to an entire class. It can be a simple "fix" or enable critical thinking. However it is delivered, it must also be part of a larger picture toward enabling students to become more observant, analytical, and self-aware.

Questions for Reflection and Discussion

1. Choose a favorite skill or task in dance. Describe in detail and/or in slow motion what happens, how it looks, how it feels (this will link to question #9 below).

2. In your own words, define **feedback**.

3. Discus use of concurrent and terminal feedback: what they are, when to use them, examples.

4. Discus use of program and parameter feedback: what they are, when to use them, examples.

5. Discuss how feedback could either make students more dependent on teachers, and how teachers can use feedback to enable students to become more independent and autonomous.

6. Give examples of the **four types of feedback**. Which do you think you prefer receiving, and why?

7. Give examples of the four **modes of communication** for feedback. Which do you think you prefer receiving, and why?

8. Discus touch in the dance studio: when and why to give it, factors to be considered, how to prepare yourself and students for it.

9. Using the skill you identified in question #1 above, develop as many ways of using different types of touch (palpation, directive/energetic, etc) as possible.

10. Using the skill you identified in question #1 above, determine ways of using self-touch for students to deepen understanding and proficiency.

11. Identify and discuss the **functions** of feedback.

12. Using the skill you identified in question #1 above, determine examples of the following feedback:
    - Intrinsic (what students should feel)
    - Concurrent (which you can give as they do it)
    - Terminal (to give after they have completed it)
    - Program (basic "what" feedback)
    - Parameter (qualities or "how")
    - Feedback delivered visually
    - Feedback delivered kinesthetically or through touch
    - Value
    - Corrective

- Neutral
- Now challenge yourself to create combinations: i.e., terminal + program + visual + value + concurrent + parameter + kinesthetic + corrective, etc.

13. Discuss factors to consider when choosing a **type or form of feedback**.

14. Discuss several reasons why it is important to know and use students' **names** in class. What examples do you have as a teacher or as a student?

15. Discuss purposes of **observation** in the dance class. How does location affect observation and vice versa?

16. Define **specific vs. general** observation, and the different **states of gaze.**

17. Why is it important to *not* dance while **observing** class?

18. Observe a class/rehearsal in a dance studio from different points. Identify what you can and can't see, what you are more aware of, from various places.

Ahead

Now let's look at practical application of the Spectrum: how is each Style actually used in class, how does an episode typically unfold?

Neutral

Now students voluntarily to create combinations: increquinal + program + visual + value + constraint + parameter + kinosthetic + proprioceptive, &c...

11. Discuss factors in choosing a type or form of feedback.

14. Discuss potent reasons why it is important to know/find out students' names in class. What examples do you have as a teacher or as a student?

15. Discuss purposes of observation in the dance class. How does location affect observation and vice versa.

16. Define specific vs. general observation, and the different states of gaze.

17. Why is it important to not dance while observing class?

18. Observe a class rehearsal in a dance studio from different points. Identify what you can and can't see, what you are more aware of, from various place.

Ahead

Now, let's look at practical application of the Spectrum: how is each style actually used in class: how does an x-style lesson typically unfold?

7 Application: The Reproduction Cluster

> *It is not so much upon the number of exercises, as the care with which they are done, that progress and skill depend.*
> *~Auguste Bournonville*

Cued Response	Practice	Reciprocal	Self-Check	Inclusion
A	B	C	D	E

Styles A-E involve learning through reproduction, concepts such as existing vocabulary, structure and rules.

The Reproduction Cluster, comprising Styles A-E, represent teaching options in which learners reproduce known information or practice codified skills. Having choices and responsibilities gives learners a greater sense of partnership in the learning process, and gives those students who don't want to assume responsibility opportunities to confront new realities. Students first become engaged in the decision-making

Giving students choices gives them a partnership in the learning process.

process in Style B: Practice, which shifts to them certain choices including where to work, when to start, pace, and when to stop. Practice Style also provides the opportunity for you to observe students individually and give private feedback, and for students to communicate directly with you. Style C: Reciprocal introduces a set of skills imperative to assessing performance. These assessment skills are then further developed in Style D: Self-Check. These two Styles are very efficient ways for students to learn how to give and receive one-on-one feedback with a peer or to self. Success at all levels is provided in Style E: Inclusion, which enables students to choose their own level of entry into the dance.

> *When first learning a skill or dance style, imitating, copying, and responding to directions are necessary ingredients of the early stages of learning. However, it is often appropriate, if not desirable, to use some Discovery Styles when first introducing some groups of learners to a new subject or topic.*

A well-planned dance class may include several episodes in different Styles. For example, you might start a technique class with a barre or warm-up in Cued Response Style, then introduce a new sequence in Practice before moving to Cued Response to perform that sequence. This could be followed by an episode in Reciprocal or Self-Check to work on a phrase done in the previous class and include a brief episode in Guided Discovery for students who are having trouble with a particular aspect of the phrase. You might then move to Convergent Discovery or Divergent Discovery and finish with a warm-down or reverence in Cued Response. The Spectrum gives you the tools to achieve pedagogic agility and achieve your objectives for the class.

> *A well-planned dance class may include several episodes in different Styles.*

Style A: Cued Response

> *The essence of Cued Response is the direct and immediate relationship between the teacher's cue and the learner's response.*

Cued Response (Style A) is so universally used in dance technique classes as to be considered *the only* teaching style. While it is desirable for teachers to learn to apply Styles other than only Cued Response, there are many reasons for and situations in which Cued Response Style would be the most appropriate Style. Aerobics, folk dance, and most technique classes rely primarily on Cued Response, and there is a beauty and exhilaration in being part of a large group of people moving together in synchronicity. The corps de ballet moving gracefully and in perfect synchronicity, a long line of dancers dancing Hasapikos at a Greek festival, doing the Hora at a bar mitzvah, a barroom dance floor full of people in a country-western line dance, an aerobics class in full swing, are all examples of the excitement and power of Cued Response.

Children often enjoy Style A activities such as "Simon Says," "Follow the Leader," "Mirror Me" or "Echo." Objectives of imitating, copying, responding to directions and precision performance are necessary ingredients of the early years when children want to learn rules and become socialized into a group. People young and old participate in Style A activities for several important reasons: learning cultural traditions and expectations, professional training, personal development.

For example, students learn about national and ethnic groups by participating in informal dance events and in international folk dance classes. In addition to steps, they learn what is considered important in that culture (individual athleticism, group cooperation, etc.); how that culture views the human body, aesthetic and social concerns such as how the arms or torso are held, how the hips move or are held immobile. Participants in social dance classes learn how a culture expects men and women to relate; for example, in couples in which one person leads and the other follows.

Dance technique classes for professional training inform the participant about the aesthetic "rules" of that genre.The basic genres of ballet, modern, jazz, and tap each have qualitative parameters for moving which define it; each main genre also has subgroups with their own rules (for example, the "schools" of classical ballet which include Cecchetti, Bournonville, Russian, and French, each have a different set of arabesques and positions). The inherent decisions and objectives of Style A: Cued Response define it as a very efficient structure to perpetuate the cultural traditions of dance movement styles.

The decisions and objectives of Style A: Cued Response are also illustrated by dance aerobics classes. The teacher makes all the decisions and cues the participants; everyone moves almost all the time, in relative synchronicity, with a degree of repetition. Given the nature of aerobic training for cardiovascular fitness (continuous use of large muscle groups over a period of time in repetitive, rhythmic motion) and need for safety (synchronicity helps prevent participants from bumping into each other), Cued Response Style is a very appropriate Style for such classes.

It is essential that teachers understand that Style A is just *one* of the options for interaction with students, especially since this is the teaching Style which is used almost exclusively in many dance classes. Style A should not be seen merely as "the quickest way to do it" or used because "if I don't use it I'm not in control of my class." Cued Response can represent an abuse of power by the teacher who harshly overuses it for control and punishment. This situation can lead to negative feelings, with the student rejecting not only the teaching Style but the teacher and the subject matter as well. Many a young child has been turned off to dance due to a too-harsh application of Cued Response Style. However, Style A can be used with humor and caring to bring a group of diverse individuals to develop a sense of unity and understand the exhilaration of moving together.

An Episode Unfolds

In Cued Response, you are the decision-maker in the Pre-Impact, Impact, and Post-Impact Sets, and your dancers execute the performance in the Impact Set. The essence of this episode is the direct and immediate relationship between your stimulus (cue or command signal) and the dancers' response. The signal or stimulus to begin a movement phrase in a technique class typically involves your saying "1, 2, ready, go" or "Come in every two measures," the beat of a drum or accompaniment of a piano. The cue needn't actually be given by the instructor: often the accompanist sets the tempo (after watching or hearing the demonstration by the teacher) and the introduction; the instructor might start recorded music and tell the students "wait two measures" or "come in every eight counts."

> *In ballet classes in the courts of France during the Renaissance, it was not unusual for the ballet master himself to play the violin to accompany classes, and in many modern dance classes the teacher accompanies the class with a drum or vocal accompaniment.*

Pre-Impact Set

You plan the interaction between yourself and your dance students, making all the decisions about how the class will be conducted including subject matter, interaction, behavior, logistics, posture, etc. This plan may be written or kept only in your head. Even when, in an emergency situation, you must teach a class "off the top of your head," you are still making decisions in the Pre-Impact Set, though it may be just a few seconds before implementation in the Impact Set. Keeping lesson plans on computer or diskette will help you in the Pre-Impact Set.

Impact Set

In this implementation set of decisions, expectations are stated and the action begins as the learners engage in active participation, following through with your planned Pre-Impact decisions. In Cued Response Style, it is imperative that your students know and understand the expectations of this episode. Dancers with previous experience understand how they are expected to respond to most given cues. However, in beginning or elementary classes, don't assume that students intrinsically know what to do, and make these behavioral expectations clear. Regardless of level or subject, when facing new students—in a master class, on the first day of a session or with "drop-in" or one-time students—explain expected behaviors. Problems may occur when expectations are not communicated clearly but such problems can be reduced when expectations are known. You "set the stage" for expected behaviors in the Impact Set.

For example, in the first dance class, you might state, "Each lesson will be made up of several episodes. Since each of you might learn in different ways, and since there are different ways to teach depending on what we want to accomplish, these episodes may be in different Styles. Sometimes I will make certain decisions; sometimes I will ask you to make certain choices. In Cued Response Style, your role is to follow my directions."

It is useful for both you and for your students to understand that you have many options for teaching and you will select an approach that is appropriate to the learning situation at hand.

Having given this explanation, you make it clear that the particular relationship between you and your students will vary from Style to Style, and that in Cued Response Style certain behaviors are expected.

This explanation is important for several reasons. First, it tells the students very clearly what behaviors are expected of them and why. Second, it lets the students know that this is one of several ways to learn, one of several relationships between teacher and learners. Third, it lets the students know that, especially in Cued Response Style, you are not an impersonal dictator, but that this is one Style in a Spectrum of Styles which are used for certain reasons and tasks, and that other Styles and behaviors will be used in class. However, students can become frustrated when the demonstration and explanation outweigh the dancing, so you spend a minimum amount of time in demonstration and explanation, and allow a maximum amount of time for active participation.

Delivery of the Subject Matter

Provide a demonstration of the whole task, its parts, and terminology, which establishes the model for performance. In most dance classes, the demonstration is by you, but may also be by a student or assistant, a videotape, a poster or a picture. Then explain any details necessary for understanding the movement, task or phrase. The amount of time for demonstration and explanation may vary; for some tasks only a demonstration is needed, while for others a detailed verbal description may be necessary. In advanced-level classes with an established movement style and vocabulary such as ballet, some teachers dispense with a full demonstration and "talk the class through" the sequence, sometimes "marking" by using the hands as feet, twirling a finger in the air to show a turn, etc. However, remember that beginners don't yet have the model for performance of the movement style or vocabulary, and do (or arrange for) as full a demonstration as possible.

Logistics

You as teacher establish the cue signal that permits the action to begin in unison performance (such as the ubiquitous "5-6-7-8"), which may vary during the episode. In most dance classes, this is tacitly understood, but beginning classes generally need some type of introduction. Consider the following examples in different types of classes:

- "We will be traveling on the diagonal by twos; if there is an uneven number the last three may go together. There is a 4-count introduction in the music; I'll cue the first pair. As soon as the pair ahead of you has started, stand in fourth position, then come in every 16 counts."
- "Please face forward and make sure you can see me as I demonstrate. We'll start standing with feet shoulder-width apart, knees slightly bent."

Although the decision for specific location is sometimes shifted to students in this way, other spatial directives and the essence of the Style keep it within the realm of Cued Response. If the rest of the episode fulfills the essence of Cued Response, then the episode is still within the landmark parameters of this Style.

- "Please escort your partner onto the dance floor. When the music begins, take closed social dance position, listen for the tempo during the four measure introduction and then begin with the basic step which we just practiced, circulating counterclockwise around the floor."
- "With your partner, make a double circle facing the line of direction; men on the inside, ladies on the outside. Stand in varsouvienne position during the 8-count introduction, then begin the polka on the outside foot: leader's left, follower's right."

Cues

Cues can be kinesthetic, visual, or verbal/audio. Kinesthetic cues include touch; visual cues include hand signals or demonstration. Verbal/audio cues include counting, names of steps, which foot is supporting, and rhythmic syllables: consider the following variety of cues for the same action in a ballet class:

- Tombé pas de boureé
- One and a two
- Right, left-right-left (or Left, right-left-right)
- Slow, quick quick, slow
- Fall, back, side, front
- DUM, dee dee dum
- Down, up, up, down

Carefully consider a variety of cue types. Some cue words or actions work better than others for different students. Some students do best by hearing the *name* of the step, others need to know the *direction*, others want to know *which foot* they're to step on, others want to know the *beats or counts* associated with particular steps, while other students respond to the *rhythm and musicality* of your voice.

> **To Do:** *Begin to identify the expectations, logistics, and cues in classes you teach, take or observe. Observing classes is extremely useful while you're studying pedagogy. Don't be afraid to go into classes to watch but do ask the teacher if it is permissible to observe and take notes. Some teachers welcome observers, while others prefer not to have observers in the studio.*

Developing Critical Thinking Skills

To encourage analysis and critical thinking and develop exploration skills in preparation for Discovery Styles, intersperse Cued Response with episodes which involve students' transposing movement. The most common transposition is right/left, when students have to figure out the "mirror image" of a learned combination. For example,

> Help students develop critical thinking skills by encouraging transposition: right/left, forward/ backward, under/over, inside/ outside.

students learn a sequence which starts on the right, then figure it out starting left. Another transposition is forward/backward (or front/back); for example, a grapevine stepping right foot to right side, stepping left foot behind right, stepping right foot to right side, becomes stepping right side, left forward, right side. A pas de bourée under (crossing back, stepping side, crossing forward) becomes a pas de bourée over (crossing front, stepping side, crossing back), or a temps lié or "scoop" forward becomes transposed to one moving backward.

Another transposition involves inside/outside turns and rotations: outside turns (turning the gesture leg en dehors, or outward away from the supporting leg) becoming inside turns (en dedans, turning the gesture leg inward or toward the supporting leg). Ronds de jambe, fan kicks, and other rotations can also be transposed inward/outward or en dehors/en dedans/

Depending on the genre of dance, there may be other transpositions. Teaching students how to approach the analysis and process for transposing will help them understand strategies for exploration for more complex problems in Discovery Styles.

Post-Impact Set

During the Post-Impact Set of decisions, feedback is given to the learner about the task performance and about the learner's role in following decisions. Style A: Cued Response is one of *action*: repeating the movement and replicating the model. Feedback can be delivered to individuals or to the group as a whole, such as:

- "Great energy!"
- "You were all together, and it looked excellent!"
- "Whoa! Nobody is using their arms, so let's do that again."
- "Some of you are doing well with that, and some still need to focus on the footwork."
- "Grace, Ahmet and a few others, be sure to take four counts for the slide."

Implications

Each Style has a certain set of implications. Each Style has a unique effect on the learner, and brings the teacher and learners together in a specific way. For Cued Response Style:

1. **The subject matter is fixed, representing a single standard.** For a ballet class you may explain that there are different "schools" of ballet, but that you are teaching Cecchetti style, thus the arabesques are numbered in a certain way and the torso uses a specific line. Or, a certain latitude may be allowed within set parameters. For example, you may explain that the focus may be either forward or to the side.
2. **The subject matter is best learned by immediate recall and through repeated performance.** This is a very physical style of learning, rote memorization, establishing the neuromuscular pathways often called "muscle memory" in dance.
3. **The subject matter can be divided into single parts that can be replicated by a stimulus-response procedure and can be learned in a short period of time.** The greater the speed of recall, the more proficient the learner will be in moving on to other aspects of the subject matter.
   - When an aerobics teacher calls out "grapevine right,"
   - When a ballet teacher says, "tombé pas de boureé,"
   - When the tap teacher tells students to do a time step,
   - When a ballroom teacher asks for a foxtrot Westchester box step,
   - When the square dance caller indicates a "grand right and left"
   - When a modern teacher asks for a Humphrey spiral fall,

   Students should have an immediate and accurate physical response. This is often called "chunking"—the student responds to a cue with a complex "chunk" of physical action that is like a sentence in motion.
4. **Replication of the model is desired over individual differences**, and through frequent replication, the group can uniformly perform the task.

> *Have you ever said, "One more time....No, I lied, one **more** time...." and repeated this process? I tell students that "One more time" doesn't really mean **one** more time, it just means, "You can't stop yet"!*

Troubleshooting

A teacher who plans an episode in Cued Response Style must be fully aware of the decision structure of this Style. These include the sequence of the decisions, the possible relationships between the cue or signal and the expected responses, the appropriateness of the task for the episode, and the memory and present ability of the learners. For example, you might be assuming that students will remember a phrase that they did last week, when in reality the intervening time has seriously eroded the memory trace. Or the technical levels of the learners might be so diverse that synchronicity of some phrases is virtually impossible, or a tempo which is too fast for the students' abilities might make staying together difficult.

Each Style represents a different reality, a different teacher-student relationship, a different set of potential problems. Teachers who are aware of these unique qualities can work proactively to troubleshoot for hazards. One person making all the decisions for others can be comforting or frustrating, so use this Style with full awareness of the emotional state of the learners, their ability to respond, and the nature of the task.

When troubles arise, rather than saying, "What did I do wrong?" analyze the situation to recognize why an episode in Cued Response Style is not reaching its objectives. This keeps you from feeling a very personal sense of rejection or blaming the students, and it enables *constructive reflection*. Here are some problems that might arise, their causes and possible solutions.

1. The class is not synchronized in the movement. Re-evaluate the chosen tempo or degree of difficulty of the phrase.

> *Also, consider your parameters for synchronicity—what is acceptable for you? I once took class with a teacher once who seemed to need absolute perfection at every moment before moving on. It felt like it took an hour to do a single tendu phrase; I thought we'd never get across the floor! Determine your "bandwidth" for acceptability; weigh your objective of having students do a phrase with adequate precision with the student's objective to get out on the floor and dance.*

2. Memories need a nudge. Keep in mind that students might not eat, sleep, and breathe dance the way you do. The problem may be anything from beginning students who haven't yet developed the vocabulary and muscle memory to retrieve a phrase, to advanced students who have so much material from classes or rehearsals in their bodies that locating the one for class today takes a few moments. Recall questions are a useful way to get everyone on the same page; these may deal with parameter or program information:
   • "Let's work on the tendu sequence we started last week. What are some things we need to remember with tendus?" (This helps students recall parameters or qualities of movement.)
   • "Next we'll add to the phrase we did last week. Who remembers what happens after the flap, flap, flap, shuffle hop?" (This "primes the pump" by giving them the first part of the phrase, which hopefully will then trigger the muscle memory of the next part.)
   • "Who remembers what torso and arms we added to the "dougie, slide, roll down, swoop, nae-nae" combo on Monday?"
3. The signals or cues seem to be confusing the students. How much information do you give in a cue? "Left!" might not be enough information, but "Step to your left front diagonal on your right foot with your arms bent at right angles on the frontal plane" might be too much information to use as a cue during a phrase. Re-think cues or signals.
4. Excessive repetition of the same task can cause boredom, fatigue, or injuries; inadequate repetition can lead to confusion or lack of training effect. As you become more experienced you will be able to "read" a class and know when repetition is adequate.
5. Stopping the action of the entire class because a couple of students are having trouble might only call attention to the inadequacies of these students. It might also frustrate other students by interrupting the flow of the movement. Such a situation might be an opportunity to engage in an episode in another Style.

> **Tip:** **The Quick Episode Sandwich.** *Sometimes while you and the class are engaged in an episode in Cued Response, you'll notice that some students are not able to keep up with the rest of the class and might even have dropped out to sit on the side. You can insert a "Quick Episode Sandwich" in which you move into an episode in Practice Style, Guided Discovery or Inclusion so that you can give such students the assistance they need without stopping the action for other students.*
>
> *For example, students are going across the floor two by two with a leap phrase, and a few students are getting onto the wrong foot somewhere. If you feel confident that the class is able to continue without your constant verbal cueing, you can multi-task: While the rest of the class continues, pull aside the ones who are having trouble and work with them briefly in Practice, help them discover how they get on the wrong foot by engaging them in a brief episode of Guided Discovery, or help them determine an appropriate entry-level alternative in Inclusion. Remember that episodic teaching enables you to shift to the Style you need to accomplish your objectives effectively.*

Summary

Cued Response, the "Do as I do, when I do it" method, is so pervasive as THE teaching method for dance that it is usually not questioned. Most dance technique teachers use only Cued Response, partly because it may be the only teaching model they know, and partly because its purpose is for students to learn the task accurately, in a short period of time, with students producing a single, immediate response. However, using this method exclusively precludes other relationships between teacher and learner and leaves the learner dependent on you for information and feedback. It also precludes discovery and creativity.

When planning classes, remember that every dance class is made up of several episodes. Determine the objectives you wish to reach, identify which part of the activity would best be achieved by synchronized performance of a predetermined model that requires the relationship of immediate response to a stimulus, but also plan for other Styles in other episodes as well. Plan an episode in Style A for its objectives of efficient teaching and learning and use it not as a symbol of authority but in an energetic and caring manner.

> **To Do:**
> *As you take or observe class, be aware of the use of cues, subject matter delivery, expectations, logistics, behaviors, roles. Watch for non-verbal as well as verbal information: demonstrations, nods and smiles, hand gestures, vocalizations, etc.*

Ahead

Now let's move on to the next Style, which will begin the process of shifting decisions to the learner.

Style B: Practice

In the Impact Set, nine decisions are shifted from teacher to learner.

Many teachers might think they are already doing Practice Style: after introducing a step or phrase in a technique class, the teacher will often allow a few moments for students to run through the phrase individually. However, Practice Style entails more than just a quick personal run-through of a phrase. The most important aspect of this Style is that, while learners are practicing the phrase or skill, they are making the specific nine decisions in the Impact Set, and as teacher you circulate throughout the room to provide individual and private attention and feedback to each student. You are still responsible for making all the decisions in the Pre-Impact and Post-Impact Sets, but you shift certain decisions from you to your students.

Using Practice Style means creating a new reality in which learners practice not only a particular dance task, but also deliberately practice making decisions. This is the beginning of an individualizing process. Practice Style gives students very clear goals and is the first step away from constant dependence on visual or verbal cues from the teacher.

> *In Practice Style, you interact with students to provide private and individual feedback.*

> *Do any of these sound familiar? Practice Style can help to reduce these problems.*
> * *"I have students who don't seem to listen or pay attention in class."*
> * *"What do I do with those students who always stand in the back and just follow everyone else?"*
> * *"It seems like I always have a few students who I never get to know in class. Sometimes those students end up dropping out or not enrolling in another dance class."*

The Nine Decisions

Here is a detailed list of the nine decisions which are shifted from you to your students:

1. <u>Location</u>. Students may choose where to practice and what direction to face. Students may at first automatically face the mirror. The first few times Practice Style is used you might even say, "Face any direction *except* directly toward the mirror." You may also tell students that facing different directions gives different learning opportunities. For example, facing sideways enables the dancer to check alignment in the mirror during pliés, and facing away from the mirror or not using the mirror at all enables the dancer to become more kinesthetically or proprioceptively aware of a movement.

2. <u>Posture</u>. Certain aspects of performance are inherent to dance and thus are not shifted to the learner; for example, if posture is intrinsic to the movement or phrase, this decision would not necessarily be shifted to students in Practice. However, while posture and alignment are codified and set for many dance forms, students may choose to focus on *part* of the posture at a time. For example, in ballet class students may sit on the floor to practice port de bras or lie on their backs with their legs straight up in the air to work on batterie. Students in a tap class might sit on the floor and clap the rhythm of a complex phrase or use their palms on the floor, using hands like feet, to practice (an example of positive transfer).

3. <u>Order of tasks practiced</u>. Students decide when to do which task. For example, students may choose to work on the hardest part of a phrase first before going on, or work on all the turns and then work on the elevations.

4. <u>When to start</u>. *Not* working in unison with everyone else can be very revealing and edifying. When students are not working in unison, they find that they cannot rely on following the person ahead of them and are challenged to actually *remember* the phrase.

5. <u>Pace and rhythm</u>. Students may choose to work very slowly and deliberately on certain parts of a skill or phrase, and may choose to "skim" or mark through other parts quickly for overall memory of the phrase. Some students may work on the phrase slowly in order to get it all at a slower pace, then gradually work it up to tempo. While rhythm is often an inherent part of the acceptable performance of a step or phrase,

dancers can also benefit from experimenting with different rhythm or phrasing of a step. In terms of using music for starting, pace, and stopping, you may wish to have the music playing throughout the Practice episode. However, emphasize to students that they may choose to work with the music or to ignore it to work at their own pace, then work up to tempo.

6. <u>When to stop each task</u>. This enables students to invest more time working on skills that are more difficult for them.

7. <u>Interval</u>. When learners practice more than one step, phrase, or action, they decide what to do in between. Some options may include writing in a dance journal, getting a drink of water, stretching, re-taping feet, doing mental practice, etc. It is often useful to inform students what you consider to be *not* acceptable behavior: talking with another student, doing work from another class, etc.

8. <u>Attire and appearance</u>. Students are not likely to change outfits for a 5-10 minute episode in Practice. However, sometimes a change in costume emphasizes an effect. Students may choose to add or remove layers of clothing, work in a long practice skirt or short tutu if available, dance with a scarf or sash, change footwear, or perform a task blindfolded.

> *I had been telling students in ballroom dance class repeatedly not to look down at their feet. So I grabbed the box of scarves (from the children's creative dance class) and blindfolded everyone dancing the role of the Follow. "OK, 'Leads', your partner can't see anything, they depend completely on you, so make sure you don't run them into anything. 'Follows', focus completely on your kinesthetic sense, on how it feels, focus on following your partner's center of gravity." It worked beautifully, and most of the students had a wonderful "AHA!" moment in which they realized that they had been using their visual sense to the detriment of their kinesthetic sense. This also works well with beginning ballet students who tend to look down during barre exercises. Use it once during Cued Response, then give studens the choice to do it on their own.*

9. <u>Initiating questions for clarification</u>. This is the first opportunity for a student to individually initiate a question during a class, have your full attention, and receive a private answer. No matter how gentle and caring you are, no matter how many times you declare "There are no stupid questions," there will always be some students who harbor questions that they are afraid to ask in front of the whole class, but feel more comfortable asking when in a one-on-one situation with you. Sometimes you'll need to invite students to ask questions. A statement such as, "Do you have any questions?" may be too general; "Do you have any questions about the footwork in the second measure" may be what is needed to get a student started.

An Episode Unfolds

In Practice Style, you make the decisions in the Pre-Impact Set exactly as for Style A: Cued Response. In the Impact Set, first give the expectations: the subject matter, behavior (decisions which students will make), and the logistics and parameters. Then the students practice the movement or phrase on their own, making the decisions that have been shifted to them. The Post-Impact Set consists of your circulating and providing individual feedback to each student.

In this Style, the focus of the episode actually changes from the performance of the task by the group, to the process of the individual practicing the phrase and receiving private feedback from you. Thus a new relationship develops between you and your students: You learn to trust them to make appropriate decisions while performing the task, and they learn deliberate and independent decision-making in conjunction with the task.

An episode in Style B must reflect this new relationship. You begin by describing to the class the shift of the decisions, present or demonstrate the task, and circulate throughout the studio to give feedback as students practice. The role of the learner is to be attentive as you give expectations for the episode and demonstrate or describe the task, then make the decisions while performing the task and receive your feedback.

In addition to the first shift of specific decision-making, two very unique features differentiate Practice and Cued Response: time and private feedback. Like Cued Response Style, the time-on-task is high, as all students can be constantly active working on a dance movement or phrase. In this Style, however, each student will set the pace for practice, and will receive individual and private feedback from you.

This individual feedback is brief and may consist only of a few words, but it is extremely important: students know that during an episode of Practice you will be watching them and them alone, and they will have a few moments of one-on-one time with you. Furthermore, you can be assured of really seeing, evaluating, and making personal contact with each dancer in class. Practice enables you to develop a new, more personal relationship with every student, not just the "good" ones or those in the front. Even if you rotate lines in class, in a Practice episode, every dancer knows that they will have your attention, even if only for a few seconds, and the opportunity to ask questions.

> *It is important to keep Practice episodes a regular part of your teaching repertoire. Sometimes a student will not feel "brave" enough to ask a particular question throughout several Practice episodes but will work up the courage after a while.*

Pre-Impact Set

Just as in Cued Response Style, you make all the decisions in the Pre-Impact Set. However, be fully aware of the decisions that are being shifted deliberately to the learner during the Impact Set in Practice Style, and select tasks that are appropriate for this Style. Most of the same phrases, tasks or skills that are appropriate for Cued Response are also appropriate for Practice:

> *Appropriate tasks for Practice Style:*
> - *Fixed tasks performed according to a model,*
> - *Skills assessed by correct/incorrect criteria.*

1. <u>Fixed tasks that must be performed according to a specific model</u>. Any alternatives are to be specified within a narrow range of choices, such as having the arms en avant or en haut for a pirouette, arms in promenade or varsouvienne position for a folk dance, etc.).
2. <u>Skills that can be assessed by correct/incorrect criteria</u>. Remember that correct/incorrect isn't necessarily a yes/no or black/white issue—dance is, after all, an art form and teaching is subjective. However, you should be able to say what is correct or incorrect about a student's performance; this will help students to understand not only the phrase itself but the dance style in general. These criteria will serve to emphasize the importance of precise performance when it is called for in class. Correct/incorrect might refer to footwork, body position, focus, movement qualities, rhythm, or anything else you feel is important in the phrase.

> *Much of what we deal with in dance is qualitative in nature and quite subjective; not everything can be assessed by correct/incorrect criteria. Ask yourself, "What can I expect students to do for themselves?" Choosing to relinquish this control and give it to students is an important step. Realize what you and your students will gain from the one-on-one contact in a Practice episode.*
>
> *Sometimes, when planning class, you'll already have decided on the phrase or skill, and then choose to use Practice Style with it. Other times you'll decide you want to do an episode in Practice Style and then create a phrase or skill that is appropriate for this episode.*

For certain tasks or phrases, you might wish to prepare a task sheet. This might be a list of the steps, moves, positions, or other features of the content of the Practice episode. It could involve your writing the sequence of the dance on a whiteboard, having a prepared poster or chart, or having copies of a task sheet to hand out to students. The end of this section has suggestions for designing task sheets.

The Impact Set

Because this is a way of working in class that is distinctly different from Cued Response, in order to assure success it is important for you to make the procedure and expectations for this Style clear to students. This is not "Everyone spread out and do whatever you want," nor is it an opportunity for students to slack off or chat (although students may see it as such unless you state expectations clearly). Set the stage for a different way of working by inviting your students to stand or sit near you. Then state the objectives of this Style: To offer time for each student to work on their own, and to provide time for you to offer individual and private feedback to each student. Describe the shift in decision-making by naming the decisions, writing them on a blackboard or using a chart, and clearly identifying the decisions for which each student is responsible. Describe your role as teacher: to observe each student, offer private feedback and be available for questions.

Next present the task or phrase. This can be a physical and/or visual demonstration by you or an assistant, a film, notation, or a "talk-through." You can clarify the footwork, rhythm, arm positions, and focus; discuss qualities and potential problems. Be sure to specify the *quantity* of each task (how many repetitions, such as 8 on each side, or the length of time, such as 10 minutes) and the *order* of the tasks (a specific sequence or student choice). An interval decision must be made to let students know what is acceptable to do if they finish the task before the designated time. This might include writing in a journal, working on another suggested step or phrase, stretching, reading ahead in a text, working with weights or elastic bands, etc. Also specify what they are *not* allowed to do, such as talk with other students, or do work from another class.

Address any questions for clarification, and tell the students to begin when they are ready. The class will then disperse and proceed. Observe the class as a whole for the first few moments of this initial episode to make sure everyone is on track, then circulate to initiate individual feedback and questions.

> ***Tip: Quick Episode Sandwich.*** *Sometimes while you are roaming about giving individual feedback, you'll notice that you seem to be making the same correction over and over. If many students in class are having trouble with a particular aspect of the task, stop the Practice and make a general announcement to all. "I see many of you taking two counts for the circle, but you hold count one, then take one count to make that circle."*
>
> *You may also do a quick "sandwich" by inserting a brief episode of Cued Response: "OK, let's all do this together: Hold 'one,' circle 'two,' step back 'three' (etc.).... Ah, good, now please continue in Practice." Remember that episodic teaching enables you to shift to whatever Style you decide will accomplish your objectives effectively.*

Post-Impact Set

In Practice Style, the Post-Impact Set begins when you move from student to student offering individual and private feedback. Observe the decision-making process of each learner as well as the performance of the task, then offer feedback and comments. Keep in mind the following:

1. <u>Identify the learners who need immediate feedback because they are making errors</u> in either the decision-making process, performance of the task, or both. Some students will still be in "follow" mode and try to copy another student. Having a task sheet will assist students' remembering the salient points of the phrase or task, and get them in the habit of attending to the initial demonstration, working on their own and initiating clear and specific questions to direct to you.

2. <u>Offer corrective feedback to each student individually</u>, then stay at least for a few seconds to verify that the errors were corrected. Some students will say, "Yeah, yeah, I know what to do," perhaps due to embarrassment, but these students need to learn how to receive and incorporate feedback.

3. <u>Be sure to observe and offer feedback to those who are practicing the task correctly</u> as well as those who need correction. All students deserve your attention and feedback, not just those who are making mistakes.

> *I remember taking class, as an adult, as a professional, as a university professor, and being surprised at the "happy little glow" I felt when the instructor said, "Good job, Liz." No matter what our level or age, receiving feedback and attention by the teacher, however briefly, is always important; it validates us.*

4. <u>For some tasks, it may take two or three episodes to observe every individual</u>, but both students and teacher will develop the patience. You may say at the beginning of the episode, "I might not be able to get around to everyone this time, but I'll be sure to see you next time." Then be sure to do it. Keeping a checklist for yourself will help you keep track of which students you've observed and who you still need to observe and initiate contact with.

5. <u>Be aware of the options for feedback.</u> Whereas feedback in this Style will be primarily corrective, remember that all forms of feedback are available, depending on what you feel is needed for a particular student in a given instance. As you begin to work more with students in Styles B-E, you'll become more aware of who needs what when, and they'll find ways of letting you know what type of feedback they want. "Do I look OK doing this?" and "Which foot comes up?" each request a different type of feedback.

> *Like many new parents I was reading various child-rearing books and worrying that I would do something "wrong." Then one day my brother Dave, having raised three children, nodded to my angelically sleeping daughter and said, "Remember, it's not about you. It's about her." When learning about the Spectrum for the first time you might feel that there are a lot of rules. Ultimately, the only important rule is,*
> *It's not about you.*
> *It's not about the Style.*
> *It's not about doing the "right" thing. It's about your students.*
> *The Spectrum gives you more ways to connect with your students, and that's what it's all about.*

Implications

Success in an episode in Practice Style involves several important implications:

- Learners can make the decisions while practicing the task.
- Learners can be held accountable for the consequences of their decisions as they participate in the process of individualization.
- You trust your students to make the decisions.
- You accept the notion that both the teacher and the learner can expand beyond the values of Cued Response Style.
- You value the development of deliberate decision-making.

The last implication is crucial. Unless you understand and value the power of shifting decisions to the learner, Practice episodes will be seen as a time for students to do whatever they want, or a time that you don't have the full and complete attention of all students. When you value the process whereby students deliberately develop decision-making skills and are willing to take the steps necessary to carry out that process, Practice episodes will be valued by you and your students as a time to make considerable progress through individual practice, attention, and interaction.

The Purpose and Design of Task Sheets

Purpose

Task sheets greatly increase the efficiency of Practice episodes. The purposes of a task sheet are:

- To assist the learner in remembering the *what* and *how* of the task,
- To reduce the number of times you must give repeated explanations,
- To help the learner develop greater concentration when listening to the explanation the first time,
- To teach students how to follow specific written instructions,
- To enhance precise performance,
- To record the progress of the learner.

Using task sheets can solve several important problems that may arise in class:

- Having a task sheet gives students something other than *you* to refer to when needed. Task sheets can enhance precision in performance by reminding students of all the important details, and also makes clear to learners that an important part of learning is listening and observing when explanations and demonstrations are made.
- Using task sheets also reduces student's manipulation of you. Manipulative students tend to ignore your initial demonstration and explanation, then ask for an additional complete demonstration. This dominates your time. Manipulation such as this takes

the control away from you and reduces your available time to offer feedback to all students.

- Finally, task sheets can provide records of student progress. Whether you grade students in college classes or just want to be able to discuss individual progress with each student, task sheets provide a written record of students' strengths and weaknesses. If you teach in a private studio you can keep the task sheets or send them home with students so that parents can track the progress of young dancers and see that dance classes are more than just "fun."

> *Tip: Here comes that student who always seems to ask a question about a point that you just covered. While you don't mind answering questions and actually encourage students to ask questions, it seems that this always happens with this student, and you have just talked about that particular point. While you're always glad to explain, this behavior takes your attention from the group: when a student can manipulate and monopolize your attention, that student controls the interaction.*
>
> *When you use a task sheet, you can say, "What is the description of the movement on the task sheet?" (You now regain control of the interaction.) The student must resort to the information available on the task sheet. You can then ask, "Is the description clear?" The student must focus on the description of the task, thus remaining task-oriented rather than manipulative. The student may respond that it is clear; then you can say, "Let me see you do it," offer feedback, and move on. The learner may respond that it is not clear; you can then ask, "Which specific part of it is not clear?" (Again, you maintain control of the interaction.)*
>
> *This process keeps the learner focused on the task and its description, and keeps the learner accountable. Effective verbal behavior can reduce manipulation and engage the student actively in the task. It can be done with warmth and a smile but firmness to enforce expectations: the expectation that students will listen, observe, and focus on the task at hand.*

Design

An effective task sheet:

1. Includes the necessary information about the task and a correct model, describing the specifics of the task.
2. Identifies how many times a task is to be performed or the length of time for a Practice episode.
3. Uses one of two descriptions of behavior:

    Infinitive: "Your task is to perform four single pirouettes on each leg finishing in fourth position back after each pirouette."

    Imperative: "Start in closed social position facing your partner. The gentleman's right hand is just below the lady's shoulder blade. Firm pressure of the heel of the hand turns her...."

4. Has space for notations concerning student's progress, feedback comments, and other information.

See the end of this chapter for examples of task and criteria sheets.

Key Points When Implementing a Practice Episode

Let your students make the decisions that are being shifted to them. They must have the opportunity to learn how to make these decisions within parameters that you set. Sometimes the most difficult part of using Practice Style is learning *not* to give cues for every movement or phrase. Avoid comments such as: "Let me see you do it again. Five, six, ready, and...." Patience will reward you with more self-reliant students.

<u>Teach them how to practice.</u> Students accustomed to Cued Response Style may not really know how to approach more in-depth practice beyond a cursory run-through, and may need guidance from you and the specifics of a task sheet. For example:

<u>Teacher</u>:

"When you are asked to begin, find a place in the room for yourself to work, and face in any direction. Please make sure that you have your own space to work and that you are far enough away from everyone else so as not to be distracted. Practice the sequence that we just did; refer to your task sheet (or the task listed on the whiteboard) as needed.

"You may practice either 'whole' (the whole phrase) or 'part' (part of the phrase at a time). Here are some suggestions for your practice:

1. Part (of the phrase): Practice only the first measure (or phrase), at least ten times on the right and ten on the left. Focus on correct shift of weight, proper arm position, alignment, and focus. Then add the second measure (or phrase): practice measures one and two, at least ten times on the right, then ten on the left. After you have practiced this until you have the sequence memorized, then add the next measure (or phrase), practicing cumulatively. With each addition practice as slowly as you need in order to do it correctly, then increase your speed until it matches the tempo of the music.

2. Part (of the body): Practice just the footwork and shifts of weight. You may do this standing up, sitting down, or even use your hands instead of your feet. Gradually work up to tempo until you have it 'from the waist down.' Next practice the same way using just the arms; again, this may be done sitting or standing. Finally, practice using the head and focus. Finally, put it all together.

3. Whole (body and phrase): Go through the entire phrase as slowly as you need to do it correctly. Pay attention to details of weight shifts, arm positions, alignment, and focus. Take whatever pace is appropriate for you; your tempo may be glacially slow or a quick run-through. Repeat it several times, gradually increasing tempo until you are able to keep the tempo of the music.

"Individual practice means you make the decisions. I'll come around to give you feedback. Please keep practicing on your own or make interval decisions until I come to you."

Some students think that practice means to do it once, or to do it until you can do it correctly once. I tell students that doing it right once is a fluke; doing it right five times is luck, doing it right ten times is skill. As a dancer, you must be able to do it well every time, whether it is in class or on stage.

Most classes have some amount of variation in skill level; some students learn more quickly and become more proficient. When you realize that some individuals in class need more challenge, you can have some students work on a different task (see Style E: Inclusion) during intervals.

To Do: *Think of a step or phrase for an episode in Practice Style. Identify how you will write it for students— step names, descriptive words, etc. It should serve as a clear but succinct reminder for students of the prominent features of the task or phrase. Dr. Ruth Day worked at Duke University and with the American Dance Festival with what she called Memory for Movement, and her research indicated that dancers are better able to retrieve a dance phrase from memory when a single word or short phrase is associated with steps or phrases. The ballet "Tombé, pas de boureé, glissade, grand jeté," the term "fat gnomes" used by the modern dance group Pilobolus, the "shuf-fle hop step fal-lap step" of the single time step, are all examples of such task cue words. Before typing up a task sheet, try an episode in which you write the task on a poster, blackboard or whiteboard, or PowerPoint presentation—this gives you a chance to "debug" the task sheet. Keep it on computer so that you can make changes as needed.*

Summary

Using Practice Style means creating a new reality in which learners practice not only a particular dance task, but actually also practice deliberately making decisions. Let your students make the decisions that are being shifted to them. They must have the opportunity to learn how to make these decisions within parameters that you set.

Practice Style also enables you to give individual attention to each student to answer questions, clarify important points, and interact one-on-one. Make it a point to include Practice episodes in class regularly and notice the change in your students and how you see your students.

> *Early in the development of the Spectrum, Style B was called "the task style," and Mosston and Ashworth had been seeking an alternative name that would be more specific to the expectations of that style. In a micro-teaching session in a workshop, a student teacher introduced the by saying simply, "Go practice." Sara writes, "Muska and I gave each other a EUREKA look and then began a decision analysis of the word "practice." Sure enough, the nine decisions delineated in Style B were intrinsic to the request "practice."* (From Muska: A biography of Dr. Muska Mosston, n.d., Tel-Aviv)

Ahead

The next Style, Style C: Reciprocal, shifts another set of key decisions to students, that of feedback.

Style C: Reciprocal

Reciprocal is the first time that the decision for feedback is shifted from the teacher to the learner.

In Reciprocal, students work in pairs; one student, the "Doer," performs the task, the other, the "Observer," observes the Doer and offers feedback by following criteria which you establish with a criteria sheet.

The purpose is two-fold: to develop feedback and socialization skills by following criteria prepared by the teacher, and to practice the task while receiving feedback from a peer. This is the first time that the decision for feedback is shifted from you to your students. The role of the Doer is to make decisions in the Impact Set and perform the task as in the previous Style; the role of the Observer is to make decisions in the Post-Impact Set and offer feedback. Your role as teacher is to make all decisions in the Pre-Impact Set, then circulate around the classroom to answer questions by and communicate only with the Observers.

Reciprocal is very useful for review purposes, and it is particularly effective for introducing a new task. Carefully designed criteria sheets will help produce an accurate initial performance. *Criteria* sheets used in Reciprocal and Self-Check differ from *task* sheets used in Practice: criteria sheets contain *qualitative information*, enabling the Observer to understand what constitutes correct performance. Task sheets

Reciprocal offers immediate and personal feedback for everyone as students work in pairs and learn to deliver feedback to a peer following criteria prepared by the teacher.

are *what* to do; criteria sheets are *how* to do it. When students are made aware of specific points concerning performance from the beginning through well-designed criteria sheets, the initial performance will be more accurate.

More decisions are shifted to the learner, specifically in the Post-Impact Set concerning feedback. This Style is based on the efficiency of immediate feedback: the sooner a learner knows how he or she has performed, the greater the chances of improving performance. The saying goes, "Practice doesn't make perfect, practice makes permanent. Only perfect practice makes perfect." A one-on-one situation is optimal for feedback, and Reciprocal Style offers this. By providing your students the opportunity for repeated performance with immediate feedback, improvement can be more efficient.

> *Cued Response is familiar to most dance students; perhaps some form of Practice is familiar as well. Some students have worked with a partner before, but Style C: Reciprocal is a new experience, and you will want to be aware of the new and different social and psychological demands and adjustments of thinking and behaving. The role of giving feedback has great implicit power that has previously belonged only to you in your role as teacher. It is often difficult for teachers to relinquish this power and for the learners to take on that responsibility. Learners must learn to respect this power when working with their peers. Both you and your students must trust each other, as well as value the place of this new reality in developing active learners.*

Pre-Impact Set
Just as in Cued Response and Practice, you make all the decisions in the Pre-Impact Set. Most of the same phrases, tasks or skills that are appropriate for the previous two Styles are also appropriate for Reciprocal:
1. <u>Fixed tasks that must be performed according to a specific model.</u>
2. <u>Skills that can be assessed by correct/incorrect criteria.</u> As before, this is less a yes/no issue than it is a way to help students clearly understand the important features of the movement or phrase. Identify the parameters that will enable you to articulate when students are on target—what causes you to say "Yes! That's it!" and what causes you to respond, "That's not quite what we're looking for now."

The end of this section has suggestions for designing criteria sheets; also see the end of this chapter for examples and suggestions for criteria sheets.

Impact Set
The Impact and Post-Impact Sets are happening at the same time: While the Doer is making decisions in the Impact Set, the Observer is making decisions in the Post-Impact Set. The Doer makes the same nine decisions as in Practice Style. The shift of decisions to the Observer concerns feedback: the Observer gathers information concerning the Doer's performance, assesses this information by comparing it against the criteria, and provides feedback to the Doer.

Remember: A diagram of the interactions in Reciprocal Style looks like this:

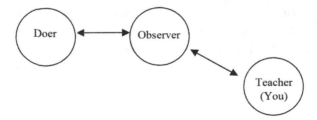

Each member of this triad makes specific decisions within a specific role. The role of the Doer is the same as in Practice Style: to make the nine decisions in the Impact Set. The difference here is that the *Doer communicates only with the Observer and does not direct questions to you, the teacher.* The role of the Observer is to observe the performance of the Doer and offer feedback to the Doer. In your role as Teacher you will communicate *only with the Observer, not the Doer.*

> **_Tip:_** *Why is it vitally important for you to communicate only with the Observer, not with the Doer?*
>
> *You are giving responsibility for delivering feedback to the Observer. If two students are engaged reciprocally and you jump in to give feedback, this usurps the power of giving feedback and strips the Observer of that role. When you come to check on a pair, if a Doer addresses a question to you, refer that question to the Observer. You may need to address the issue of your not communicating with the Doer during your introduction to Reciprocal Style by saying, "Let's ask your Observer, who has the criteria and has been observing your performance. I am not ignoring you. Doers should direct questions to their Observer. Observers, if something isn't clear or if a question arises that you can't answer, please feel free to ask me." Remember that you are enabling independent students; you are giving your students the skills they need to provide feedback.*

The following are the steps that each member of the triad follows in Reciprocal Style.

Doer
The Doer makes the nine decisions in the Impact Set as in Practice. Questions for clarification should be directed to the Observer.

Observer
1. Receives the criteria for performance, usually on a criteria or task sheet, from you.
2. Observes the Doer's performance.
3. Compares and contrasts the Doer's performance with the criteria.
4. Concludes where the performance was correct or incorrect by making decisions in the Post-Impact Set.
5. Communicates the results with the Doer; gives feedback.
6. Initiates communication with you, if necessary.

Teacher
1. Circulates and is available to answer questions by the Observers.
2. Initiates communication only with the Observers.

Depending on the nature of the task, the Observer may give feedback either *while* the Doer is performing or *after* the task. During slow or repetitive tasks, the Doer may be able to hear and make corrections while moving, as in an adagio or during a series of repeated steps in ballroom dance. With rapid movements such as jumps, hops, and leaps or with a quickly-moving sequence, the Doer would not be able to make corrections during performance, so it would be more appropriate for the Observer to give feedback after the Doer has completed the task.

> *This is a difficult behavioral adjustment for most dance teachers to make, especially when the Doer asks questions of you which are directly related to correct performance. Having a clear and accurate criteria sheet will help reduce problems. If a Doer addresses a question to you, refer the question to the Observer. Sometimes you will need to turn to the Observer and ask the question yourself, "Alexis, which arm should be up?"; sometimes a look and a raised eyebrow are enough for the Observer to initiate a response. If the Observer is unable to answer the question, you'll need to make an adjustment decision: you may need to tell the Observer the answer or engage in a brief episode of Guided Discovery with the Observer.*
>
> *If it is a question that has arisen with other pairs, you may interrupt the Reciprocal episode with a "Quick Episode Sandwich" in Cued Response or Guided Discovery: "Class, let me have your attention. This question seems to be coming up for everyone, so let me clarify...." Then, as the pairs return to their work in the Reciprocal Episode, make a note to re-think the criteria sheet, your introduction or your demonstration.*

Expectations: Behaviors and Roles

It is essential for you to prepare students for an initial episode in Reciprocal Style. The following is a sequence of events for a first episode:

1. **Tell** your students that the purpose of this Style is to work with a partner and learn to offer feedback to that partner.
2. **Identify** the Doer, Observer, and Teacher triad and explain that each partner has a specific role. Each partner will have the opportunity to be both the Doer and the Observer.
3. **Explain** the roles of each person in the Triad:
    *   **The Doer** is to perform the task as in Practice Style, and may talk to and ask questions of the Observer, but not address you.
    *   **The Observer** is to observe and give feedback to the Doer using the criteria sheet. The Observer may ask you questions if needed.
    *   **The Teacher** is to be available for any questions and clarification by the Observers. Make it clear that you will not give feedback to or answer any questions from the Doers; this is the role of the Observer. You can explain that you're not being rude, but that you will not take over the role of the Observer.
4. **Discuss feedback**. In the beginning episodes in Reciprocal Style, feedback should be discussed, and sample feedback needs to be provided so that all students will learn how to give appropriate feedback. The feedback chart in Chapter 3 may be reproduced on a poster or photocopied as a hand-out for this purpose. Explain that the better and more specific the feedback, the better the improvement.

Expectations: Subject matter

*   **Present the task.** Now that everyone is clear on the new structure of this Style and each role and lines of communication, present the task. As for Cued Response and Practice, this presentation may be via demonstration, description, or video.

    Have a poster of the different types of feedback in the studio.

*   **Explain the criteria on the criteria sheets.** Here it is extremely important that all students understand that they are to apply the criteria as a tool for assessing a partner's performance. Most students will want to resort to personal preferences: "It looked good to me!" Therefore, it is important to emphasize that they are to use the criteria sheet as a guide for *informed* content observance and *specific* feedback.

<u>Expectations: Logistics</u>
- **Give the logistical information** such as where to get the criteria sheets, time limits, number of repetitions, interval tasks, how many times they are to change roles, etc.
- **Have the class select partners.** Partner selection may be by student choice, randomly assigned, etc.

<u>Action</u>
- Have the pairs decide who will be the Doer and Observer first, then tell them to disperse and begin. When the Doer completes the task the specified number of times or when the pre-set time limit is up, Doer and Observer switch roles and repeat. Observe the class as a whole for the first few moments of the initial episode then circulate throughout the studio to initiate feedback with the Observers.

A class that has learned to work in Reciprocal Style is a joy to watch and will make you proud of the new abilities of your students. Partners develop new facets of their relationships such as making new decisions, offering feedback from praise to correction, connecting, succeeding and providing feedback for a peer to succeed.

Implications
The new reality, relationships, roles, and new social and psychological demands of Reciprocal Style produce a unique set of implications.

<u>It is implied that *you*</u>:
- Accept the socializing process and interaction between Doer and Observer as a desirable educational goal in the dance studio.
- Recognize the importance of teaching students to give accurate and objective feedback to each other.
- Are willing and able to shift the power of giving feedback to your students during Reciprocal episodes. Again, this is usually a very difficult behavior change if you are accustomed to being the sole source of information in class. Refraining from direct communication with the Doer takes restraint!
- Understand the benefit and have the patience to take the needed time for learners to learn these new roles and decision-making.
- Prepare the students adequately and trust the students to make the additional decisions shifted to them.

<u>It is also implied that *your students*</u>:
- Can expand their active role in the learning process and engage in the reciprocal roles of doing and observing.
- Can accept you in a new role.
- Can adjust to spend time learning without your constant watchful eye.

The Criteria Sheet
The criteria sheet is the single most important factor in predicting the success or failure of an episode in Style C: Reciprocal. The criteria sheet gives students a definite target that is fixed and observable. It tells the Observer exactly what to look for, it tells the Doer about individual abilities and progress, and it provides you the basis for interaction with the Observer.

When my daughter was very young she was always saying, "Look at that, Mommy!" and she expected me to know instantly exactly what she was seeing, which was frustrating for both of us especially when I was driving the car in rush-hour traffic! If someone simply says, "Look!" your response is likely, "Where do you want me to look?" The criteria sheet informs and guides students' looking; it helps to tell your students what to look for. This is a particularly effective way to train dancers' observation skills.

Although preparing criteria or task sheets takes time initially, they are very efficient and valuable for several reasons. First, in the long run criteria sheets can save you much time and explanation. Second, a thoughtfully designed criteria sheet can be implemented in several Styles. Third, it keeps your teaching consistent; you can be assured that every class that uses the criteria sheets is receiving the same important information in the same way. Finally, it is also an excellent way to validate and document dance teaching as an important aspect of arts education, a written document that can be included in applications for teaching positions, promotion, tenure, and/or grants as an example of your organized and thoughtful teaching strategies.

The criteria sheet includes the following parts:
1. *Description* of the task, including a detailed description of each sequential part of the activity.
2. *Specific key aspects* or trouble spots to look for during the performance. Experience will help you identify these; just think of the corrections you seem to make over and over in class.
3. *Drawings* or sketches, if necessary, to illustrate the task.
4. *Examples of feedback*, which are particularly useful in the early episodes of Style C.
5. *Reminders* of the Observer's role, which are particularly useful in the early episodes of Style C. Examples of feedback and reminders of the specific roles for Style C can be listed on the back of a task sheet or on another sheet.
See the examples of criteria sheets for different classes at the end of this chapter.

Young children as well as adults enjoy working together; they also benefit from the empowerment inherent in giving feedback. College dance majors who plan on teaching, choreographing, or performing will benefit from learning to assess performance and give accurate and constructive feedback. Adult beginners enjoy the expanded cognitive level of Reciprocal Style as well as being able to give feedback to a peer. All students will benefit from the increased awareness and assessment skills in addition to the immediate, external feedback.

Examples for Using Criteria Sheets

Develop criteria for the movement or phrase, then give these to the students. How the criteria are delivered will vary and may include:
1. **An impromptu checklist written on the board from suggestions elicited from students in class**. For example, after a run-through of movement or dance phrase in a technique class, character class, repertory class or rehearsal, you might ask students to enumerate the parts of the phrase and salient features (this is informative because it tells you what the class has and hasn't picked up). In a choreography class, you might ask students what are some of the previously-discussed basic elements of composition or design which should be applied to the current assignment.
2. **Photocopied criteria sheets that are given to the students**. For specific international folk dances or technique sequences that you use each year, you may keep the criteria sheets on file or on computer and update them when needed. Examples of these are presented at the end of this chapter.

3. **Classroom posters or charts that are posted on the studio wall**. For example, many studios display posters of the basic arabesques and attitudes in the Russian, Cecchetti, and Vaganova schools of ballet. These posters may be used as visual criteria sheets or in conjunction with written criteria sheets.
4. **Written descriptions available in texts.** Written descriptions in texts can offer instant criteria or task sheets. If you use such a text for a class you may wish to have students work directly from the text or use the description as a point of departure for creating your own criteria or task sheets.

How the task and criteria sheets are applied will vary according to the Style being used. In Practice, students use task sheets to work individually and receive personal attention and feedback from the teacher. In Reciprocal, students work in pairs in roles of Doer and Observer, giving and receiving feedback according to the established criteria. In Self- Check, students apply the criteria and the skills developed in the previous Style, those of analyzing performance accurately and delivering effective feedback, to self-assessment.

Criteria sheets are especially useful when considering assessment of students. A student might not have understood the many factors that combine to make the grade received for a movement test, a mid-term or final exam, and may question your grading method and come to you to discuss the grade. Use of criteria sheets will enable you to sit down with individual students, review progress and identify areas that need work. You might open such a conference with a student, "Let's take a look at your work in class. On this checklist for Practice, I commented that you needed to work on_____. On this checklist for Reciprocal, your partner mentioned the same thing and worked with you on it. Did you see it on the videotape that we used with the Self-Check sheet? How do you feel about your progress in this area?"

> *When you present workshops, students will appreciate having criteria sheets as something tangible to take with them. Presentations at masterclasses, workshops, and job interviews will appear more professional if you include criteria sheets, and participants and reviewers appreciate having something written. Criteria sheets are also documentation of your preparation as a teacher, and should be included in a portfolio for job interviews or for promotion and tenure.*

Tips

For the first episode, choose a simple task so that the focus will be on the new roles rather than on a demanding task. Emphasize and reinforce the criteria process: observe, compare, contrast, and give feedback. If you are worried about your ability to handle the initial episode of Reciprocal Style, you might try these two strategies:
1. Try using this Style with part of the class first. Have the whole class engage in Practice Style, but choose a small group to work with in Reciprocal. Let this group experience the new roles under your observation and feedback. Go through the class group by group and after a few episodes the whole class will have been introduced to it.
2. Introduce Reciprocal Style by using a model, demonstrating the process with one pair of students: Select a couple in advance who are secure enough to try a new idea in front of the class. Present the Style by going through the process step by step as each partner experiences the roles of Observer and Doer while the rest of the class watches, listens, and follows along with their criteria sheets. Stop the action if necessary to explain, answer any questions, clarify and emphasize the roles and expectations.

Reciprocal Style is an excellent way for students to learn to engage the cognitive operations involved in *comparing and contrasting performance with criteria*. It is also an excellent way for students to learn how to give clear and objective feedback.

Troubleshooting

During episodes of Reciprocal Style, some problems emerge immediately and are resolved after the teacher addresses them; others may continue to emerge due to the new social and emotional landscape of this Style. The more familiar you become with this Style, the more you can anticipate problems and deal with them gracefully and often pro-actively.

The "Pretty Good" syndrome: This problem occurs when an Observer doesn't refer to the specifics of the criteria sheet and relies instead on personal values. The phrase "pretty good" is very ambiguous. The Doer may interpret this to mean that whatever they're doing is "good enough." Deal with this by asking specific questions of the Observer to get both partners on track. For example:

    T: "How is your partner doing?"
    O: "Pretty good!"
    T: "What does 'pretty good' mean? *Specifically*, how is your partner doing?"

A better way to initiate communication with the Observer is:

    T: "What is your partner *doing well*?" This verbal behavior reduces the "pretty good" syndrome by immediately asking the Observer to focus on specific criteria.
    Then the exchange may continue:
    O: "She's keeping her pelvis aligned and head up during the demi plié."
    T: "Your observation is accurate, you know how to follow the criteria sheet. Did you tell your partner what she was doing well?"
    O: "No."
    T: "An important part of your role as Observer is to give feedback to your partner. Please use the criteria sheet to give specific feedback to your partner."

Inaccurate or Faulty Feedback. Sometimes the Observer offers inaccurate feedback to the Doer or may not catch an error. It may take all your restraint not to jump in and make the correction to the Doer yourself. Be sure to communicate only with the Observer and refer to the criteria sheet.

    T: "Let's look at the criteria sheet again. What is the second point?" (This makes the Observer focus on the criteria sheet and the information contained on it.)
    O: "The second point refers to the…."
    T: "Did you partner do it?"
    O: (to Doer) "Let me see you perform it again. (Observes). Oh, I see!"
    T: "Now please give your partner specific feedback on how she did it."

Manipulation

Don't let yourself get surrounded by students, Doers or Observers, who demand your attention. "I will come around to each pair. Please be patient and continue working with your partner." Students will, over time, develop patience with each other and with waiting their turn. Young children often vie for a teacher's attention; in older classes some students will try to avoid it. In Reciprocal Style, *everyone* receives attention from his or her partner and from you. Make the parameters clear; tell students that you will get to all couples and will answer Observer's questions.

Circulation
Move to pairs randomly rather than in a pattern such as circling the room clockwise. As you communicate with each Observer, scan the entire class, to keep an eye on how the whole class is handling that episode. If you notice that one pair is in conflict, you can finish your communication with that Observer and deal with the problem immediately.

Verbal abuse
The Observer may use verbal abuse ("No, dummy!"). In this case, your role is to give parameters for acceptable behavior.

> T: "I won't let you talk to your partner this way; I wouldn't let her talk to you this way. Your role is to follow the criteria sheet and give feedback to your partner. Now, let's look at the criteria sheet again...."

When confronting a problem, don't ask, "What's the problem?" This only invites accusations and denials. Rather than become the judge or arbiter, *re-focus the Doer and Observer on the task at hand*: their roles and application of the criteria sheet:

> T: "OK, let's watch together as the Doer performs the phrase and the Observer follows the criteria sheet to give constructive and effective feedback."

Your interaction with the Observer will focus on how he or she understands the criteria, observes the Doer, and presents feedback to the Doer. Many students have not yet learned how to really give constructive feedback to a peer. Feedback is not destructive criticism; even using the word "constructive criticism" may permit a negative focus. Using established criteria and offering specific, objective feedback is a new experience. It is a situation that creates a new relationship between two people, a relationship that necessitates honesty and mutual trust. It will take practice and your guidance.

> *It is important for the Doer, Observer, and you to understand that Reciprocal Style is not designed to differentiate levels of ability; the major contribution of this Style is that it creates a condition in which both partners are equal in their roles. Almost every class includes more and less experienced sstudnts, and a beginner may not at first feel comfortable providing feedback for a student that they perceive as more advanced. However, you can help everyone understand that both partners contribute to the social context and learning content of the interaction process. Think now how you will address this in class.*

In addition to presenting a new situation for students, Reciprocal Style also represents a very new situation for *you*. If you have been accustomed to using Cued Response Style, it may be difficult to relinquish the power of feedback to the Observer. The focus of this Style is on the behavior of the Observer, and you will take on a new role, as an enabler rather than as a cuer. However, after you (and your students) gain facility with moving along the Spectrum, you'll realize that this gives you more flexibility, more freedom, and more powerful teaching.

After an episode in Style C, you will offer feedback to the entire class, addressing their performance in their role as Observers. You might say, "We need more time to learn how to compare performance against criteria," or "You all offered specific feedback to your Doers effectively today." Your feedback to the class as a whole is essential; learners always need to know that you have observed their performance.

Pairing Techniques

The most appropriate technique is often self-selection. Students like working with someone they know, and the first episodes begin more quickly and continue productively if they are allowed to select the partner that they want. The trust needed for this Style comes more readily with partners who know each other. Since the primary objective for this Style is the appropriate behavior in roles of Observer and Doer, self-selecting partners tend to reach this objective with minimal conflict. Random or teacher-selected pairings may produce conflicts that you have to deal with before working with the new roles. Partners who are comfortable with each other will be more comfortable with the roles of giving and receiving feedback. After several episodes you may observe that all participants are skilled in these roles, and can announce that everyone is to get a new partner. After a few more episodes, new pairing techniques can be introduced, so that everyone is able to expand their contacts. The increase in social tolerance and communication among class members is a hallmark of Reciprocal Style.

Uneven Numbers

When you have an uneven number in class, several options are available.
- Ask the extra person to perform the task in Practice Style (or Self-Check, if you have already introduced it). Offer feedback as you circulate to interact with the other pairs.
- Have a group of three work together. If the task is not very complex, one Observer may work with two Doers.
- If the task is complex, one Doer may have two Observers: Observer1 can observe one portion and Observer 2 can observe the other portion. For example, one Observer will watch the footwork while the other observes the arms and focus. However:
  o Having one Doer and two Observers who confer and give feedback to the Doer is the <u>least</u> effective arrangement and often results in the most unwanted behaviors.
  o Sometimes a given pair develops conflicts that necessitate separating that pair; they may each move to make threesomes with other couples. Threesomes have different dynamics than pairs, but things like this happen in the real world, and what is important is that you make a deliberate decision, preferably beforehand, about how to deal with situations such as these.

The Benefits of Reciprocal Style

The first five steps in the Post-Impact Set of 1) receiving criteria, 2) observing performance, 3) comparing and contrasting performance with criteria, 4) drawing conclusions and 5) communicating the results, are essential for dancers on several levels. First, many dance students have a way of growing up to be dance teachers, and this process will prepare them for that eventuality. Most dancers and teachers also choreograph, and this process is as essential for choreographers working with their dancers as it is for teachers with students. Second, these skills are important to those students who will eventually analyze or write about dance and dance performances, including notators, dance critics and historians. Third, dancers need these skills objectively analyze their own performance. They develop the tools to develop greater self-awareness. Fourth, all students, even those who never take another dance class but go into careers in other areas will benefit from being able to use criteria to observe and compare performance and communicate feedback. This last benefit is a life skill for all learners.

Summary

In Reciprocal, students work in pairs; the Doer performs the task while the Observer observes the Doer and offers feedback by following criteria supplied by you the teacher. The purpose is two-fold; to develop feedback and socialization skills by following criteria prepared by the teacher, and to practice the task. This is the first time that the decision for feedback is shifted from the teacher to the learner. Not only is Reciprocal very useful for review purposes, it is particularly effective for introducing a new task. When students are made aware of specific points concerning performance from the beginning through well- designed criteria sheets, the initial performance will be more accurate. Learning to use criteria, develop observation skills, compare performance and communicate feedback is an important skill that will benefit anyone.

1. *Identify a movement or phrase that will be appropriate for an episode in Reciprocal. Choose a simple exercise, phrase or skill that you do frequently in class. If it is the same one you used for the To Do in Practice Style, this exercise will be an extension of the previous one: you will be working from a task sheet to create a criteria sheet. Just as you did for the task sheet in the To Do in Practice Style, write down your chosen exercise, phrase or skill in the detail you believe is necessary for that skill and the chosen level of ability.*

2. *Identify how you will articulate the salient features of this movement or phrase in written form: what aspects are important to you as an artist, what aspects do you want your students to attend to? Think of the reminders or corrections that always seem to be needed for that task. If you're currently teaching that class, take your "rough draft" into class and, as you do it, note to the comments and reminders that you make and jot them down (a clipboard is useful for this; you'll feel like a jock but it is useful). Your criteria might focus on the qualities or Efforts, particular use of the body, or other aspects of the phrase.*

3. *Implement the updated draft via a list of criteria written on a whiteboard, a large sheet of paper, or photocopied to use with a part of the class. Take a copy with you as you circulate and update it as you see necessary.*

4. *Keep all criteria and task sheets on computer. This way, you can easily adapt and update sheets for different classes, different tasks, different levels.*

Ahead

In Style D, Self-Check, we see the next set of decisions that are shifted to the learner to develop a greater awareness of one's own performance.

I enjoy this anecdote concerning Style C: Reciprocal, taken from Muska: A Biography of Dr. Muska *Mosston (n.d.,* Tel-Aviv*):*

From 1963 to 1970, Muska Mosston hosted the SHAPE UP television program on CBS-TV. CBS had wanted a program that would help children achieve and maintain physical fitness, but with Muska they got much more, and each week the station received letters from adults as well as children who enjoyed Muska's approach to learning. Muska used the show as his own vehicle for involving children in thinking and moving as he tried out his emerging ideas that became the Spectrum.

In one show he was using the Reciprocal Style, and told the children that they were to watch their partners perform a particular movement and give them feedback about how they were performing. The students eagerly began working, one as "Doer" and the other as "Observer" with a list of "things to look for," an early form of the criteria sheet. However, the problem was that Observers weren't giving any feedback to their Doers! Muska called the children together and asked if they understood that they were to tell their partners how they were doing. One little girl said, "I don't want to say anything bad about my partner's performance in front of all these people." Muska asked, "Well, is there anything else you could say besides bad things?" She replied, "Yes, I could say good things about the movement." Muska agreed, saying, "That's right, so please go back and practice that." The little girl became indignant, saying, "I thought you said this was about teaching and learning." Muska replied, "Yes, I did." The little girl stated with conviction, "But teachers don't say nice things!" From then on, Muska said, we made sure to emphasize the importance of providing feedback about what the Doer is doing well in addition to correcting errors.

In this biography Sara Ashworth also wrote that in Style C: Reciprocal, the term "little teacher" too frequently evoked unwanted behaviors. Altering the name to "observer" alleviated the invitation to counterproductive behaviors.

Style D: Self-Check

The essence of Self-Check is that learners perform the task individually and privately, and provide self-feedback by using criteria provided by the teacher.

In Self-Check the power for providing self-feedback is shifted to the individual student. In this Style, students develop an awareness of their own performance, enhancing kinesthetic awareness and becoming more able to accurately assess performance based on criteria which you provide. You make decisions in the Pre-Impact Set as in previous Styles, and are available for questions from learners as needed. The learner makes decisions in the Impact Set, performs the task and makes decisions in the Post-Impact Set by providing self-feedback according to your criteria. This is a further shift of decision-making of the previous Styles.

The main objective of Self-Check (Style D) is for each student to develop an awareness of personal performance by learning to observe his or her performance and make assessments based on criteria. Enhanced kinesthetic awareness and objective self-observation mean that the learner is becoming weaned from total dependence on outside sources of feedback (the teacher or a peer), develops the ability to provide an internalized schema of accurate performance and thus becomes more able to rely on self-feedback.

This Style continues the individualizing process by shifting decisions in the Impact and Post-Impact Sets to the learner. The learner thus learns to apply criteria for self- improvement, to maintain honesty and objectivity about performance, and to accept discrepancies and personal limitations.

The carryover of skills learned in the previous Styles enables this Style to follow in a smooth progression. In Style B: Practice, students learn to practice the task on their own using a task sheet; in Style C: Reciprocal, they learn to use a criteria sheet to give feedback to a peer, and in Style D: Self-Check, they learn to apply given criteria to their own performance.

Learn to respect the pauses that occur during Self-Check as very important: students are negotiating and learning.

You still make all the decisions in the Pre-Impact Set, dealing with what to cover and anticipating all decisions. As in Practice and Reciprocal, the learner makes the decisions in the Impact Set while performing the task. However, in the Post-Impact Set, instead of making decisions for someone else, these decisions are made for oneself. Episodes in Self- Check provide learners with opportunities to practice *self-reliance*.

An Episode Unfolds

After you introduce and describe the procedure for a Self-Check episode, tell your dancers to disperse in the studio and begin working on the task, as in Style B: Practice. As they practice the task, they will frequently refer to the criteria sheet, comparing their performance with criteria. Learners may choose to either repeat a certain task to correct or maintain performance, or to go on to a new task.

Self-Check is the first Style that gives time for learners to make these kinds of decisions for themselves. The pauses that occur during Self-Check are very important: Pausing to read and internalize the criteria, pausing again after performing the activity to reflect on performance. You will be able to observe the process of self-negotiation as they work. You will see students expressing concern or joy as they identify, practice correcting, and deal with discrepancies between theory and reality: between the criteria for correct performance of a movement or phrase and how they actually perform it. A good deal more than "just going through the motions" is occurring in the dance studio when your students are engaged in Self-Check.

Pre-Impact Set
You still make all the decisions in the Pre-Impact Set: you plan the lesson, anticipate the decisions shifted to the learners, decide which tasks are appropriate and develop the criteria sheet for this episode. The same skills which are appropriate for the previous Styles are appropriate for Self-Check.

Impact Set
Especially for the first episode in this Style, explain the purpose and expectations of this new Style and the roles of the learner and teacher. Your introduction might go something like this:

"The purpose of Self-Check is for you to develop a greater awareness of your own performance, enhance kinesthetic awareness and become more able to accurately assess your performance. Just as in Practice Style, you will practice individually but now will also use the criteria sheet to provide self-feedback.

"Your role is to make the decisions as we have done previously in Practice and Reciprocal and practice the phrase. You will also provide your own feedback according to the criteria provided on the criteria sheet.

"I will come around and be available for questions."

Present, describe or demonstrate the task, explaining any logistics or parameters needed. Then tell the students to find their own space and begin. Each dancer decides where to start, continues making decisions as in Styles B and C, and adds the new decision of self-feedback.

Post-Impact Set
As they follow the criteria sheets, observe students' performance and how they implement the criteria sheet for Self-Check. Communicate with each student about his or her proficiency and accuracy in the Self-Check process. It is important that your verbal behavior reflects the intent and essence of this Style and supports the change in roles and relationship between you and your students. This is *not Practice*. When watching a student, ascertain whether that student can *compare, contrast, and draw conclusions* concerning personal performance and criteria. When discrepancies exist, lead the learner to see these accurately. Talk with the student and really listen to what the student is saying. If the student is unaware of certain discrepancies, it is important to frame questions carefully, pointing out problem areas without increasing the frustration that can occur with questions that the learner cannot answer.

Tip: Quick Episode Sandwich. *If you sense a student becoming frustrated, you may need to make an adjustment decision: do a quick episode sandwich by going to Style B to offer feedback to the learner about performance of the task and how to fix it. You may also do a quick episode sandwich in Style F: Guided Discovery to give the student hints which will enable him or her to discover how to fix the problem.*

You might approach a student and ask a general question such as "How are you doing?" This enables the learner to decide how to respond, such as:
1. "Fine!"
2. "I can't get it, and I don't know why."
3. "I can't get it, but I know how to fix it."
4. "I can do it and I understand the criteria sheet."

The first response is too general; it may mean that the student has problems but doesn't want you to know, or may mean that the student is able to do it. You must ask questions that invite the student to focus on criteria and performance, as in Style C. The second statement tells you that the student is unable to identify or correct an error, and you need to tell (or guide) the student. The student should be able to verbalize specifically what she or he is doing, as in the third and fourth responses; then you can verify it, give encouragement, and move on. A better way to initiate communication is to refer to a specific aspect of the task such as, "What are you doing well and what are you having trouble with?" or "How are your elevations?"

<u>Logistics</u>

It is important that learners attain the basic competency in a task for this Style to be appropriate. It is difficult to perform an accurate self-assessment when learning an absolutely new skill, and beginning students who are still in the first awkward phase of dance are not yet ready to move to Self-Check. In addition, some movements, such as leaps or other elevations, go by so quickly that the learner doesn't have a lot of time to assess the performance. If asked, "Was your back leg bent or straight when you landed from the tours jeté," the student might not know. Therefore, for new skills or actions that are performed very quickly, Reciprocal Style would be a more appropriate choice.

In a class some students may be working in Practice, some in Reciprocal and some in Self-Check Style at the same time. This can be accomplished if you design your criteria sheet to be utilized with different Styles (see examples at the end of this chapter).

Video is an excellent tool to accompany Self-Check. Students can be recorded as they perform the task and the video can then be a resource in two ways: students can view and critique themselves outside of class time, using the criteria sheets to assess and record areas that need more work in the next class; or the video can be available at a station in class for students to refer to as they work.

Professional educational videos or CD-ROMs can also be useful in Self-Check. Educational videotapes or DVDs detailing particular steps, phrases or exercises may be set up as a station in class for students to refer to as they work, providing a tireless and constant demonstration for students that need a reference model.

Implications

Style D: Self-Check implies that *you*

- Value the independence to be given to students,
- Value the learner's ability to develop a personal monitoring system,
- Trust the learner to be honest and accurate during this process,
- Have the patience to ask questions focusing on the student's process of assessment, self-check and on the performance of the task.

And that *your students*

- Can work privately and engage in the self-checking process,
- Can identify personal limits, successes, and failures,
- Can provide personal feedback for improvement.

> ***Tip****: You can learn a great deal about your students by watching them work in this Style. Students reach a comfort level with Self-Check at different speeds. Some students enjoy independence and are immediately ready for the demands of individualization inherent in Self-Check, while others will need more time before they develop the skills, work habits and confidence to work successfully in Self-Check. Be patient and focus on the learning process.*

Student Observation Forms and Techniques

It is said that learning is a covert activity. It can't be seen or directly measured, but we infer it is happening by a change in behavior: while previously a student couldn't answer a question correctly, now they can; where once a student couldn't do a grand fouetté, now they can. In dance classes, it's often easy to see when a student has learned something. But sometimes learning in dance is more cognitive than physical. Often students, especially beginning adult students, are quite engaged cognitively, though their physical skills may be at the very basic level. You can't always tell what they're thinking, but like an iceberg, there's a lot more under the surface. Observation forms are a tool to enable students to share what they're thinking.

In addition to learning how to observe for episodes in Style C: Reciprocal and Style D: Self-Check, students may find themselves temporarily unable to physically participate in class. In academic classes, students may be required to participate in order to receive

> *Observation forms enable an exchange of cognitive information.*

an attendance or participation grade; students in recital and competition studio classes may be required to attend a certain number of classes in order to perform. When a student isn't able to participate *physically*, let them know that you expect them to participate *cognitively,* and use this as an opportunity to guide their seeing and sharpen their observation skills; give them an opportunity to show you what they understand. Rather than have them sit in a corner or just run the music, use this as an opportunity to participate mentally and enhance their observation abilities even more. Telling a student to "just watch class" isn't enough; tell them what you want them to notice and watch, and guide their seeing and thinking. Take the time to craft clear, thoughtful observation forms and keep them on hand for those times when a student has a sore knee, menstrual cramps, or other "I'm not up for dancing" days. Examples of observation forms are at the end of this chapter.

> *Be sure that these forms aren't seen as "busy work". Read them, and let students know that you read them. In a ballet class, while the rest of the class is working in Practice or Reciprocal, or is engaged in individual stretching, I come over to the observer(s) to touch base, chat about what they are noticing, and call their attention to certain aspects of class. This lets them know that their observation is important, brings their observation to a new level, and gives me the chance for some one-on-one or small-group interaction, to see on what cognitive level they are engaged. I always take a moment to peruse the forms after class; these student observations are often informative. I might discover that the student who seems to be perpetually disgruntled in class is actually working with deep concentration; the student who seems to be a klutz is actually noticing line and design and making lots of internal connections.*

Summary

In Practice, you as the teacher are responsible for providing feedback; in Reciprocal, students provide feedback to a peer based on criteria, and in Self-Check, the power for providing self-feedback has been shifted to the individual student. Through application of each of these Styles students develop an awareness of personal performance, which serves to enhance kinesthetic awareness. From the criteria that you articulate, students learn how to internalize and apply criteria for performance improvement; they learn how to deal positively with discrepancies between their abilities and established criteria.

Several distinctions are key to Self-Check. Your verbal behavior reflects the intent and essence of this Style, which is distinctly different from Practice and supports the change in roles and relationship of teacher and learner. When watching and interacting with students, determine whether each student can compare, contrast, and draw conclusions concerning personal performance and criteria. When discrepancies exist, lead your dancers to see these accurately.

Ahead

In any dance class it is rare that all students are at the same level of performance. The next Style, Inclusion, will prove very useful for every teacher who has a class of students with a wide range of abilities.

> ### To Do:
> *Identify a dance phrase or skill that would be appropriate for an episode in Style D: Self-Check. Remember that most learners are not aware of the details concerning their performance in the early stages of learning movement, and that it is difficult to perform an accurate self-assessment when learning a new skill or one that goes by very quickly. Using the skills you developed in the two previous To Do tasks, develop a criteria sheet for your chosen skill or phrase that will reflect what you feel is important in that dance phrase. Do keep the artistic facet of your teaching engaged!*

Style E: Inclusion

The purpose of Inclusion is for all students to be active independent of their level of performance, learn to choose an appropriate level of entry and learn when to move to another level.

In the previous four Styles, every task was designed by you as the teacher and represented a single standard with each learner working to perform at that level. However, in any dance class it is rare that all your students will truly be at the same level of performance. In Style E: Inclusion, the major decision shifted from you to your student is which level of difficulty to choose.

154

This Style will prove very useful for you every time you have a class with a wide range of abilities.

Here it is useful to discuss the concept of level of entry. Think back and try to recapture a moment when trying a dance phrase or skill wasn't easy, didn't come as second nature. Remember playing "double Dutch" jump rope? Gaining entry into those two twirling ropes was terrifying and exhilarating. Remember showing up at a social dance and everyone else already had a partner? Did you worry about how to enter the swirling sea of dancers? In order to "enter" or be a participating member of the class, each student learns how to identify a *point of entry*. Remember that example of the slanted rope? Each student chooses the height of the rope for what they believe is an achievable level. "Will you join the dance?" in this Style becomes an open invitation to find an achievable level and join the dance.

Objectives
The objectives of Inclusion Style are:
- Inclusion of all learners and continued participation,
- Accommodation of individual differences,
- The opportunity to enter the activity at one's ability level,
- The opportunity to step backward to succeed in the activity,
- The opportunity to step backward to re-explore the basics of a complex activity,
- Enabling learners to see the relationship between one's aspirations and the reality of one's performance.

Individualization is greater than in previous Styles, because choices exist among alternative levels within each task.

One application of Inclusion in ballet classes is for teaching and practicing pirouettes. Consider the following center floor exercise for pirouettes en dehors:
1. Start in fifth position, right foot front. Tendu the right foot á la second.
2. Plié in 4th position, right foot back.
3. Relevé passé retiré with one of the following options:
   a. No turn
   b. Quarter turn
   c. Half turn
   d. Full turn
   e. Double turns or multiple turns
4. Finish in fifth position, right foot front. Repeat for a total of four times on the right, then with four on the left.

Students may choose any of the options, from the "no turn" to "multiple turn" version. Thus, with the same basic exercise, students may choose the level that they feel is appropriate for their level of performance at that moment.

Using the example of the pirouette, let's examine the decisions a learner makes when given the multiple-level conditions of an episode in Inclusion Style. Here is the sequence of steps that a dance student goes through:
1. The dancer looks at the options described or demonstrated by the teacher.
2. The dancer makes a decision of self-assessment and selects a level. Usually the level is one that the student knows will ensure success.

3. The student performs the task.
4. Now the student has three options, based on performance of the task:
   a. To repeat at the same level,
   b. To choose a greater degree of turning,
   c. To choose a lesser degree of turning.
5. The student repeats the phrase with the selected degree of turning.
6. The student assesses the results. Again, three options are available: stay with that level, choose a greater degree of turning, or choose a lesser degree of turning.
7. It is important for you to remember to refrain from saying, "Do your best." This is a vague admonition, and learning isn't always best served by doing the most difficult task. The decision for the appropriate level must belong to the student. You can tell a lot about students as to the initial

> The purpose of Inclusion Style is for the student to make the decision about the appropriate level.

level they choose and their response to the results. Students may choose to remain at a particular comfort level for many reasons; again, it is important for the instructor to respect and honor the student's decision for choosing that level. On the other hand, some students may be driven to attempt a level beyond their abilities.

For example,
Teacher: "Which level have you chosen?"
Learner: "I'm doing the phrase on level three."

Teacher: "And how is your performance on this level?"
Learner: "I'm OK."

Teacher: (Observes for a moment) "Tell me about the second part of that phrase."
Learner: "I seem to be getting off-balance there and can't get all the way around to get into the next part of the phrase."
Teacher: "Let's take a look at your balance. Why do you think you're getting off?" At this point you may engage the learner in an episode in Guided Discovery, to help the student either to discover how to accomplish this level or to select a more appropriate level.

An Episode Unfolds
Inclusion is a time for students to reflect on their level of ability and choose an entry point that they feel is appropriate for them. Helping them see options, guiding them to choose what is best for them, and also honoring their decisions, are at the heart of Inclusion. Keep all this in mind as you plan an episode in this Style.

Pre-Impact
Your role is to make all the decisions in the Pre-Impact Set. The learner makes the decisions in the Impact Set, including the decision about the level of the task. In the Post- Impact Set, the learner makes assessment decisions about performance and decides which level to continue using. To introduce this Style for the first time in a class, prepare a demonstration of the concept of inclusion using the slanted rope mentioned previously, the sequence of the Inclusion episode, and appropriate questions and statements. Also prepare the various options for students to select for the degree of difficulty.

Impact

Expectations: Behaviors and roles.
The concept of multiple levels, choice, differences in performance, self-correction and changing one's mind are all new concepts. Set the stage by presenting the concept: tell the students or ask questions that guide them to discover the concept of Inclusion. The best method for initially introducing classes to Style E is to actually do it using a slanted rope: nothing can match the impact for class members of really doing it, the experience of everyone being included and choosing their own level. Whether they are children or adults, nothing is as powerful as having all students go through this experience. It will be a smooth transfer to other dance movements and phrases. Such a presentation is usually so powerful that in subsequent episodes using Style E this preparation is not needed; learners do not need to see or hear it again, they just need to experience it.

To review the slanted rope activity: Have two students each hold one end of a rope, each end about a foot off the ground, and ask all members of the class to run and leap over it. Chances are that all of them will clear it, thus all are successful. Raise the rope a few inches and most would be successful again. Continue to raise the height of the rope, and at each subsequent height a few students will fail to clear the rope, and be excluded from the experience. Continue to raise the rope until the number of students not excluded and experiencing success is only one, and eventually none.

Now have one student hold one end of the rope at floor level and the other student hold the end of the rope at shoulder level, and ask students to choose where they will run and leap over the slanted rope. After they have done it once, tell them that they should evaluate their performance; they can choose to try a higher level, a lower one, or to stay at that same level. What is important is that they *evaluate their performance and choose a level.*

> *This Style is equally appropriate for children's technique classes, university classes, multi-level classes.*

After your class has experienced the concept of inclusion, identify the dance activity that is to be performed. Then tell the students the main objective of this Style: the inclusion of all learners by providing different degrees of difficulty within the same dance phrase. As with previous Styles, each student chooses a location and all disperse with task sheets in hand. Then they will look over the levels for the task and decide on their individual entry points.

Clearly describe behavior expectations by explaining to students their role. They are to survey the choices, select an initial level of performance, and perform the phrase. They will then assess personal performance against the criteria that you have provided, and decide whether the same level or another level is desired or appropriate. Define your role as teacher: you will initiate communication with each student and answer any questions.

Expectations: Subject matter.
Present the dance phrase and discuss the factor or factors that determine the degree of difficulty. Explain logistics and any necessary parameters; answer any questions, then tell the class to disperse and begin to work on the task.

You will see your students performing the tasks on different levels, assessing their performance, and making decisions about the next step. Just pause and observe for a moment to give them time to experience this new process. Then circulate through the studio to offer individual feedback to each student as in the previous Styles.

Remember that you will respond to the student's role in decision-making, *not* to performance of the task. For example,

    <u>Teacher</u>: "What are you performing well?"
    <u>Learner</u>: "I'm doing well with the phrase on level three."
    <u>Teacher</u>: "I see that you know how to make that decision."

When you detect an error when a student is practicing, no matter what the selected level, ask the student to review the task description and check performance again. Be patient and wait to see if the student can identify the error. If not, tell him or her.

Be sure to pay attention to learners who stay at their initial chosen level. The purpose of this Style is to reduce the gap between aspiration and reality, and sometimes this gap is emotionally based rather than physically based. With some students, the ability is high and the desire low: the student is capable of more than is attempted. Sometimes the reverse is true: the desire is high and the ability is low: the student is trying to bite off more than he or she can chew. It is your role to help your students understand the nature of the gap and work to close it. Deal with this issue using tactful support, allow time to develop an understanding of each student, and develop rapport so that each learner will come to understand his or her gap and be willing to reduce it.

<u>Verifying vs. Approving</u>

Avoid using value feedback referring to the selected level (i.e., "Excellent choice," or "You can do better than that!") It is the student's role to learn to select a level that is appropriate, not to please you. It is not your role to tell the learner whether or not you like their selected level. However, it *is* your role to guide students if or when they constantly or repeatedly make inappropriate level decisions. This Style offers learners opportunities to learn to accurately self-assess their level of performance. Focus on using neutral feedback and on being patient. Remember that the objective of Style E is for students to learn to make appropriate decisions about which level in the dance activity is most appropriate for them. Sometimes this is a valuable "reality check" for students.

> *My husband asked me to teach him to knit. He had a rather complex project in mind—a pair of wool socks-- and wanted to get started on it right away. I suggested starting with something easier—a scarf. After stopping and undoing it several times due to errors of various kinds (yes, it's harder than it looks), frustration was starting to set in—"Why do I have all these holes and twists in my work and how do I fix them?" Because I could feel immediately when I made a mistake, I hadn't made beginners' knitting mistakes for many years and so didn't know how to tell him what to do. So I started a small piece of my own, in which I would practice making mistakes of various kinds, then systematically figure out what was wrong and how to fix it. He did the same, and gradually became more adept, both at fixing mistakes more easily and also at feeling when a mistake was made, and reducing the number of mistakes. Dance is like that: Mistakes provide usable data. Permission to fail is important for success.*

Post-Impact

As in the two previous Styles (Reciprocal and Self-Check), the Impact and Post-Impact Sets are interwoven as learners assess their performance using the criteria sheet. Observe your class for a bit, and then circulate to make private contact with each dancer, offering feedback about their participation in the role. This will work as in Styles B and D with the added dimension of verifying (not approving) to the learner the appropriateness of the selected level. After learners make their assessment comments it is appropriate for you to make positive value statements concerning the appropriateness of their selected levels.

> *Tip: It is appropriate, and sometimes very important, for you to ask a student why a particular level was chosen. ("Tell me about your choice of this level.") For example, using the example of the pirouettes, when you encounter a fairly advanced student doing the "no-turn" version; you might be tempted to encourage the student to do a different level. However, this student might be attempting multiple turns but has made a conscious decision to practice the "no-turn" version in order to identify problems with balance, arm position, alignment, or push-off, and will use this information when performing the multiple-turn level. Harder is not necessarily better, and working at a simpler level will often yield information for the student.*

Implications

Each Style of the Spectrum has a unique function and power in the development of the individual dance student. Style E has tremendous implications for dance pedagogy. Whether your motto is "Every person has a dancing soul" or "Only the strong survive," Inclusion can be a powerful tool in the dance studio. If inclusion is a goal of dance education, especially when teaching children and adult beginners, then the inclusion of *all* students by creating conditions for successful entry points into dance is important, and Style E accomplishes this goal.

The concept and application of Inclusion contain a cluster of implications:
1. Most importantly, use of this Style implies that philosophically you support the concept of Inclusion and accept that there are differences in performance.
2. It also implies that some episodes may tend to *exclude* while others are specifically designed to *include*. This dichotomy occurs in all aspects of dance education.
3. It implies that you have created conditions for the class to experience the *relationship* between aspiration and reality, desire and ability.
4. It implies that students have the opportunity to learn to accept the *discrepancy* between aspiration and reality, between desire and ability, and can learn to reduce the gap.
5. It implies that it is legitimate to do more than or less than others. It is OK to be on a different level of performance than the person next to you. Legitimizing this difference between individuals validates a reality based on intrapersonal rather than interpersonal competition: not measuring what others can do but "what I can do." In episodes in Inclusion, the competition is against *oneself* rather than against someone else.

> *"You are in competition with the person you want to become." -- Martha Graham*

The five points listed above are essential factors that invite teacher and learner to examine self-concept, including a learner's ability to choose an appropriate level of skill, independent from the teacher's decision. Inclusion can help students gain an authentic picture of where they are in class. Some students in classes have an unrealistic picture of themselves, either that they are not as good as everyone else when in fact they are average or above average, or that they think their abilities are very high, when in fact they are below par. Episodes in

Inclusion, used in conjunction with other Styles, can help students to see their dance abilities more realistically.

It is extremely important to give careful thought and planning to create legitimate options in entry points to a dance task, recognizing differences among students in terms of factors such as ability, physical attributes, energy levels, and cognitive understanding. This Style is appropriate for children, university non-majors and multi-level classes.

> *Inclusion obviously isn't appropriate for every objective in dance teaching. In many upper-level technique classes, one of the objectives is specifically to prepare students for the professional world: to exclude those who aren't able to do the most complex or physically rigorous training. Auditions for the Broadway stage are obviously not inclusion situations. And many teachers believe that the selection process should begin at the elementary level: those students who can't do it shouldn't be kept on and given "false hopes." Whereas Style E would generally not be the only Style used in teaching dance, it is extremely important in children's classes and beginning adult or recreational classes. Inclusion can be used appropriately even in professional preparation technique classes: remember that one important objective of Style E is to enable learners to see the relationship between one's aspirations and the reality of one's performance.*

Degree of difficulty: Designing the task

The main question which will confront the dance teacher who wants to use an episode of Inclusion is, "How do I identify what determines the degree of difficulty in the selected task?" Degree of difficulty may involve flexibility, balance, strength, endurance, speed, agility, precision, rhythmic ability, projection, application of qualitative features (Efforts), and others, depending on subject matter. Some suggestions include:

1. Turns: varying the degree of turn (partial, multiple) or adding a turn in a phrase;
2. Adding elevations or changes of level (deepening a level or adding a fall; putting in a hop, such as doing a relevé or a cabriole instead of a simple arabesque);
3. Taking the body off-balance while turning;
4. Varying use of arms or legs during the turn;
5. Changing the spatial relationship within the room or within the body;
6. Varying use of arms or torso during an elevation;
7. Adding batterie (beats);
8. Balance, static or dynamic alignment, "center;"
9. Varying timing of a movement;
10. Changing alignment or center of gravity during a balance: adding a twist, tilt, "twilt," penché or cambré to a balance;
11. Qualitative features (Efforts), for example:
12. Vary or intensify the inherent qualities in the phrase: (for example, extreme lightness or strength), or application of a constellation of Efforts;
13. Change the phrase to use Efforts that may be the opposite of what seems natural for the phrase or for the student;
14. Focus, projection, performance.

For some students, Style E can be disturbing. Some very good dancers have difficulty with this approach to learning because they are more comfortable in situations in which they are told what to do, in which they know their "place" in the hierarchy of the class and are recognized by the teacher for their abilities. Their goal is to be the best and they feel comfortable when the dance studio classroom facilitates that need. They are accustomed to being singled out as "the best" in class; emotionally they feed on positive public feedback that calls attention to them. Breaking the emotional dependence for attention and feedback from the teacher can be unsettling for such students; accepting that all learners are equal (in episodes in Style E) can shake their sense of self as "the best."

For students who are less skilled, the opposite reaction often holds: they usually love this Style. For many, it is the first time they have been included; they identify with this Style because they have an entry point that allows them to participate and succeed, and they see a chance for progress and development at their pace. Also, teachers who have "special needs" students or who teach multi-level classes will find Style E especially useful.

> **_Tip_**: *For students, learning to become more independent takes time. Having infrequent episodes in Style E may be frustrating, whereas regular episodes in Style E will give the opportunity to gain the full benefits.*

Summary

In any dance class it is rare that all students are truly at the same level of performance. In this Style, the teacher designs a task with different levels of difficulty, and each student decides which level of difficulty to choose. The purpose of Inclusion Style is to include all learners, accommodate individual differences, give students the opportunity to enter the activity at one's ability level and enable learners to see the relationship between one's aspirations and the reality of one's performance.

> **_To Do_**: *Create a dance phrase that includes at least three different levels. Write a "script" for how you will present these as choices or options for students. Be proactive in anticipating how you'll work with students in the following situations:*
> * *A student who chooses a difficult level and is frustrated about his or her inability to perform it.*
> * *A student who chooses a simple level and seems to be performing the same level repeatedly with no change.*
> *Reflect on the kind of feedback you'll supply and how you'll deliver or phrase the feedback.*

Chapter Summary

Styles A-E are used primarily for reproduction: for practicing "known" information: codified movement pattern or styles. You give the steps, provide the model to be followed by the students. The Spectrum brings you and your students from Cued Response, which represents a single criteria that all must follow, through the socialization process of Reciprocal to the increased cognitive and kinesthetic awareness of Self-Check to the level of Inclusion, in which students learn to accurately assess their own level of ability.

Following are examples of task sheets, criteria sheets, or checklists from modern dance, ballet, jazz, ballroom dance, and folk dance classes. They are designed to be used in Practice, Reciprocal, Self-Check and/or Inclusion Styles. The ballet grand allegro gives examples of multiple levels for almost every step of the 8-measure phrase, just to give examples of how many ways a step can be varied.

Ahead

The next section deals with the Production cluster of Styles, inviting the discovery of solutions.

Questions for Reflection and Discussion

Style A: Cued Response

1) Define "**quick episode sandwich**" and give an example.

2) Identify the **characteristics or examples** of an episode in this Style.

3) Define **decisions** in the Pre-Impact, Impact, and Post-Impact Sets and give an example of each.

4) Define **cueing, expectations** and **logistics** and discuss why they are particularly important in Style A: Cued Response.

5) Give examples of different types of **cues**, discuss which are your favorites and why you think you gravitate toward these.

6) Discuss some **problems** that might arise during an episode in Style A: Cued Response, and identify possible **solutions**.

Style B: Practice

1) Identify how an episode in Style B: Practice differs from just having students do a quick individual run-through.

2) Identify the **nine decisions** that are shifted from teacher to student in Style B: Practice.

3) List examples of **appropriate tasks** for Style B: Practice.

4) Discuss the **implications** of Style B: Practice.

5) Discuss **problems** that might arise during an episode in Style B: Practice, and possible solutions.

6) Discuss the purpose of **task sheets**, and some factors to keep in mind when designing a task sheet.

7) Give examples of how using task sheets can pro-actively head off certain problems.

Style C: Reciprocal

1) Identify the **decisions** which are made by the Observer.

2) List the **roles** of the Doer, the Observer, and the Teacher, and discuss the dynamics of the Doer-Observer-Teacher triad. Why is it important for the teacher to communicate primarily with the Observer and not the Doer?

3) Identify **appropriate tasks** for Style C: Reciprocal.

4) Discuss the **implications** for Style C: Reciprocal.

5) Give examples of the different forms a **criteria sheet** might take.

6) Identify some of the **benefits** of using Reciprocal Style.

7) Discuss how to introduce the concept and importance of Reciprocal for all students, addressing the issue of students who are more and less experienced working together.

Style D: Self-Check

1) Identify how **Self-Check** differs from **Practice**.

2) List the **decisions** which are shifted to the learners.

3) Discuss the **implications** of Style D: Self-Check.

Style E: Inclusion

1) Define **level of entry**.

2) Identify the **objectives** of Inclusion.

3) Identify the **decision** that is shifted to the learners.

4) Discuss why you think there is a distinction between *verifying* and *approving* a learner's choice of level in Style E: Inclusion.

5) Give reasons why some students might be disturbed by Style E: Inclusion. How could you proactively troubleshoot for this?

Examples of Task and Criteria Sheets

Following are some examples of task and criteria sheets for a variety of dance styles in a variety of formats. Note the differences between *task* sheets and *criteria* sheets. Try out different formats and see what works best for you! You may also wish to print hand-outs or posters of the Classroom Charts to put on the backs of task and criteria sheets that you give to students during episodes of Practice, Reciprocal, Self-Check and Inclusion.

Criteria Sheet: Polka
Style C: Reciprocal or Style D: Self-Check

Name (Doer) _____ Date _____

To read "Direction" cues, read down the column marked, "Direction"; for reading "Foot" cues, read down the column marked, "Foot", etc.

1. Face any direction.
2. Start by practicing moving forward.
3. Start by working through each part at the speed you choose.
4. Gradually work until you can consistently match the tempo of the music.
5. Once you are able to consistently match the tempo of the music moving forward, practice moving in different directions: forward, backward, sideways, turning.

Direction	Foot	Rhythm	Beat	Cue
Place	Left	Ah	ah	Hop
Forward	Right	Quick	1	Step
Together	Left	Quick	and	Together
Forward	Right	Slow	2	Step
Place	Right	Ah	ah	Hop
Forward	Left	Quick	1	Step
Together	Right	Quick	and	Together
Forward	Left	Slow	2	Step

Date	Feedback by	Rhythm Correct?	Matches music?	Pathway straight?	Weight shift correct?	Directions correct?

Name_____

Date_____

<u>Modern Dance</u> Spiral Extension Series

Repeat each sequence, phases 1-4, alternating right, left, right, left.

		Progress notation, etc.
Phase 1. Spiral roll A. Sequential action through body: foot, knee, hip, torso, head. B. Finish in contraction with elbow pulled in to hip. Phase 2. Full extension A. Hips as high as possible B. Arm extended directly to ceiling C. "Energized" hand D. Extended leg completely straight E. Head supported and extended (not dropped) back Phase 3. Contraction A. Initiate in abs and elbow B. Fist, elbow, and abs used strongly, don't "sag" into gravity C. Take all counts to arrive; don't "sit" Phase 4. Spiral release to floor A. Sequential action through body: chest, hip, knee, then head & foot. B. Start with other foot to other side Correct rhythm 4 counts for each phase 2 counts for each phase 1 count for each phase		

Name_____		
Date_____		

Tango (American/International, 8-count basic)

Working individually or with a partner, practice through an entire song.

INDIVIDUALLY	Progress notation, etc.	Feedback by:

1. FEET AND LEGS
  –A. Correct step pattern and rhythm: S, S, Q Q, S
  –B. Feet parallel
  –C. Feet step directly forward, backwards, sideways
  –D. Reach forward or backward with extended knee; smoothly with
    no bounce or excessive knee bend.
 	
2. DANCE FRAME
  –A. Elbows lifted, arms parallel to floor
  –B. Shoulders relaxed
 	
3. FOCUS
  –A. Spine erect
  –B. Chin level
  –C. Eyes focus parallel to floor
 	
WITH PARTNER
1. FEET AND LEGS
  –A. Feet move in parallel lines, feet facing directly toward each other
    without stepping outside partner's feet.
  –B. Leg reaches directly forward or backwards, leg reaching from
the hip
 	
2. DANCE FRAME
  –A. Bodies face directly toward each other
  –B. Lead's R hand rests on Follow's back, just below shoulder blade,
    fingertips on the spine, with light pressure.
  –C.Follow's L hand gently holds Lead's bicep
  –D. Lead's R upper arm contacts Follow's L forearm, supporting
    it slightly.
  –E. All elbows are slightly lifted
  –F. Extended arms are buoyant, extended but relaxed. Lead's L hand
    is palm up, Follow's R hand palm down resting on Lead's hand.
 	
3. FOCUS
  –A. Spine erect
  –B. Chin level
  –C. Eyes focus parallel to floor		

Name			

MISERLOU

To the student:
Start by working through each part at the speed you choose. Then practice with a speed that matches the tempo of the music.

Description of the task	Quantity of the task	Progress notation, etc.	Feedback by:
Phrase 1: Facing center of circle – 1. R foot: Step side – 2. Pause – 3. L: touch toe FD – 4. Circle L toe around behind R foot	Practice phrase 1 eight times		
Phrase 2 – 1. L foot steps behind R – 2. R foot steps to R SD – 3. L foot steps across in front of R – 4. Turn ¼ turn to L on L foot to face reverse LOD	Practice Phrases 1 and 2 in sequence eight times		
Phrase 3 – 1. R foot steps across in front of L – 2. L foot steps a little behind R (on ball of L foot) – 3. R foot steps across in front of L – 4. Pause	Practice Phrases 1-3 in sequence eight times		
Phrase 4 – 1. L foot steps behind R – 2. R foot steps to right, beside L – 3. L foot steps in front of R – 4. R foot touches next to L, no weight on it Or, Practice individually the four sequences of this dance, then practice the four phases in sequence.	Practice the entire dance eight times through, practicing to reach the proper tempo		

Task Sheet for **Plié Sequence**

First Position:
- Demi plié, straighten. Demi plié, straighten. Grand plié, straighten.
- Port de corps: Roll all the way down, roll up to vertical.

Second Position:
- Demi plié, straighten. Demi plié, straighten. Grand plié, straighten.
- Port de corps: Curve and stretch to the right, lift to vertical. Curve to the left side, lift to vertical.

Third Position:
- Demi plié, straighten. Demi plié, straighten. Grand plié, straighten.
- Port de corps: Flat back, release all the way down. Flat back, straighten to vertical.

Fourth Position:
- Demi plié, straighten. Demi plié, straighten. Grand plié, straighten.
- Port de corps: Curve forward, lift to vertical. Cambré back, return to vertical.

Fifth Position:
- Demi plié, straighten. Demi plié, straighten. Grand plié, straighten.
- Port de corps: Arrondi: Curve side, down, across the body, back, side, vertical.

Criteria Sheet for Style C: Reciprocal or Style D: Self-Check

Name _____

Plié Sequence

In all positions: Two demi pliés, one grand plié, then a torso variation. Do once, receive feedback, repeat, incorporating feedback.

Plies in each position:	Progress notation, etc.	Feedback by:
a. Thighs rotated out: active outward rotation		
b. Abs engaged to keep pelvis aligned		
c. Arch of foot lifted (no rolling in or pronation)		
d. Heels remain on floor during demi plié		
e. Chest lifted and open		
f. Straighten knees completely after each plié		

First position
Pliés: See criteria above
Port de corps: Rolling forward and return to vertical
1. Sequential action starting at head, not pelvis
2. Maintain integrity of shoulders; don't lift or "hunch" shoulders
3. Lift spine to vertical on return, don't let lower back to arch or sag
4. Arms lift to 5th high and open 2nd at end

Second Position
Pliés: See criteria above
Port de corps: Tilt side, curve front, tilt side, then to vertical
1. For right side:
    a. Right arm to 5th low (en bas)
    b. Left arm to 5th high (en haut)
2. Diagonal lines in tilt
3. Curved spine when forward

Third Position
Pliés: See criteria above
Port de corps: Flat back, release, flat back, vertical
1. Arms in line with spine, not "winging" back
2. Entire spine (cervical, thoracic, lumbar) straight
3. Release head in the drop over
4. Entire spine straight again, arms in line
5. Up in "one piece"

Fourth Position
Pliés: See criteria above
Port de corps: Cambré back and return to vertical
1. Maintain integrity of shoulders: don't lift shoulders
2. Pelvis straight
3. Neck lifted and extended, not "dropped"
4. Arms reaching forward, horizontal line from fingertips to crown
5. Knees straight throughout

Fifth Position
Pliés: See criteria above
Port de corps: Spiral (port de corps arrondi)
1. Reach side then down with top of head & fingertips
2. Reach fully to each cardinal point: side, down, side, back, side, vertical
3. Reverse spiral: reach fully to each cardinal point again
4. Knees straight throughout

Name: _____

Intermediate Jazz
Pirouettes

Task:
1. Tendu Side
2. Plié in 4th position back, parallel
3. Relevé in parallel, forced arch
4. Finish in 1st position.

For Styles C, D: Criteria:
1. Tendu side:
   a. Elongated spine, abs engaged, tailbone lengthened downward
   b. Hips level
   c. Arms energized

2. **Plié in 4th position**
   a. Elongated spine, abs engaged, tailbone lengthened downward
   b. Hips level
   c. Back foot in parallel 4th position
   d. Entire back foot on the floor
   e. Arms in proper position, parallel to floor

3. **Relevé in parallel forced arch**
   a. Elongated spine, abs engaged, tailbone lengthened downward
   b. Hips level
   c. Shoulders and forearms square and level
   d. Adequate push-off from back foot
   e. Head moves appropriately with degree of turn

4. **Finish in 1st position**
   a. Return to 1st position, with control.

For Style E: Inclusion: Choose Entry Level
1. No turn, relevé only.
2. Quarter turns
3. Half turns
4. Single turns
5. Double turns
6. Triple turns

Name _____

Elementary/Intermediate Ballet
Grand Allegro phrase

Instructions:

Description of the Phrase	Progress notation, etc.	Feedback by
Measure		
1. Piqué on right		
2. Pas de boureé,		
3. Temps lié,		
4. Tombé to left foot front in 4th position.		
5. Relevé in 4th,		
6. Plié,		
7. Relevé passé,		
8. Finish in 5th position R foot front.		
Levels for measure 1:		
1. Piqué in first arabesque		
2. Step sauté in first arabesque		
3. Step cabriole in first arabesque		
Levels for meas. 2:		
1. Pas de boureé		
2. Pas de boureé entournant		
3. Step pas de chat		
Levels for meas. 3:		
1. Temps lié to point tendu en arrierre		
2. Temps lié to relevé in first arabesque		
3. Temps lié to sauté in first arabesque		
4. Temps lié to sauté in passé		
Levels for meas. 4:		
1. Step to 4th position L foot front		
2. Tombé to 4th position L foot front		
3. Single frappé of L foot to pointe tendu front, plié in 4th position		
4. Double frappé of L foot to pointe tendu front, plié in 4th position		
Levels for meas. 5-8:		
1. Relevé 4th, plié, relevé passé, finish in 5th position R foot front.		
2. Relevé 4th, plié, 1 pirouette en dehors, finish in 5th position R foot front.		
3. Relevé in 4th, plié, double en dehors, finish in 5th position R foot front.		
4. Two single pirouettes en dehors, one double, finish in 5th position R foot front.		
5. Single pirouette en dehors, single fouetté, double fouetté,		

Examples of observation forms.

The following are observation forms which I use in classes. Observation forms need to be general enough for any point in the timeframe of the class, yet focus students' attention on key aspects of class performance.

Ballet Observation Form

<u>A few ballet terms:</u>

Port de bras	*Retiré*	*Coupé*
Plié	*Passé*	*Cou de pied*
Tendu	*Pas de cheval*	*Chassé*
Degagé	*Grand battement*	*Sauté*
Relevé/elevé	*Temps lié*	*Tombé*
Rond de jambe	*Arabesque*	*Reverence*
Sous-sus	*Pas de boureé*	

For these observations, don't "name names." You are not "spying" ot "tattling" on peers, you are observing classroom behavior so you can better understand how it contributes to learning. Use the back of this page or additional pages as needed.

1. Observe for instances when students are actively engaged in information-gathering: when they ask questions (of the professor, of each other), answer questions (of the professor, of each other), seek information, or other appropriate learning behavior.

2. Observe for instances when students disengage from class (i.e., talk unnecessarily, "space out").

3. Observe for instances when students do not seek information when it seems to be needed (are passive, wait for others to figure things out then follow, seem clueless).

4. Identify evidence of students who are participating in class completely (mentally, physically, emotionally).

5. Discuss individual differences that you observe between dancers and they perform barre or center floor combinations and enchainements.

6. Reflect on your class participation and behaviors. What do you think you do well, and what do you want to focus on for improvement?

World Dance Observation Sheet

Student Name: _____ Date: _____

For these observations, don't "name names." You are not "spying" or "tattling" on peers, you are observing classroom behavior so you can better understand how it contributes to learning and overall atmosphere of learning.

1. Observe student behavior when a dance is called for review. Identify the types of behaviors you notice. Which are productive to learning?

2. Observe student behavior when dances are taught for the first time, for instances of active engagement during instruction: when students pay attention, when they practice actively and productively (as opposed to listlessly going through the motions). What is productive to learning?

3. Observe for instances when students are actively engaged in information-gathering: when they ask questions (of the professor, of each other), answer questions (of the professor, of each other), seek information (looking in the book or cue sheets), or other behavior.

4. Observe for instances when students disengage from class (i.e., talk unnecessarily, doodle, "space out").

5. Observe for instances when students do not seek information when it seems to be needed (are passive, wait for others to figure things out then follow, seem clueless).

6. Identify evidence of students participating in class completely (mentally, physically, emotionally).

Modern Dance Theory
Observation Form

Name _____   Date _____

Class topic: _____

For these observations, don't "name names." You are not "spying" or "tattling" on peers, you are observing classroom behavior so you can better understand how it contributes to learning and overall atmosphere of learning. Use the back of this page or additional pages as needed.

1. Observe for instances when students are actively engaged in information-gathering : when they ask questions (of the professor, of each other), answer questions (of the professor, of each other), seek information, exploring aspects of the exercise or task, practice, or other appropriate learning behavior.

2. Observe for instances when students disengage from class (i.e., talk unnecessarily, doodle, "space out").

3. Observe for instances when students do not seek information when it seems to be needed (are passive, wait for others to figure things out then follow, seem clueless).

4. Identify evidence of students who are participating in class completely (mentally, physically, emotionally).

5. Reflect on your class participation and behaviors. What do you think you do well, and what do you want to focus on for improvement?

8 Application: The Production Cluster

Discovery Threshold	Guided Discovery	Convergent Discovery	Divergent Discovery	Learner-Designed Individual Program	Learner-Initiated	Self-Teaching
	F	G	H	I	J	K

Production Cluster

Now you and your students together explore terra incognita via the Production Cluster of the Spectrum, from Style F: Guided Discovery to Style K: Self-Teaching.

Style F: Guided Discovery is the first Style in which your students become engaged in discovery. You design and present a series of questions designed to bring your students, step by step and discovery by discovery, to arrive at an answer which was previously unknown to them. Style G: Convergent Discovery, the second Style past the Discovery Threshold, engages the learner further in reasoning, using the rules of critical thinking[19] for the specific discipline (i. e., dance), "trial and error", and logic to discover the one correct answer or solution. Divergent Discovery (Style H) is related to what has also been referred to as *lateral thinking*[20], which asks the learner to generate multiple solutions or responses. However, in Style H, learners do not simply generate numerous responses but also apply various analytical skills to determine which of the multiple responses answer the question or are solutions to the problem, and it is this process of generating multiple options and choosing which are appropriate that is at the heart of artistic process (which will be explored further in Chapter 9). Style I: Learner-Designed Individual Program is another step along a pathway of increasing levels of independence and discovery; it is the first Style in which the *learner* designs the task or problem, which is, again, essential to artistic process. In Style J: Learner-Initiated, the individual learner initiates the Style or Styles for the episode or series of episodes, and this is the first time that your student, rather than you, makes all the decisions in the Pre-Impact Set. Style K: Self-Teaching occurs anytime an individual initiates a learning experience, designs it, performs it, and evaluates it, and is the mark of an independent learner.

Remember that, although the Spectrum is presented here sequentially, it need not be applied sequentially. Any Style may be implemented at any time. While some Styles do build on previous concepts, such as Styles B: Practice, C: Reciprocal, and D: Self-Check, you may, as I do, start the first day in a beginning-level class with an episode in any of the Production Styles. For example, you may start a class by posing the question, "What is dance?" using questions to guide the students to an answer which defines the subject for that class, whether it is ballet, ballroom or Baltic dances. You could start a class with an episode in Style H: Divergent Production by asking each student to design five movements for the word "travel" to introduce the concepts of axial and locomotor. So, keep in mind that application of the Spectrum is not a one-way street, with you and the students starting at one end and finishing at the other end

Remember the Zen garden analogy for the Spectrum? Walking through the garden is not a goal-oriented event. Since every stepping stone affords a different view of the garden, all stones are equal; it just depends on what you want to see or experience. You may walk along the path in any direction or even skip from one stone to another depending on where you want to go. You and your students may move to any step along the path depending on the goals for the class or lesson at that moment.

Style F: Guided Discovery

In Guided Discovery, you bring the students, by way of a well-designed sequence of questioning, along a path of discovery to a single correct answer.

Guided Discovery is the first Style that crosses the Discovery Threshold and invites the learner to engage in the discovery process. You bring your students along a path of discovery, by way of a well-designed sequence of questioning, to a single correct answer. This Style is rather like a dialectic or Socratic dialog.

This Style introduces learners to the concept of discovery. In all previous Styles, information or the answer to questions was known or immediately revealed to learners; feedback was designed to correct a learner's response or performance. Guided Discovery uses neutral and/or value feedback with the question sequence to guide the learner along the cognitive path that converges on a single correct answer.

As in the previous Styles, you as teacher still make all the decisions in the Pre-Impact Set. Your decisions concern objectives, the *discovery target answer*, and the *design of the questions* that will guide the learner to the discovery of the target answer. The Impact Set in this Style is the sequence of decisions made by you and your students. In the Post-Impact Set, you use value or neutral feedback to verify the student's response to each question or hint. The dialectic form is unique to this Style.

Discovery is more effective than demonstration to commit a concept or phenomenon to memory for a long period of time.

An Episode Unfolds
In an episode in Guided Discovery, you deliver each question as designed, wait for and listen to the learner's response, offer feedback (neutral and/or value), then move on to the next question gradually guiding the learner to the anticipated target answer.

Pre-Impact Set
Developing an effective sequence
The first Pre-Impact decision concerns the specific subject matter—what law, principle, rule, kinesthetic action, et cetera, do you want them to discover in this episode? Dance students can discover many different things, including:
- How
- Why
- Concepts
- Relationships
- Order or system
- The reason for something
- Limits or parameters
- Principles or governing rules

Example of a Guided Discovery question sequence
Episodes in Guided Discovery are often short; they may only include a few questions. However, what is important is that *the sequence of questions leads to discovery* of a pre- determined target. The following example is from a ballet class, but could be adapted to be applicable to most classes in technique, improvisation, choreography, and kinesiology. The specific purpose is for dancers to discover the source of torque or force for initiating turns. This is a good one to use when you notice that students are having trouble completing a full axial turn such as a pirouette, or increasing from a single turn to multiple turns.
- Question 1: "So, you're trying to move from doing a single to a double pirouette. What do you need in order to make that change?
- Anticipated response: "Get more force" or "go faster" or "push harder," etc.

- Question 2: "What propels you in a pirouette?"
- Anticipated response: "The arms."

- Question 3: "Try doing a turn without pushing with your feet: stand in passé relevé, then use your arms to propel you in a full turn."
- Anticipated response: Students try this method and realize that actions of the arms alone do not provide adequate torque for a turn. Notice that, in this instance, *the movement itself provides intrinsic feedback.*

- Question 4: "Now try doing a turn without pushing with your arms: stand in 4th position (or 1st, or 2nd, or whichever you choose for this episode) with your arms held crossed over your chest. Now push against the floor to propel you in a full turn (students do it). So, which gives you more force, the arms or the feet?"
- Anticipated response: "The feet!"

- Question 5: "Which foot?"
- Anticipated response: (Students will try each one several times. Again, experimenting with movement provides feedback.) "The foot that comes up," "The back foot," etc.

- Question 6: "So, in order to get more force for turns, what do you need to do with that foot?"
- Anticipated response: "Push harder," "Push with the whole foot," "Make sure the whole foot, not just the ball of the foot, pushes against the floor," etc.

The process of developing an effective sequence design may seem time-consuming, but just like the process of developing an effective task sheet, once you've made it you can use it over and over. After your "target" has been determined, the next step is to develop the sequence of steps, the questions or clues that will bring students to discover the end result. Experimentation and experience will help you develop effective dialectic sequences.

An effective design can be used as the model or prototype for that same target in different levels and different styles of dance (such as turns in modern, jazz, or ballet). Once you start thinking in the dialectic form and applying these in classes, it becomes easier. See the end of this section for examples of Guided Discovery sequences.

> *Often the most difficult aspect of Guided Discovery, for the teacher, is to wait for the learner's response. Fight that urge to "Just tell them the answer and get on with it!" Be patient and you will be rewarded.*

Impact Set

The Impact phase in this Style involves an interweaving of subject matter and the cognitive and emotional aspects of the relationship between teacher and student. It involves actually using the question sequence, the road-test for your sequence. If students have a lot of trouble with responding, you'll want to stop and re-work either an individual question or the whole sequence.

Being aware of the following will help direct your delivery:
  a) Objective or target of the episode. What do you want the to learn?
  b) Direction of the sequence of the steps. Where are you going with this?
  c) Size of each step. Are they appropriate for the skill level and cognitive level of the students?
  d) Interrelationship of the steps. Do they relate logically with each other, is the pathway clear, does step each build on previous ones?
  e) Speed of the sequence. Are you giving enough time to enable the learner to engage in mediation?
  f) Emotions of the learners. Are they engaged and challenged or becoming frustrated?

What should you do if a response is incorrect or tangential to the planned direction of the sequence? Repeat the question or hint that preceded the incorrect answer; if the response is again incorrect, ask a question that represents a smaller, intermediate step. Your verbal behavior is very important in maintaining a supportive climate. "Have you checked your answer?" or "Would you like to think some more?" indicates that you are patient, value the time needed by the student to engage in discovery, and consider the learner to be the focus of the relationship.

Guidelines for Delivery

In addition to a thoughtfully designed question sequence, it is important to follow four guidelines:
1. **Do not tell the answer.** To tell the answer eliminates the "discovery" and defeats the purpose of Style F: Guided Discovery. This will derail the entire process of connecting one small discovery step to another. If the student seems unable to form an answer, insert an appropriate intermediate step or hint, and be sure to note this in your lesson plan, a personal Post-Impact analysis for re-design.
2. **Wait for the student's answer.** This waiting time is necessary for the learner to engage the cognitive process of mediation. If you get impatient and give the answer, students will learn that they don't need to think of a response because you'll give it anyway, which defeats the purpose of Guided Discovery. Waiting time is often only a few seconds for each answer. However, research literature in several studies has revealed that some teachers are unable to wait more than two seconds for an answer. Relax and wait; an extra second or two will not slow down class, and you and your students will be rewarded.

However, when the task involves remembering a known, correct answer, waiting too long will not produce the answer, only frustration.

3. **Offer frequent feedback.** This can often be reinforcing with a "Yes!" or a smile and nod. The feedback can also be built in to the task. In the example of the pirouette, the experience of doing the turn in different ways provided the feedback. The movement itself provides the feedback; you need only confirm it. The purpose of offering frequent feedback is to provide encouragement, to indicate to learners that they are on the right path.
4. **Maintain affective awareness.** This means keeping a climate of *acceptance and patience* that will keep the discovery process flowing. Impatient reprimands will trigger frustration and will eventually bring the sense of discovery to a halt.

> *Key Points for Delivering a Guided Discovery Sequence:*
> 1. *Do not tell the answer.*
> 2. *Wait for the student's answer.*
> 3. *Offer frequent feedback*
> 4. *Maintain affective awareness.*

Post-Impact Set

The unique nature of the feedback in this Style is that, in a way, feedback is built into every step of the process. You are providing positive feedback or reinforcing behavior with each response to each question, which is encouragement for the student's accomplishment at every level. Continuous motivation is provided by the immediate, positive reinforcement; this spurs the student on to seek solutions, explore and investigate more.

If you have not used this teaching-learning Style in class previously, it may take some time to develop this form of dialog; students who have previously been taught to "shut up and dance" may not readily think and respond. As you use this Style in class and students begin to understand your expectations, as students begin to feel secure and less afraid to respond, the willingness to participate and offer overt verbal or physical responses becomes contagious.

In small classes it may be easy to observe all students for signs that they are at or near the current step; this may be more difficult in large classes. However, the excitement for discovery learning will soon permeate even a large class.

Especially the first couple of times you use Guided Discovery, it will be very helpful for you to do a quick analysis immediately after the episode or at the end of the class. Often all you'll need is a few notes or suggestions for improvement. The following is a brief checklist for you to evaluate your application of this Style.
1) Were you able to follow the sequence you planned?
2) Did you wait for every response?
3) Did you deliver the appropriate feedback (value and neutral)?
4) Did you need to clarify or insert questions?
5) Did you reach your target?
(Examples of Guided Discovery sequences, worksheet and checklist are at the end of this section.)

Some teachers find that they have already been using a form of Guided Discovery; others will find this Style initially frustrating. You might be thinking, "I usually use this Style; I often ask questions." Simply asking questions does not mean that you are using Style F. Several key points are essential to effective use of Guided Discovery:
1. The questions are in logical sequence, related to the structure of the episode's subject matter, and bring the learners along the path toward the answer. Random, isolated questions are not a part of this Style.
2. You wait for the student's response. If you wait for a few seconds and give the answer, students will learn that they don't need to think of the answer because it will be given. Waiting is an important part of Styles that engage the student in discovery.
3. The topic and target must be unknown in order to be discovered. Questions that have to do with memory or recalling a known answer are not part of this Style.

You want the learner to discover the answer but not become frustrated. Each question and response is a step toward an answer. If the step is too big, the learner will not be able to get to it. Sometimes questions for a smaller step need to be inserted as "hints."

> *Tip: It seems like a lot of work, but once you've gone through the process of creating a question sequence in Guided Discovery, it is intensely rewarding, not only for your students but for you as well. I remember a friend who, sighing about teaching elementary-level classes, once said, "If I have to teach 'pas de boureé' one more time I'll just go crazy." When dance teachers get burned out it is generally because they get stuck on teaching at a purely physical level and teaching in a single style. This becomes too much like repetitive factory work. Vary it for yourself (and for your students) to keep the act of teaching interesting cognitively, creatively and artistically!*

Implications of this Style
Using this Style implies that you are willing to cross the Discovery Threshold: to take risks and explore terra incognita. It also implies that you are willing to invest the time in studying the structure of the activity, identify a concept appropriate for discovery, and develop the cognitive path that will lead your students to the goal or target.

If you are accustomed to using solely Cued Response in class, this Style may be a challenge for you. However, if you have already been courageous enough to implement episodes in Practice, Reciprocal, Self-Check and Inclusion, you have already made several important transitions in your teaching, so give up the role as the sole source of knowledge and trust the cognitive capacity of your students.

An important implication of Guided Discovery is that the learner is capable of making the cognitive steps that lead to the discovery of the target concept. Guided Discovery can be used when working one-on-one with a student or with a whole class. You can insert a quick episode in Guided Discovery with one student while the rest of the class is engaged in Practice or Self-Check or at the end of class with a small group of students. If you give your class a break after the barre or warm-up to do self-directed stretches, you can use this time to work with individual students on key problems by using Guided Discovery. Choreography and composition classes are an excellent time to use it; so are tutorials and seminars.

Also remember that an important aspect Guided Discovery is the cognitive engagement and positive reinforcement in the affective domain. A three-minute episode may make the difference between a student quitting in frustration or realizing that you notice them, value them, and that many concepts in dance are awaiting their discovery.

> *A colleague remembers Muska telling her proudly about one student who came running up, exclaiming, "I can think, I can think! Muska, you made me realize I can think!" "That was her reaction to solving one of the infamous cognitive challenges he was forever posing so students could experience the joy and confidence building of 'Aha' moments" (Mueller in Simri, p. 138).*

Examples of Guided Discovery dialectics

Example #1:
Subject matter: Rules, concepts, principles which are applicable to most classes in technique, improvisation, choreography, kinesiology
Specific purpose: to discover the relationship between balance, base of support and center of gravity.[21]

Question 1: "What is balance?"
Anticipated response: Children as well as adults will generally have a response that demonstrates balance, either by giving a verbal answer or by showing a balance position.

Question 2: "Find a position which is very balanced (or stable)."
Anticipated response: Some dancers will stand on both feet, some will lower their center of gravity slightly while standing as in a plié, some will widen their stance.

Question 3: "Now become even more balanced, the most balanced possible!"
Anticipated Response: Moving to a more stable position. Check student's solutions to the problem by pushing each dancer slightly to upset the position of balance. This will cause students to realize that getting lower and adding more points of support will afford greater stability. Some may even lie on the floor, which is the anticipated target answer because this will be the hardest position to upset by a slight push.

Question 4: "Now move to a position that is *less* balanced."
Anticipated response: Most will find a new position with a smaller base of support or higher center of gravity. If they're lying flat on the floor they might roll onto one side; if they're on all fours they might remove the support of a hand or foot.

Question 5: "Now move to a position that is even *less* balanced!"
Anticipated response: Now they're probably starting to experiment, challenging themselves to find new, more precarious balances. This question can be repeated several times until most are on relevé on one foot with their arms in the air; some might suggest standing on one hand.

Example #2
Subject matter: Ballroom dance.
Purpose: To discover how to lead from closed to open position and from open to closed position.

Demonstrate closed position and open position.
Question 1: "So you want to get from closed position to open position. Leaders, how are you going to get your partners to do what you want to do?"
Anticipated Response: "Tell them!"

Question 2: (Smiles) "No, that's cheating! Ballroom dance is non-verbal communication. How will you tell them non-verbally?"
Anticipated Response: "Give them a secret signal?"

Question 3: "Well, think about where you want your partner to go. How do you want them to change their relationship to you?"
Anticipated Response: "They have to turn out (or turn away or turn right, turn clockwise)."

Question 4: "Yes, they have to turn away from you. Good. So, how will you them her to do that—how do you turn their body? Try several ways and see what you come up with to clearly communicate where you want them to go."
Anticipated Response: "Use the heel of your right hand to turn their body."

Question 5: "Good! What else do you have to do with your right arm so that it's not awkward?"
Anticipated Response: "Drop the elbow?"

Feedback: "Correct! Also, relax and drop your left arm slightly. Please practice this several times."

Question 6: "Now, let's figure out how to reverse those signals to get from open to closed position. How does the follower's relationship to the leader change?"
Anticipated Response: "The follower turns to face the leader again."

Question 7: "Good. And how will a leader turn their partner to face them again? (prompts: If you used the heel of your hand to turn them out…..)"
Anticipated Response: "Use the fingertips to turn her to them you again!" etc.

Example#3
Subject Matter: Elementary modern dance, children's dance
Purpose: To identify, categorize and name the five basic elevations and derived elevations.

Question 1: "What is an elevation?"
Anticipated Response: "A rise, getting higher, etc."

Question 2: "You can rise onto your toes, yes, but how would you get even higher?
Anticipated Response: "Jump, hop, etc."

Question 3: "Good! Yes, jumps and hops definitely get you off the floor! Some people use these terms loosely or interchangeably, but actually all elevations are classified or named according to the number of feet you use to propel yourself off the floor and the number of feet you use to land. Let's identify these. Somebody show me a jump."
Anticipated Response: Several students do various kinds of elevations; some are jumps and some are not.

Question 4: "Terry, do what you just did again. Does it push off with two and land on two? Hold onto that one and we'll look at it again in a moment. Ashton, do what you just did again. Let's all look at it—how many feet does Ashton use to push off the floor?
Anticipated Response: "Two."

Question 5: "Correct! Any time you're using two feet to propel yourself off the floor and land with both feet, that's a jump. Everyone, take a moment to make up a different type of jump—remember that a jump is two feet to two feet. You can turn, travel or stay in one place, do anything else with your arms or legs, but a jump is two feet to two feet."
Anticipated Response: (Students perform various types of jumps, and the teacher observes for correct responses, notifying students who produce incorrect responses, such as, "Blair, how many feet did you land on? Try it again; yes, you landed on one and *then* closed the other one, so that's landing on one foot.")

(Note: Although students are doing different types of jumps, which may appear divergent, all responses which are jumps are correct.)

Question 6: "Now, let's come back to Terry's elevation; please watch as he does it again. How many feet does he use to leave the floor?"
Anticipated Response: "One."

Question 7: "Correct. And how many does he use to land?"
Anticipated Response: "One."

Question 8: "Yes. What is that?
Anticipated Response: "A hop."

Question 9: "Yes, that is a hop—one foot to the same foot. Try out some hops—try some turning, some traveling; as long as you push off and land on the same foot."
Anticipated Response: (Students create various types of hops, and the teacher observes for correct responses.)

Question 10: "OK, what is another way to get off the ground?"
Anticipated Response: "One foot to the other!"

Question 11: "Do it (student does a leap). "Good, and what is that?"
Anticipated Response: "A leap!"
"Yes, a leap goes from one foot to the other" (Repeat having students try different leaps)

Continuing with the questioning, students can identify the remaining two elevations: sissonne (two feet to one foot) and assemblé.

Question 12: "Are there other elevations?"
Anticipated Response: "A skip."

Question 13: "Let's look at a skip. It's actually a combination that includes one of the elevations we've named so far. Do a skip very slowly (or have them work in pairs to watch someone else do a skip), and see if you can identify it."

Here students discover that a skip is a combination of a step and a hop, that a gallop is a combination of a step and a little leap back. Some students ask about certain elevations that they may have done in another dance class, such as a tours jeté (leap) or grand fouetté (hop), and may be surprised to discover that the step called a "switch leap" is really a hop!

Example #4
Subject Matter: College introductory modern dance
Purpose: To introduce side falls, work with the concept of balance and off-balance.

Teacher: Today and all this week we're covering falls.
Anticipated Response: (Various groans)

Question 1: What is the one essential element for a fall? What is necessary for a fall to be a fall?
Anticipated Response: To go down, to get bruised, to land on the floor.

Question 2: Watch these two demonstrations and tell me which is a fall and which isn't. (Kneels, then lowers down to prone position using hands. Comes back up to kneeling. Balances on knees and falls into prone position.) And this one. (Sits, hugging knees, then rolls into supine position on back. Comes back up to sitting. Hugs knees and balances on tailbone then falls, rolling, to supine position.) Which one in each demonstration was a fall and why?
Anticipated Response: (Sometimes students are unsure, can't verbalize the difference).

Question 3: Try the front version: kneel and *let* yourself down, then kneel and *fall* forward onto your hands. (Students try it out). Try the back version: sit on your tail and do a controlled roll down, then sit and balance, then *fall* onto your back. (Students try it out). What is the difference?
Anticipated Response: One of them lost control.

Question 4: Do either the front fall or back fall and control exactly when you fall. *You* control the moment of the fall, so it's not loss of control....
Anticipated Response: Loss of balance!

Question 5: Right! It isn't loss of *control* but temporary loss of *balance*. Those of you who have had kinesiology know the terminology: when your center of gravity moves outside the vertical line of your base of support, you will lose balance and fall." Falls can begin at any level and end on any level that is the same or lower. (Have students explore falls in different directions such as side, back, front falls; from different levels such as kneeling, sitting, and standing; to different levels such as standing to fall from one foot to the other, standing to fall to support against a wall or a partner.)

To Do:
Develop a sequence for the concept, "What is the relationship between tempo and size of step?" (Yes, you can probably just ask this question and most students will be able to answer it, but having them actually go through a sequence will be a stronger, more memorable experience).

This concept can be used in ballroom, international folk dance, ballet, modern or other dance styles. Determine what class you want to introduce to this concept, and develop a Guided Discovery question sequence. The sequence that you develop from this starting point can then be used to illustrate how dancers must apply different strategies in performing balancés in ballet class, the two-step in country/western dance, a waltz step in ballroom dance, a jazz pas de bourreé, running steps in a modern work, etc.

Summary

In Guided Discovery, you bring the learner along a path of discovery, by way of a well-designed sequence of questioning, to a single correct answer. Your students will begin to develop a sense of discovery process which, combined with the ability to provide self-feedback developed in Style D: Self-Check, will enable them to explore, analyze, and check solutions to movement questions.

Ahead

Style G: Convergent Discovery, takes the student further into terra incognita. The learner goes through the process of discovery without hints or guiding clues from the teacher. This is the next step into the Discovery Zone, on the path toward independence.

Subject matter: Purpose: Question:	Notes
Anticipated Response:	
Question:	
Anticipated Response:	
Question:	
Anticipated Response:	
Question:	
Anticipated Response:	
Question:	
Anticipated Response:	
Question:	
Anticipated Response:	
Question:	
Anticipated Response:	
Checklist for application of your Guided Discovery dialectic: • Did you reach your target? • Were you able to follow the sequence you planned? • Did you wait for every response? • Did you deliver the appropriate feedback (combination of value and neutral)? • Did you need to clarify or insert questions? (Update your sequence)	

Style G: Convergent Discovery

For Style G: Convergent Discovery, the student is engaged in exploration, reasoning, and critical thinking in the process of discovering the one correct answer to a question, the one solution to a problem.

For Style G: Convergent Discovery, each student is engaged in the process of discovering the one correct answer to a question, the one solution to a problem. How does this differ from Guided Discovery? You present a question and the learner goes through his or her own discovery thinking process without the benefit of a series of questions, guiding clues or hints that lead the learner to the anticipated target response. In Guided Discovery you provide the questions which lead to the discovery; in Convergent Discovery the learner constructs their own series of questions to make logical links that leads to the anticipated answer. Through this process, the dancer makes more decisions about the use of cognitive operations or "thinking in movement" to solve the problem at hand. The dancer also makes more decisions about the discovery process itself, the one correct solution, and the verification of the appropriateness of the solution.

To illustrate this, take a moment to solve the following problem:

Problem A

"An elevation, sometimes generically called a 'jump,' is anytime you push off from the floor and land on your foot or feet. Given that elevations are classified or typed according to the number of feet you use to propel yourself off the floor and the number of feet you use to land (and, when using one foot, whether it is the same or opposite foot), how many types of elevations are possible?"

This task is similar to the example used previously for Guided Discovery. However, as you can tell from the wording and tone, the one for Guided Discovery was designed for less experienced or younger students.

If you didn't already know the answer, you might solve it in a number of ways. As an energetic young dancer, you'd probably stand up and start jumping, hopping, leaping, and otherwise bouncing about until you arrived at the answer, "Five!" Or, you might sit and work it out with your feet or hands. Or you might write out all the possible combinations.

If students have already covered this material, if they already know the following:
- Jump = 2 feet to 2 feet,
- Hop = 1 foot to the same foot,
- Leap = 1 foot to the other foot,
- Sissonne = 2 feet to 1 foot,
- Assemblé = 1 foot to 2 feet,

then this will be Style B: Practice, as they simply recall the terms. However, many students, even advanced dancers, have either been accustomed to generically calling everything a "jump," or have a different, precise term for every different elevation and haven't studied them analytically. While having different terms for every elevation is useful, so is understanding broad categories, to understand that a pas de chat, saut de chat, glissade, tours jeté (grand jeté en tournant) and grand jeté all belong to the broader category of leaps. This knowledge will be useful when students encounter new knowledge: when they either learn a new elevation or see an elevation in a new context, they will be able to analyze it and tell whether it is a leap or a hop.

An Episode Unfolds Pre-Impact Set

As with previous Styles, you make all the decisions in the Pre-Impact Set: you choose the subject matter, design the problems or challenges for the episode, and determine the logistics appropriate for the episode.

Choosing tasks and Designing Episodes

Many of the same concepts which you might deliver with Guided Discovery are also appropriate for Convergent Discovery. Keep in mind the following criteria:

> *The difference between Guided Discovery and Convergent Discovery is that in Convergent Discovery, the learner constructs the series of questions to make the logical links that lead to the answer.*

1. The question, situation, or task must invite convergent thinking,
2. It must engage the learner in cognitive operations other than memory,
3. It must have a single correct response, answer, movement, or solution.

Impact Set

The shift of decisions comes in the Impact Set. The learner makes the decision about engaging in the cognitive operations that will lead to the discovery of the solution. In this process, the learner asks himself or herself questions concerning the presented problem. In Convergent Discovery the learner is autonomous during the search for the solution. Your role is to present the problem to your students, then observe them as they proceed through the process of exploration and discovery. This requires patience and restraint; sometimes teachers have a tendency to jump in and intervene, but restrain yourself!

The first few times you present an episode in Convergent Discovery, address your students and state the objectives of this Style:[22]

- To discover the one correct answer to the presented question or problem and the cognitive operations appropriate for the task at hand, and
- To examine the answer for its correctness, by using an answer sheet or answers at the end of the text, or by consulting with you.

Then introduce the role of the teacher:

- To present the question, allow time to work and think, and verify the solution and/or offer corrective feedback.

Describe the role of the learners:

- To receive the content question or problem, engage in mediation by searching to discover the single correct answer, and
- Verify the answer or solution and, if necessary,
- To call upon the teacher to participate in the verification.

Especially in initial episodes in Convergent Discovery, present behavior expectations *before* you introduce the subject matter. The more relevant and challenging the task, the more captivating it is, and the more students will want to jump in and start working on the problem *now*! But not only do you want your students to engage in the more independent problem-solving process of Convergent Discovery, you also want them to focus on the cognitive capacities they possess, and how to exercise and apply them in the future.

Initiate the episode by stating,

> "The main objective of this episode is for you to discover the solution to a problem by using logical, converging, and reasoning cognitive skills. Your role is to examine the problem and discover the solution or target answer; my role is to present the problem, follow your thinking process, and offer feedback or clues if needed but to allow you to discover the solution. You may ask relevant questions for clarification at any time while you are working." Explain the logistics and the parameters (time, space, and any others), present the problem, and have students begin.

> **_Quick Episode Sandwich:_** _If you observe several students making the same error in thinking, you can stop the action to repeat or clarify the task, procedure, or cognitive operation. You can address the whole class or only the students who were involved in the common error._

The solutions to the problems may be expressed in writing, notating, drawing, verbally, through movement, or other modes of communication, depending on the subject matter. You remain available for questions or verification after students begin working. Students who needs clarification or who have questions may individually request information. This initiation of communication gives you, in turn, an opportunity to learn about students' ways of approaching cognitive tasks: listen to students, answer questions if necessary (using Style F) that will guide them on the path to discovery. This private and cognitively intimate interaction is unique to this Style.

> **_Tip_**: _In the dance class, you will be able to see what paths students choose to follow and explore; not all paths will lead to the solution of a given problem. It is imperative that you wait; thinking takes time, and learning from failure is a necessary aspect of Convergent Discovery. It is this "waiting" time in which students examine and evolve ideas, sort through the many possibilities, and decide on the appropriate solution. You are waiting but your students are actively engaged in critical thinking. And although you can observe it when the dancers are in motion, when they aren't moving they're still cognitively engaged; allow them time and space. This process is private; don't intrude!_

Post-Impact Set
In Convergent Discovery, students are engaged in the Post-Impact Set interactively with the Impact Set; in the process of exploration and trial-and-error the movement provides its own feedback.

Circulate from one learner to the next, offering individual feedback about the correctness of the solution and about the cognitive process that leads to the solution. Use neutral feedback to acknowledge appropriate thinking and correct solutions, and corrective feedback to address inappropriate thinking—flaws in reasoning and judgment—and errors in the solutions. In some tasks you can observe students' process of discovery, but in some tasks this is not observable. You can initiate the contact with students by asking, "How are you doing?" "Have your verified your solution?" "How did you arrive at the answer/solution?" or "Do you have any questions about or problems with the task?" You have the opportunity to engage the learner in dialogue for the purpose of clarifying and guiding the flow of the discovery.

During closure at the end of the episode, offer positive value feedback to the entire class about the way they approached the task, their engagement in eliciting the cognitive operations necessary for the convergent discovery, how they searched for the solution and solved the problem. "Hey, everyone did a great job in working through that problem! I could see different learners using different sequences, but you all arrived at the same answer at the end."

191

Objectives

Style G: Convergent Discovery has specific subject objectives and behavior objectives that can only be accomplished in by this Style[23].

The subject objective is:
- Discovering the single correct solution or answer.

The behavior objectives include:
- Crossing the discovery threshold by discovering the single correct response,
- Engaging in a specific sequence of cognitive operations (thinking in movement) that lead to the solution,
- Becoming aware of one's engagement in problem solving, reasoning, and critical thinking.[24]

In the Post-Impact Set, the role of the learner is to verify the rightness of the solution by rechecking the reasoning process; sometimes simply by recognizing that the solution did indeed solve the problem. At this time, after the dancer has spent time in inquiry, exploration, decision, and testing the solution, you may participate in verifying the rightness of the solution by asking questions.

> *Suzanne Farrell, former soloist with the New York City Ballet, provides an example of a spontaneous application of convergent discovery, at the end of a rehearsal for* Vienna Waltzes. *She relates that she had already taken off her long practice dress, when Balanchine asked to see her solo. "So for the first time I danced my solo just wearing tights and leg warmers. I found myself taking tiny, tiny balancés. It felt so delicate, so beautiful. I said to myself, 'Mmm, Farrell. Remember this. It's a nice effect. Something you haven't done before.' I was so excited about my discovery. But that evening when I put on the costume and felt the weight of it, I knew I couldn't do those tiny steps because they wouldn't produce enough momentum to move the dress as dramatically as I'd like. I just stored away the memory of that effect and told myself, "Some other time, Farrell. Some other ballet" (Daniel 1979, p. 7).*

Although in theory the Styles of the Spectrum can be done in any order, it is advisable to have done episodes in Guided Discovery prior to working in Convergent Discovery, so students have seen the process of applied logic in action. Let's look at some more examples:

Problem A

"OK, now transpose the phrase from front to back (or inward/outward)."

Problem B8

"What is the rule that governs balance positions?"

This rule consists of three interacting principles that govern one's ability to maintain balance. Students might be at a loss as to how to approach this, so you might try what I call Style F.5 (halfway between Style F: Guided Discovery and Style G: Convergent Discovery): Give students a bit more information but let them go through it by themselves. For example:

"Explore the following positions; try to maintain your balance in each position for a few seconds:
1. Start with a position close to the floor, with 6 points of contact between your body and the floor,
2. With four points of contact between your body and the floor,
3. With two points of contact between your body and the floor,

4. With two points of contact in as high a vertical balance as possible,
5. With one point of contact in a non-vertical position.

Using the information about your balance from each position, state the rule that governs balance positions."

In order to solve this problem, the student must engage in exploration and trial-and-error, trying these balance positions. The experience of exploring the positions provides the student with information needed to discover the solution. This discovery process involves the activation of the following cognitive operations and critical thinking processes:

1. *Comparing* the information gathered from exploring these balances
2. *Organizing* the information into categories,
3. *Drawing conclusions* about each category, and
4. *Identifying* the relationship among the three principles involved in the sought, single rule.

Problem C

Question: "How is torque (rotational force) affected by size of a dancer's base of support during turns[25] such as pirouettes?"

The target answer is that the greater the size of the base of support, the greater the torque or rotational force; thus it is easier to accomplish multiple turns from fourth position (large base of support) than from fifth (smaller base of support), and almost impossible to do even a single turn when starting from a relevé retiré (passé) position (the smallest base of support).

Students need to understand the concept of base support. If they've already encountered the term in a physics or kinesiology class, or if you previously did Problem B above with them, or if you did the Guided Discover for falls with them and used the term "base of support," then they're cognitively prepared for a further application of this concept.

Initiate this episode by asking the class to do pirouettes en dehors from two feet in various positions and from one foot, from flat and from relevé. "Based on this information, draw a conclusion about the relationship between size of base of support and torque."

Students may initiate questions as they seek the answer, so be prepared for questions such as,
- "What positions can I do the pirouettes from?" (Answer: try all possible positions)
- "What arm positions can I use?" (Answer: keep the same arm position, so that the only variable is the size of the base of support)
- "Does the size of my feet matter?" (Answer: yes, even though students can't change this; bigger feet will mean a larger base of support).
- "Does the size of my fourth position matter?" (Answer: yes. Technically and theoretically speaking, the wider or larger the fourth position, the more torque can be produced. However, beyond a certain point, the bigger that fourth position becomes, the harder it is to maintain correct alignment, which can affect the dancer's ability to maintain balance throughout the turn).

In a pure Convergent Discovery episode, you would state the problem and students would start working to solve it. However, if you feel they need Style F.5, then you could give them the following task sequence and questions to answer on their own.

Instruct the class to do pirouettes en dehors from different positions:
1. From fourth position,
2. From fifth position,
3. From fourth position en élevé,
4. From fifth position en élevé,
5. From retiré (á terre),
6. From retiré en élevé.

Questions:
1. As you went from fourth position to fifth position, how did the degree of turn in your pirouettes change? Did you find it easier or more difficult to do a single (or multiple, depending on level of class)?
2. As you went from á terre to en élevé, how did the degree of turn in your pirouettes change?
3. As you went from two feet to one foot, how did the degree of turn in your pirouettes change?
4. As you went from á terre to en élevé on one foot, how did the degree of turn in your pirouettes change?
5. Based on this information, draw a conclusion about the relationship between size of base of support and torque.

__Quick Episode Sandwich:__ If you observe several students making the same error in thinking, you can stop the action to repeat or clarify the task, procedure, or cognitive operation. You can address the whole class or only the students who were involved in the common error.

Summary
In Convergent Discovery, the student is engaged in reasoning in the process of discovering the one correct answer to a question, the one solution to a problem. It is essential that you allow your students the time to engage in this process.

Ahead
In Style H: Divergent Discovery, students do not create only one answer to a question, they are invited to generate multiple responses in response to the same question.

Style H: Divergent Discovery

In Divergent Production, dancers are engaged in creating multiple responses to a single question, problem or task.

Innovation depends on divergent thinking, which is the basis for Style H: Divergent Discovery. The essence of Divergent Discovery is that learners are engaged in producing multiple discovered responses to a single question, problem, or task. The purpose of this Style is to engage in discovering and producing divergent responses.

An Episode Unfolds

Your role as teacher is to design suitable tasks, questions, or problems that invite multiple responses. The role of the dance student is to go beyond the known and create something new.

Pre-Impact Set

You determine the specific topic that will be the focus of the episode; for example, a topic for an improvisation or choreography class with divergent possibilities might be use of time, space, relationships, etc. Then you design the specific problem or series of problems that will enable learners to generate multiple solutions.

Impact Set

In this set the learners produces divergent solutions, then based on criteria set by the teacher, decide which divergent solutions are appropriate to the problem. The solutions generated by the student in the process of experimentation become the content of the episode (more on experimentation, thinking in movement, and artistic process will be discussed in the next chapter).

Post-Impact Set

As in the previous Style, the learner is engaged in the Impact and Post-Impact Sets interactively: the learner assesses the discovered solutions while seeking to generate multiple solutions. For each possible solution, the learner asks, "Does this particular solution answer the question?" If it does, then the learner knows that it is one possible option to keep in their growing "bank" of answers. If it does not answer the question, it can be discarded or re-worked, and the learner can continue to seek more solutions. When the learner can see the solution, external verification is not needed. However, given the subjective and aesthetic nature of dance, the learner may not be able to see certain aspects of the solutions. Feedback by video, teacher, and/or peers is valuable.

Examples include:
- Technique class: "Design four ways to finish the phrase we have been working on."
- Improvisation: "Generate six ways to do the action, 'turn.'
- Ballroom: "Make up three ways to get into the swing move called the 'Pretzel.'
- Notation: "Write the position demonstrated in three different ways."

Tip: The reason for the very directed ("Design three ways to....) language above is to prevent the self-limiting behavior on the part of some students when confronted with divergent tasks. If you say to a student, "How many ways can you..." and he or she answers, "One way. This way," that pretty much brings things to a screeching halt. "This is all I can do" usually means, "All I want to do and all I'm going to do just now, thank you very much and go away"). "I'm sure you can come up with another way" can invite the student to respond, "No, that's all I can do" and the exchange becomes a power struggle. Yes, in the perfect world all students want to be in dance class and all students have an innate desire to create, but reality sometimes has another agenda for us, one in which students engage in self-limiting behavior and thus challenge us as teachers. "Find three ways to..." lets the student know that you expect that they will all be able to produce three alternatives; this is the behavior expected of everyone in class.

On the other hand are those wonderful students, bless 'em, who will not only be creating alternatives until the custodian comes to lock the studio doors but will still be creating new alternatives when class meets again tomorrow or next week. When you ask for a set number of alternatives, you are establishing this as an activity that will take place in a certain time frame and that something specific will be done with the movement material that they have produced. Parameters thus provide a structure for students: knowing how many, how long, how much will enable them to make better choices.

Getting Past the Roadblock

During an initial episode in Divergent Discovery, most learners will start by doing things they've done before, working from memory and/or muscle memory. Then they will pause, as though they've run out of things to do. At this point they will cross the Discovery Threshold and begin to produce new responses. Some learners reach this point and stop, reluctant to risk the unknown, but recalling previously learned responses or actions triggers *divergent memory responses in Practice Style*, not Divergent Discovery. In order to get past this mental road-block, elicit that first cluster of predictable memory responses from the whole group, which reinforces the meaning of divergence and leads the class toward the discovery point. When the lag or hesitation occurs, stop the group action and restate the objective of Divergent Discovery: to produce unfamiliar, new ideas or movements. Then shift your students to working individually or in small groups to continue producing responses *but not repeat any already done by the group.*

*Avoid using the phrase, "Do whatever you like." If Divergent Discovery experiences lack adequate direction or purpose, students may feel that **they** direct the content, or that they can stop anytimet. Remember that students do not direct this learning experience, you do. Also, when students' responses aren't relevant to the task, or if their responses are not acknowledged in a meaningful way, they may feel that the experience lacks direction or that producing multiple solutions is a waste of time. Be sure that when you introduce an episode as Divergent Discovery, it has relevance and purpose. The following are examples of tasks which are too undefined, and are **not** examples of Divergent Discovery:*
- *Get a hula-hoop (or scarf, or other prop) and try different things with it....*
- *Make up your own movement today....*
- *Do your own leap and ending shape for the end of the phrase....*
- *Make up a dance....*

PFD Reduction: Possible, Feasible, Desirable[26]

While the essence and importance of Divergent Discovery is to move beyond the known and familiar by producing multiple solutions, in dance it is often essential to make choices, selecting certain responses and discarding others, to reach a conclusion, ending, or final product (the nature of choices and strategies will be discussed more in artistic process, Chapter 8). So, how are these choices made—how are the multiple solutions generated in Divergent Discovery reduced?

The reduction process involves several stages. The first stage is brainstorming: Certain parameters are defined in the task itself ("Design three ways to move from standing to sitting while you continue to hold both hands with your partner"), but other than those parameters, the solutions produced are relatively free from restrictions.

Learners explore the subject matter by asking, "What is *possible?*" Some students will really try to push the envelope; in theory, students could design responses which are physically impossible given limitations such as gravity, muscular strength and flexibility.

After *possible* responses have been generated, the second stage involves reducing all possible choices to the *feasible.*

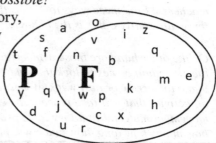

This level examines the possible ideas according to a specific criterion, selected by the teacher in initial experiences in theis process. For example "Using the criterion of X, which of these *possible* solutions are *feasible?*" Determine that this this criterion will reduce the possible to the feasible.

> *Ever hear of a corporation, school or organization doing a feasibility study? The purpose is to reduce the possible solutions to the feasible.*

Once students have reduced the possible to the feasible, the next step involves further selection, reducing the feasible to the *desirable*, by applying another criterion.
"Now, using the criterion of Y, which of these *feasible* solutions are *desirable?*"

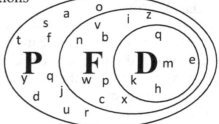

Although this is presented as three stages, there could be severeal more stages of criteria inserted for further reduction, depending on the number of divergent responses originally produced and the criteria used in the original PFD reductions.

> *In some situations, personal opinion serves as the criterion for the last reduction. As in the phrase, "de gustibus non est disputandum," (there is no disputing about tastes), sometimes it just feels right. Developing and trusting this intuitive judgment is important in the arts.*

This process of reducing by criteria is important in that it teaches learners the importance of establishing criteria for choosing ideas, responses, movements, so that they learn that the selection process is guided or governed by criteria. Divergent Discovery and reduction work together in artistic process. "Divergent thinking leads to no agreed-upon solution. It involves fluency, or the ability to generate a great quantity of ideas; flexibility, or the ability to switch from one perspective to another; and originality in picking unusual associations of ideas. These are the dimensions of thinking that most creativity tests measure and that most workshops try to enhance....Divergent thinking is not much use without the ability to tell a good idea from a bad one—and this selectivity involves convergent thinking." (Csikszentmihalyi, 1996, pp. 60-61) In dance, as in the other arts, these criteria often have aesthetic, sometimes cultural or traditional, sometimes physical limitation (again, more about these choices and criteria in the next chapter).

Examples of Divergent Discovery Episodes
Following are suggestions for use with Divergent Discovery and PFD reduction. The first is designed for a class in international folk dance, the second uses action words, and the third uses Motif Writing, a symbol system for writing dance allowing for multiple options and latitude in performance.
International Folk Dance Class
This could be used to "wrap up" a unit on a particular geographic region or culture, such as Israeli and Jewish dances, after several dances from that area have been studied. It could also be used at the end of a course which studied several regions, with the class divided into several groups and each group assigned a different region.

Divide the class into small groups, and have each group discuss and identify characteristic movement qualities, positions, formations, steps, purposes, and any other special features of the dances of a particular area. Using these elements as criteria, students will start by producing ideas for a dance representative of that region. Other parameters might include the number of learners working together, length/time of the sequences, music or attire.

Each group will present their dance in a class performance or "lecture-demonstration," and should have a name for the dance, the country or region it represents, the purpose for the dance (where, when, why or by whom would it be done?), its formation and the steps used. Each group might also teach their dance to the entire class.

Action Words

Action words have many applications. I've developed this collection of action words over several years. Entering these into your computer will enable you to add new words and create a personalized collection. Depending on the number of students in your classes and how many words you want them to use, make several copies of each sheet of words, cut them apart into slips of paper and keep the slips in a container such as a manila envelope, coffee can, or costume fedora.

Action Words may be used in any type of dance or action. These words do not name any specific movementor step, but are chosen to allow students to produce a variety of alternatives. Collections for use in specific classes, such as a collection of the ballet, modern, tap or jazz terminology that you use, could be kept in separate containers.

You may "re-cycle" the words by asking that students return the slips to you after they have their phrases memorized, but sometimes the slips get crumpled or discarded, so you might keep several copies of each sheet on hand to re-stock your supply. These are fun as an occasional assignment in technique class, for use in improv or choreography class, or as a one-time workshop with a special group of students.

Using Action Words (a few suggestions)
1. Have each student pick a single action word and produce five different movements for that word (using the technique described above to "get past the roadblock"). After producing these five options, use PFD to reduce to a single option. Then have students pick three more slips, doing the same with each one: produce five options, then reduce it to one. Ask students to put these in any order, then work on transitions to get from one action to the next. **OR....**
2. Have each student pick five words and put them in any order. Produce a movement "sentence" with those words. Direct students to experiment with putting the words in a different order and producing another "sentence" with those words. You may either have the students use personal opinion to choose between the two, or perform both phrases sequentially in a single long movement phrase. **OR....**
3. Put on a piece of music while the students work on their phrases. You may want to set parameters such as specifying that their phrase take a certain number of measures, or randomly assign time values to each word (i.e., word 1 takes one measure of four counts, words 2 & 3 take one measure, word 4 takes two measures, etc.). **OR....**

4. With the entire group, pull out four words. By consensus, have the group suggest the order they'd like. Now everyone produces actions for each word—everyone is doing the same word at the same time but in their own ways. **OR....**

5. Have the students work in pairs. For each word the pair picks, the partners must relate to each other in some way: moving toward or away from partner, moving together in synchrony, or one move and the other responds to the partner's movement. **OR....**

6. Create your own variations!

In addition to using the Action Words in class for student projects, these movement words can be a very useful tool for you. Use them when *your* well of creativity runs dry and you need to produce a new technique phrase or dance, or when you just need a little nudge to get you going again. If you find yourself doing the same phrases or movements over and over, get out your collection of words and experiment with them. Challenge *yourself* in an episode of Divergent Discovery to create several different variations for each word, to go beyond *your* known.

shake	open	turn	stretch
wring	flick	dab	press
float	glide	slide	pull
fall	descend	rise	scatter
gather	wiggle	flatten	fly
slither	explode	twist	bend
grow	shrink	reach	contract
extend	contract	travel	go!
carve	slash	under	over
around	through	hop	skip
jump	leap	sissonne	assemblé
drop	pause	scatter	turn
spin	patter	run	rise
narrow	widen	swing	hang

melt	drip	walk	wander
push	tap	arch	curl
collapse	expand	point	draw
pour	rotate	hide	crawl
creep	bound	soar	sail
wave	touch	whisper	shout
beat	kneel	sit	listen
spread	balance	wipe	climb
lie	squeeze	pass	kick
fall	shoot	swim	hold
weave	bounce	peek	look
run	chase	spring	wilt
descend	ascend	bend	spin
grasp	release	break	bump

Motif Writing

Another suggestion for working with Convergent Discovery and Divergent Discovery is to use Motif Writing, developed from the work of Rudolf Laban. This is a form of dance notation which allows latitude of performance: dancers can perform each action in a wide variety of ways. Motif Writing can be used as a stimulus to enable students to contribute to choreography of a dance work, or as a way to introduce the symbols used in Labanotation (Kinetography Laban). For more information on Motif Writing please see *Your Move: A New Approach to the Study of Movement and Dance* by Ann Hutchinson Guest.

> *Be aware that differences exist in use of symbols among Ann Hutchinson Guest, Valerie Preston-Dunlop, and others who teach Laban studies in the United State, Great Britain, Europe and other areas of the world.*

A Few Suggestions

When introducing students to the symbols, I've used episodes in Cued Response, Guided Discovery, Convergent Discovery and Divergent Discovery. Remember that if you're using these as Divergent Discovery, students need to produce multiple options before moving on.

1. Produce a class score. Ask students to call out symbols while you write them, very large, on the board. The whole class will be engaged in the same score, but it will look very different on everyone.
2. Have the class produce group scores. Divide the class into groups of 3-5 students; have each group produce its score and perform it as a group dance. All members of the group might perform the same action but in different ways, or they can perform the same action in unison. For example, for the "elevation" symbol, one person in the group might jump, another person might hop, another leap, assemblé or sissonne; or everyone in the group could do the same elevation in unison.
3. Have each individual produce a score and the dance that goes with it. Then take up the papers and give each score to a different person or assign partners and have partners exchange scores. Each student now creates a new dance to a new score. Select student pairs at random to perform their individual solos simultaneously; the class members observing the pairs offer suggestions on changing facing, timing or actions to blend the two into a duet.

Guidelines for using Motif Writing

1. Like Labanotation or Kinetography Laban, Motif Writing is written from *bottom to top*, reading "up" the page. Start with a double bar line at the bottom of the page and finish with a double bar line at the top of the page; the double bar lines defines the beginning and end of the score.
2. The length of the symbol gives the time element: a very long symbol is done for a longer time than a shorter symbol. Time is relative and open to students' interpretation. The width of the symbol does *not* increase with the length.
3. Symbols should not touch; leave a little space between symbols for clarity.
4. Two symbols side-by-side show *simultaneity*: two things are happening at the same time. For example, turning while jumping (a turn symbol and an elevation symbol written side by side) or twisting while traveling (a twist symbol beside a path sign).
5. A single parenthesis or bow which ties two symbols together indicates a *blended* action: an expansion which smoothly becomes a fall, a turn which blends into a twist.

		Action
○	Pause
⊙	Axial movement
(⎮)	Elevation
▱	Turn or rotate
▱	Twist
◇	Shape
	Transfer Weight
V (x)	Contract
V (И)	Expand
♪	Accent
▯	Balance
▱	Lean
)	Fall

Pathways

	Any Pathway
	Straight
	Circling right or cloclwise
	Circling left or counterclockwise
	Circling either way
	Spiraling in
	Spiraling out
	Curving

Motif Writing

Guidelines for using Motif Writing

1. Like Labanotation or Kinetography Laban, write from bottom to top, reading "up" the page. Start with a double bar line and finish with a double bar; the double bar defines the beginning and end of the score.

2. The length of the symbol indicates the time element: a very long symbol is done for a longer time than a shorter symbol (the width of the symbol does not change with the length)

3. Symbols should not touch; leave a little space between symbols for clarity.

4. Two symbols side-by-side show simultaneity: two things are happening at the same time. For example, turning while jumping or twisting while traveling.

5. A single parenthesis or bow which ties two symbols together indicates a blended action: an expansion which smoothly becomes a fall, a turn which blends into a twist.

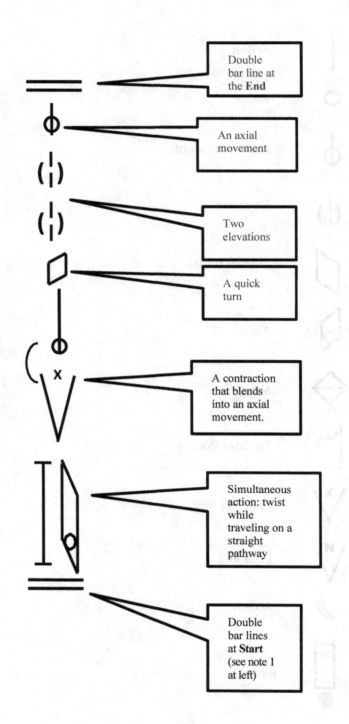

Double bar line at the **End**

An axial movement

Two elevations

A quick turn

A contraction that blends into an axial movement.

Simultaneous action: twist while traveling on a straight pathway

Double bar lines at **Start** (see note 1 at left)

Summary

In Divergent Discovery, your students are engaged in producing multiple discovered responses to a single question, problem, or task. As teacher, you design suitable tasks, questions, or problems that invite multiple responses, and your dance students seek to go beyond the known and create new phrases, ideas, or movements.

Through the process of generating multiple solutions and assessing each solution, your students are not only learning to create options for themselves, but are also learning important thinking skills which are involved with determining which solutions are appropriate. This process is at the heart of artistic process (which will be discussed more fully in the next chapter). Given the subjective and aesthetic nature of dance, the learner may not be able to see certain aspects of the solutions, and feedback by videotape, teacher, and/or peers is valuable; help your students know when to seek such feedback. This Style is often used in creative movement, improvisation and choreography classes.

Ahead

Through the Spectrum, your dance students are learning more about the parameters involved in making choices and decisions within and about the art form of dance. Learner-Designed Individual Program (LDIP) represents an important shift in the process, as the learner discovers and designs the questions or problem within the subject matter determined by the teacher, and seeks the solution.

To Do:

Start to recognize how often you use PFD reduction (with and without Divergent Discovery in your everyday life). Examples:

1. *You're sitting in a restaurant perusing the menu. How to choose from so many options? Maybe your first thought is, "Well, I had a big lunch, so I'm not very hungry." Click; first criterion. Maybe your next thought is, "And I've decided to eat more vegetables and less red meat..." Click; second criterion. Perhaps then you peek in your wallet and think, "I'm running low on cash, so something relatively inexpensive..." Click; third criterion. And perhaps you still have lots of choices, so your next thought is, "I know that the portions here are huge, so I'll get something that I can take home half in a doggy bag, something that will heat well for lunch tomorrow..." Now you know what to order!*

2. *You're in the store with your birthday gift certificate from your grandmother: The gift certificate is for $50 (first criterion), it's winter so you're looking for a sweater (second criterion), and it's February and you're so tired of wearing black, brown, navy and charcoal grey that you're ready for some bright colors (third criterion). OK, so that narrows it down, doesn't it?*

3. *And how often do you do this with a group:"Hey, gang, where shall we go for dinner?" Well, there are lots of possibilities; how to choose? Beck has a long drive home and wants something close by, so that limits things considerably. Charlene doesn't like sushi, Jack likes Italian but Suze had pizza for lunch and doesn't want that for dinner, so, we've narrowed our choices again. Jurgen is doing that low-carb thing and Gabrielle says if she doesn't get a glass of wine with dinner she's going to hurt somebody. Hey, look--Dinner and PFD Reduction!*

Style I: Learner-Designed Individual Program (LDIP)

> Now the learner discovers and designs the details of the program within the broad topic or problem set by the teacher, and seeks the solution.

Learner-Designed Individual Program is another step past the threshold of discovery along a pathway of increasing levels of independence and discovery: it is the first Style in which the *learner* discovers and designs the details within the broad topic or problem set by the teacher, produces an individual program, and seeks the solution.

The cumulative effect of experiences in the previous Styles makes LDIP possible, and success in this Style depends on successes in the previous Styles. In Style I: LDIP, although you make the decision concerning the general subject matter, such as a particular aspect of dance, your students achieve greater independence by identifying and designing the question or problem within the subject matter and seeking the answers or solutions. It is the first Style in which the learner designs, develops and carries out an organized personal program.

> An important difference between Divergent Discovery and LDIP is the nature of given vs. found problems, which will be discussed more in Chapter 9.

You as teacher designate the general subject matter area, such as a particular aspect of dance notation, a certain period in dance history, or an aspect of technique. Your student discovers and designs the specific problems or questions within that subject matter area and seeks the solutions.

It is *not* "do whatever you want" or "anything goes." It is an approach to evoke and develop the creative capacities of an individual who is motivated and disciplined, one who takes the initiative for generating ideas, who takes the opportunity to develop a program based on his or her cognitive and physical capacities in the specific topic and who can follow projects through to completion.

Style I is a highly disciplined approach to the process of *problem finding* which is at the heart of artistic process. This Style is a paradigm for exploring, examining, and making choices concerning an issue in dance in order to discover its components, the relationships among the components, and the possible structure or order for the components. Style I enables the dancer, choreographer or researcher to discover the unique structure for the chosen problem. The structure could be spatial, temporal, emotional, or involve any other possible way of organizing and ordering the selected components.

The project for LDIP requires a series of episodes rather than a single episode, as it provides the individual dancer the opportunity to practice the cumulative experiences and skills acquired in the previous Styles A-H and inter-relate them over a longer period of time. LDIP requires certain abilities of the learner. A dancer must have some knowledge of his or her physical abilities and familiarity with the processes of discovery, both convergent and divergent. The dancer must be aware of and understand certain concepts concerning the dance medium, be able to categorize and analyze these concepts, and be able to construct an overall structure. The dancer must also have the maturity and tenacity to endure the development and use of this longer-range program.

While this Style seems to emphasize analysis, categorization and structure, this does not exclude intuition, spontaneity and serendipity. Planned sequences along with those odd bits that sometimes burst forth randomly can be woven into an overall structure, the logical and the intuitive finding a relationship which enables the project at hand to develop into a coherent, unified work.

The previous Styles of the Spectrum help prepare your students for this level of responsibility by teaching them the skills and cognitive understanding necessary for working at this level. And while students may develop ways of organizing material on their own through idiosyncratic work, random exploration is not enough. This Style gives learners the opportunity to practice all the previous skills and find ways of interrelating them over a longer period of time. It is important to re-emphasize that Style I: LDIP is not done in a single episode. It requires a series of interconnected episodes over which learners explore an issue deeply, create multiple solutions, explore alternatives, and develop an overall organizing structure.

An Episode Unfolds **Pre-Impact Set**
You, in your role as teacher, decide the general subject matter and the learner selects the topic.

Impact Set
The shift of decisions occurs in the Impact Set. The student identifies and designs the problems and multiple possible solutions within the general subject matter chosen by the teacher. The student then formulates the overall idea for the completed program. This may take the form of an internal imagined idea, a written outline, a synopsis or libretto. In the arts it is recognized that this original idea will probably change form along the way to the completed work. However, developing the original, seminal concept as a point of departure is a very important step and one that will provide guidance toward the final product.

Your role in the Impact Set is to be available when your student initiates questions about the project. You also initiate contact with your student to verify where he or she is, the direction he or she is taking, how progress is going, reexamine connections and relationships, etc. Therefore the process is:
1. The learner selects the topic that will be the focus of the study from within the general subject matter area (decided by you).
2. The learner develops an answer to the question, "What will constitute a completed program?" This answer provides guidelines to develop criteria for the Post-Impact Set.
3. The learner generates the questions, concepts and/or issues appropriate for the chosen topic, organizes the tasks involved and designs the program.
4. The learner collects information about the topic, answers the questions, and organizes them into a suitable framework.

These steps do not necessarily occur sequentially. The process of identifying the concepts and issues, designing the program, and collecting information will probably be interactive with the process of developing criteria for successful completion. During this time you initiate contact with your student to observe the work-in-progress, listen to or observe periodic presentations, answer your student's questions and initiate questions yourself.

Betsy Blair writes of the open-ended and exploring approach of both the student and the teacher embarking on discovery together. "I began to see my teaching as a figure-eight with a creative pause existing at the cross of the eight. It was in this moment of 'creative pause' or 'full silence' that I perceived the possibility for a new idea to break in or to be grasped or for the question to be transformed. For me, the deepest and truest moment of learning happens simultaneously when both teacher and student recognize that something fresh or insightful has been seen/grasped/felt/intuited by both simultaneously. This can happen in the context of a group too."[27]

Here is a version of Betsy's drawing:

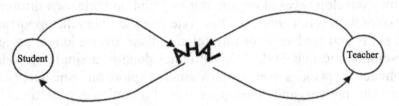

> **An Example of LDIP**
>
> *A student comes to you with an idea for choreography. Rather than saying, "OK, go ahead and get started and show me something in a few weeks," you sit down together to discuss parameters such as genre or style or other aspects ("I've seen your work in jazz and ballet, but I'd like to see you develop more in the modern genre, particularly by using the weight and flow factors....") or guide the student through a dialectic ("What styles are you most comfortable with? The modern class seems to be a new and different style for you. What do you find most challenging about it?") to determine a fruitful direction to pursue.*

Post-Impact Set

As in the previous discovery Styles, the Impact and Post-Impact Sets are interwoven. The role of the student is to examine the work, validate it in relationship to the original problem, establish connections and relationships, organize them, and maintain the development of the work in progress. Your role as teacher is to dialogue with students concerning progress and trouble spots, and to answer questions. This will include changes in the overall shape of the work, criteria, and discrepancies in the work as it progresses. Help your student to understand that the process isn't necessarily linear, and that the project, writing, research, choreography or whatever it is will change during the process.

Choosing tasks for LDIP

Think in terms of a research project, thesis or choreographic project. The general subject matter might be a delimited aspect of dance history such as "Female post-modern dance choreographers in the latter half of the 20th century." In choreography or composition class, the teacher might make an assignment such as, "Choreograph a solo study which approximates 3 minute; you choose the criteria." LDIP can also involve a project in dance notation, pedagogy, history, kinesiology, or many other subjects.

It is at the level of LDIP that the threshold marking *artistic process* occurs: that line of demarcation between *presented problems* and *found problems*, and this will be discussed more fully in Chapter 8. Up to this point, problems have been the sort that have been presented by the teacher. It is in Style I that learners, themselves, must formulate the exact nature of the problem to be solved. When the learner is able to engage in problem-finding and organize a schema for the work, the learner is engaging in artistic process.

Be patient in your introduction of learners to this Style. Students are gaining independence but still need your guidance; they must clearly understand their role and your expectations, so don't be afraid to give detailed instructions. Remember that the project for Style I will unfold over a series of episodes, over a period of time during which the learner engages in activities including thinking, moving, implementing, exploring, experimenting, performing, writing, and recording. This process cannot be hurried. In addition, you will need time to observe the process of your student: time to listen, time to think and assess, and time to conduct periodic individual dialogs.

> *Students need a great deal of independence to be successful in this Style, and not every student achieves that at the same rate. That quality of independence in the medium is often independent of physical skill or age. As an undergraduate dance student I was full of ideas for projects and independent studies. Some panned out and others didn't. I am grateful that my professors did not give up on me!*

Student readiness

The most important consideration in choosing this Style is the readiness of the learner. A student must be proficient in certain aspects of the chosen topic; the student must also be comfortable with the processes of discovery, exploration, and providing self-feedback. While non-dancers may be able to produce sequences of movement and children can use movement expressively, these activities are very different from creating a thoughtful, well- structured work.

> ***Tip:*** *LDIP is not appropriate for every class, and not everyone in a class will be ready for this Style at the same time. Some students who start LDIP with enthusiasm and many ideas will not yet be able to endure the rigor of this Style: continuous experimentation, discovery, and analysis. With such students, switch Styles and wait for a more appropriate time for LDIP.*

Summary

LDIP is an important step along the pathway of discovery and independence. The cumulative effect of experiences in the previous Styles makes this Style possible: the learner designs, develops and performs an organized personal program. While it is not for everyone and some students will never initiate this Style, it is a big step forward for the individual who is motivated and disciplined, who takes initiative, and who can plan and follow projects through to completion.

> ***To Do****: Identify a research or choreographic topic for a class or small group of students. Reflect on how you can structure it so that students can identify and design the problems and multiple possible solutions within the general subject matter that you delineate. Reflect on the students' level of preparedness.*

Ahead

In the next Style, the learner makes all the decisions in the Pre-Impact Set for the first time.

Style J: Learner-Initiated

> This is the first time that the learner makes all the decisions in the Pre-Impact Set.

In Style J: Learner-Initiated, the individual learner initiates the Style or Styles for the episode or series of episodes. However, this is the first time that your student, rather than you, makes all the decisions in the Pre-Impact Set. The purpose of this Style is for the learner to initiate a learning experience, design it, perform it, and assess it, based on established criteria. The student comes to you with a willingness to conduct a project which may have a series of episodes. Having recognized his or her readiness to move forward, inquire, discover, and examine solutions, the individual student creates a total learning experience from idea to completion.

Although this Style is similar, in some aspects, to the previous one, the significant difference is that it is the first time that the *learner* initiates the Style. The student comes to *you* and says that he or she is willing to work independently. Just as the defining point between Divergent Discovery and LDIP is the nature of given vs. found problems, the defining point between LDIP and LI is that *you don't go to the student, the student comes to you*. You may plant the seed for such an event in the fertile ground of a student's mind, but the student decides to start the process. This difference is crucial. The readiness and ability to initiate such a situation creates a very different reality for the relationship between teacher and learner. In LI, the learner is taking even more responsibility for initiating and conducting the episodes for teaching and learning. Like LDIP, LI necessitates a series of episodes. Students may require weeks or more for immersion in the process of discovery and experimentation.

> *I love working with students in LI! Projects that students have initiated have included the student dance organization president organizing a dinner dance performance, student choreographic works, graduate theses, and some intriguing pedagogy projects. Once you have helped students prepare the fertile ground in their minds, you may be surprised and pleased with what they grow. You'll probably find that you get to know a whole new facet of a student and, in turn, that the student gets to know you on a different level as well, which is a learning experience as valuable as any other.*

An Episode Unfolds Pre-Impact Set

For the first time in the Spectrum, the Pre-Impact decisions shift from you to your student. Your student makes all the decisions in the Pre-Impact Set, including selecting the general subject matter, the specific topic, methods and tools for dealing with the issues, and the rest of the Pre-Impact decisions including how to assess the process in the Post-Impact Set. The attitude that brings about LI reflects an attitude of readiness to take charge of the entirety of a project.

Impact Set

In the Impact Set, the role of the learner is the same as for LDIP: to discover, examine, and assess solutions and develop a schema for the work. In addition, however, the learner touches base periodically with you, to share information about the work in progress, how ideas change, etc. During the Impact Set the learner responds to each found problem by experimenting, exploring, examining, and discovering the possible solutions to the problems. Some responses will be purely cognitive, others primarily physical or motional; some responses are a product of the cognitive and motional processes, "thinking in movement."

Your role as teacher in the Impact Set is to listen, observe, ask questions, be a sounding board, and alert your student to any decisions that may have been omitted. In short, your role is to be supportive during the creative process. As with LDIP, this process may require several weeks or more for the student to become immersed in the process of discovery over a series of episodes.

Post-Impact Set

In the Post-Impact Set, the learner makes all decisions concerning assessment and evaluation. Assessment uses learner-produced criteria, which was developed during the Pre-Impact Set. This assessment is performed by and for the learner. Your role is to listen, observe, be supportive, and be available to the requests and questions of the learner. If you identify discrepancies, it is not your role to evaluate, tell or judge, but it is appropriate to ask questions that will enable the learner to identify those discrepancies (another useful application of neutral feedback). Often just being available to be a sounding-board, asking for clarification, or "playing devil's advocate" is very useful to the student as she or he develops and hones ideas.

Summary

The *student* comes to *you* and says that he or she wants to work independently. The readiness and ability to initiate such a situation creates a very different reality for the relationship between teacher and learner. The attitude on the part of a student that brings about LI reflects an attitude of readiness to take charge of the entirety of a project. Your role is to be supportive and help your student identify discrepancies; it is the student's role to develop assessment criteria and make all decisions concerning evaluation.

Ahead

Maximum decision making is the definitive characteristic of Style K: Self-Teaching.

__To Do:__

My favorite chocolates come individually wrapped with a line of inspiration or philosophy printed on the foil wrapper, and one reads, "To do great things one must not only act but dream." Take a moment to dream in Divergent Discovery. Generate several ideas for projects for yourself that you would want to pursue under the guidance of a mentor. Brainstorm. Daydream.

Don't be afraid to be completely outrageous; the purpose is not to be practical but to dream: "Live under the stars on a beach at the foot of a volcano and create a dance about the movement of the sun, wind, water and lava with Deborah Hay or Anna Halprin," "Collaborate with Merce Cunningham and NASA scientists to develop the first dance in zero-gravity," "Under the direction of Ivor Guest, interview Filippo Taglioni and George Balanchine and compare dance training throughout the centuries." It doesn't matter that the person you want to study with or meet has long since passed away; don't worry about how you'd pay the rent on that grass hut. In other words, refrain from unconsciously editing out a wild idea by thinking that it would be impossible to do. We're talking about a big dream here, and really fun ventures are often generated from wishes and dreams.

OK, so the purpose of this "To Do" wasn't to really do anything. However, if you want to actually do something, the next step might be to determine how close you can actually get to accomplishing that dream.... What might actually be achievable, and how? Do PFD reduction and see where it gets you.

Style K: Self-Teaching

Self-Teaching occurs any time individuals are engaged in teaching themselves.

Self-Teaching occurs when an individual initiates a learning experience and designs, performs, and evaluates it. It is the mark of an independent learner. The learner decides how much external feedback (if any) to seek. The artistic process involved with choreographing a dance, preparing for a role, writing an article for publication, notating and/or reconstructing a work, are all examples of Self-Teaching.

This Style almost speaks for itself. The beautiful internal logic of the Spectrum as it was designed leads us to realize that this Style has always existed. This Style typically does not exist in the classroom but in situations in which an individual is engaged in a personal heuristic process. Choreography, performance, notating, writing about dance; all these have the capacity to be learning processes, to teach the artist something about the medium of dance, about the work in progress, about dancers, about the self.

In Self-Teaching, the artist participates in the roles of both teacher and learner. Sometimes the interplay of these roles is sunconscious; sometimes it is in the front and center of one's thought processes, listening to that internal critic which is the "teacher-self" speaking.

In any and all creative endeavors including writing, dance, music, and painting, most artists ask a colleague or peer to read, watch, see, listen to their work; "Here, friend, let me show you my work and tell me what you think." We recognize that we need the fresh eye, another point of view. We are not asking a teacher's approval, we are asking a respected peer for their thoughts, and in Style K: Self-Teaching the individual may request feedback.

Chapter Summary

The individual Styles and clusters of Styles can be applied to a variety of subjects in the dance curriculum. All subjects can employ the entire range of the Spectrum, depending on when the teacher wants students to acquire information and principles, discover single correct concepts, or new variations on concepts and multiple possibilities. The versatile dance teacher can develop mobility along the Spectrum, applying teaching strategies appropriate to the task at hand.

Styles A-E are designed for the efficient acquisition of fixed or codified information, such as in classes in dance technique, folk & square, aerobics, ballroom, and dance notation. Styles F-G are options that foster discovery of single correct concepts, and could be used in technique, folk & square dance, ballroom, and notation as well as other courses such as dance kinesiology and dance history or in any course to deliver concepts and principles. Styles H-K are designed for discovery of alternatives, new concepts, and to foster creativity, and can be applied to the previously mentioned courses plus choreography, composition, and improvisation. Styles F-J especially engage the student in reasoning, inventing, problem solving activities, and invites the learner to go beyond given information; Style K moves outside the classroom per se.

In Style F Guided Discovery, you guide the learner's responses according to a planned sequence of questions and "discovered" answers.

In Style G: Convergent Discovery, the learner discovers a single correct answer without guiding questions or clues from you at each step.

In Style H: Divergent Discovery, the learner produces divergent ideas, responses or answers to the problem that you present.

In Style I: Learner-Designed Individual Program the student discovers and/or designs the task or problem within the topic that you define.

In Style J: Learner Initiated, the student initiates the learning situation making all decision and keeps you informed about the progress.

In Style K: Self-Teaching, the learner determines how much, if any, external feedback to seek.

Questions for Reflection and Discussion

1. Reflect on and discuss appropriate forms of **feedback** in the various Discovery Styles.

2. Reflect on why **patience** from the teacher is mentioned and needed more in the Production cluster of Styles, and is needed more as teachers and learners move through the Spectrum.

3. Identify the important **four guidelines** mentioned for an episode in Guided Discovery, and discuss why they necessary.

4. Identify the **three key points** that will help you create the steps for a Guided Discovery episode and direct your delivery.

5. Discuss the forms of **feedback** which are appropriate (and not appropriate) for Guided Discovery.

6. Identify how a **Guided Discovery sequence** differs from just asking questions.

7. Discuss how **Convergent Discovery differs from Guided Discovery**, including decisions shifted from teacher to learner, the roles of teacher and learner, and appropriate tasks.

8. Identify **criteria** which will help you choose tasks and design episodes in Convergent Discovery.

9. Identify **situations** that might arise during an episode in Convergent Discovery and discuss how to handle them.

10. 10. Consider the anecdote of Suzanne Farrell's spontaneous Convergent Discovery. What made it Convergent Discovery? Have you had something similar happen?

11. Identify a **concept or movement problem** for an episode in Convergent Discovery. Determine how you will present it to the class. Identify ways to encourage the process that enables each dancer to converge on a single solution, and remember that students need time to engage in the discovery process.

12. Identify differences between **Divergent Discovery and Convergent Discovery**.

13. Identify the **roadblock** that you may need to help students surpass during initial episodes of Divergent Discovery.

14. Discuss why the following not examples of Divergent Discovery, and how you could change each of the basic ideas for an episode in Divergent Discovery:
    • Design a phrase that includes three of the five types of elevations.
    • Create a twisted shape which balances on one leg.
    • Design a phrase that includes five of the action words written on the board.

15. Define **PFD reduction** and give examples.

16. Identify a **concept or movement problem** for an episode in Divergent Discovery. Design how you will present it in class, considering any potential problems, roadblocks, pitfalls. Include criteria for PFD reduction.

17. Identify the **decision** shifted from teacher to learner in Independent Program: Learner's Design (LDIP).

18. Identify the **four steps in the LDIP process**.

19. Discuss the **roles of the teacher and learner** in LDIP.

20. Identify and discuss the significant difference between Learner-Initiated and LDIP —focusing on the decision shifted from teacher to learner.

21. Identify and share times when have you engaged in Self-Teaching.

Ahead

The upcoming chapter is almost the most important aspect of teaching dance. All the nuts and bolts of lesson planning and implementation aside, the elusive spirit, the white-hot lucent flame that burns throughout the art form of dance is that of discovery. Not only is discovery important for teaching, but it is at the heart of what defines creation in art and separates it from all other activities. Creativity and the nature of artistic process are essential to understanding dance, its reproduction and production. While teaching dance, we can never forget that we are teaching an art form: Dance is not just a task, a skill, a set of movement phrases; it is art, and all who participate in it are engaging in the creation of art.

I remember my own impromptu Self-Teaching episode at age 11. My father, combining multiple roles as parent, teacher, gardener, and tease, said that he would be planting pickles in the garden on Saturday and I was to help him. Well, I had assisted with the laborious process of soaking cucumbers in brine and dousing them with hot vinegar enough to know that pickles didn't just grow that way. After helping him put seeds in the ground all afternoon, and enduring his teasing that he was "planting pickles" while I adamantly held that the vegetable that he was planting was a cucumber, I stomped up the hill from garden to house and pulled out reference materials from our home library including several dictionaries, two encyclopedias, Joy of Cooking, *and a book on gardening. I dashed off a pithy but complete comparison of the terms "pickle" and "cucumber" and presented him with it. He continued to tease me about "planting pickles" for many years, which may explain why I still love researching, comparing, analyzing, and writing (and eating, but not making, pickles)!*

Tips: Other suggestions for Discovery tasks include:
- *The role of the center of gravity (lower, higher) in performing turns*
- *Changing momentum, such as traveling forward then hitting a half-toe or piqué balance in arabesque, or how to tell a waltz partner to change from the streamline to the hesitation.*
- *Factors affecting stability in a variety of balances: for example, exploring tilting or "off-center" balances, turns and other actions especially in modern dance.*
- *Factors affecting height of different elevations.*
- *The relationship among head, shoulders, and legs to maintain balance in turns.*

Many excellent ideas can be gathered from books such as,
- *Physics and the Art of Dance by Kenneth Laws and Martha Swope*
- *Human Movement Potential: Its Ideokinetic Facilitation by Lulu Sweigard*
- *Dance Kinesiology by Sally Sevey Fitt*
- *Taking Root to Fly by Irene Dowd.*

9 Discovery, Creativity, Artistic Process

> Dancing: The Highest
> Intelligence in the
> Freest Body.
> ~Isadora Duncan

As we have been learning, what differentiates reproduction activity from production activity is *discovery*. Production engages the learner in the discovery of new ideas and movements through problem solving, categorizing, synthesizing, hypothesizing, extrapolating, and creating. This chapter examines the nature of discovery, creativity, and artistic process: what these terms refer to, how are they used in dance, and how the Spectrum can be applied to enable students to discover ideas, concepts, and joy in dance. Let's take a closer look at various aspects of production activity.

Discovery, Creativity, Flow, and Artistic Process

Discovery

Discovery is enjoyable. Children finding the hidden Easter eggs, playing "Marco Polo" and hide-and-seek; the archaeologist searching for a legendary hidden tomb, the paleontologist uncovering dinosaur fossils, and the bird-watcher happening on the nest of a rare species; these are examples of adults engaged in discovery. When people are asked to choose the best description of what they find most pleasurable about doing what they enjoy, whether it is reading, playing, dancing, mountain climbing, or whatever the activity, the most frequent answer is "designing or discovering something new." We derive pleasure from learning and making something new.

Creativity

According to Hindu tradition, the god Shiva created the world by setting its rhythm in motion with his dance. Creativity has long held a fascination and mystery: the artist has the ability to take inert matter and shape it into meaningful form. Once a work of art is created, it takes on a life of its own, existing apart from the artist. Paul Taylor has said of choreographing a dance, "I find that it takes over if you let it" (Hodgson, 1976, p. 13).

The word "creativity" is very broad, often vague, sometimes confusing or intimidating. Definitions may range from personal ingenuity or insight to the process sometimes referred to as "creativity with a capital C." The former type of creativity refers to a process that almost everyone can perform, from children who explore use of color, sound and movement to adults who

> *Creativity, the ability of the artist to take inert matter and shape it into meaningful form, has long held a fascination and mystery.*

achieve insight, experience epiphany, and produce ideas or artworks that change the world. The latter type, the "capital C" Creativity, represents a thought, process or product that changes or transforms the art form; this type of Creativity is achieved only through years of experience in the art form or field of study. However, the daily, "garden-variety"-type of creativity is the basis for the more culturally important Creativity that permanently alters the topography of an art form.

Flow[28]

The optimal experience involved with the process of discovering and formulating something new is called "flow" (Csikszentmihalyi 1997). Flow is an almost effortless yet highly focused state of consciousness that can occur in almost any setting. The following are key elements of flow (with examples specific to dance):

- **Clear goals every step of the way**. Whether it is a choreographed phrase or an improvisation, you, as the dancer, "know" the next step or movement. The creative process may begin with a goal of solving a problem that may be assigned by someone else, or defined by you, but in all cases you perceive the clarity of the goal.
- **Immediate feedback to your actions.** You can feel the rightness of each action. The movements become motion; they have a cohesive, internal logic that links one inexorably and inevitably to the next. This sense comes when you have succeeded in internalizing criteria or judgment and can give self-feedback.
- **A balance between challenges and skills.** Challenges that are too great will result in frustration; abilities that are far in excess of the demands of the job will result in boredom. In flow, you are balanced on the fine wire connecting skill and challenge. Rather than panic there is the sense of excitement and exhilaration.
- **A merging of action and awareness.** You become the dance. Concentration is focused in a single-mindedness that is required by the close match between skill and challenge, made possible by the clarity of the goals and the internal delivery of feedback.
- **Exclusion of distractions.** You aren't thinking about what to make for dinner that night or problems in your love life. Distractions interrupt flow, so it is essential to "get lost" in the problem, the project, the dance, the act of moving. Intense concentration on the present results in mindful, intentive action, a moment-by-moment unfolding of motion.

- **No worry of failure.** The complete involvement in the unfolding action precludes distractions and worries of failure. You have clear goals, know that your abilities match the challenge at hand, and are so completely focused that failure is simply not an issue.
- **No self-consciousness.** In flow, the submersion in the action keeps out thoughts involved with protecting the ego. Through the loss of self-consciousness associated with flow, the sense of self paradoxically expands to allow you to develop a stronger self-concept, knowing that your abilities are equal to a challenging situation.
- **Distorted sense of time.** Time is not an issue when you are submerged in the flow of motion. Attention to the unfolding action may mean that time slows down and you can sense, attenuate, and shape every gesture; it may also mean that an improvisation lasting for an hour can seem to go by in a few minutes.

> *Jacques D'Amboise has said, "I've had two or three times in the course of dancing where everything so worked that time slowed down, that I felt as if I was outside myself watching myself move in slow motion and I could enjoy myself. And at the same time I was doing it and in control of it; I was in control of the two aspects. I still can feel.... the joys of those moments" (The Power of Dance video 1992).*

- **The activity as an end in itself.** The activity is performed not solely for an external goal, but because it is, in and of itself, pleasurable.

> *Why do dancers take several classes a day when a single class will achieve the necessary training effects? Why do even accomplished dancers continue to take class? Why do professional teachers, who have "retired" from a performing career, continue to take class? We say it is because we have to maintain our technique or to keep in shape, and that is true, but deep down, it really has less to do with training than pleasure. We do it because it feels so good to dance. It is our breath, our sustenance, our heaven on earth.*

Artistic Process

Artistic process is the process of discovery, experimentation, exploration, and shaping.

When studying discovery and production in dance (or any of the arts), it is necessary to discuss the aspect of production known as *artistic process*. Dance education may have two distinctly different purposes. At the college or conservatory level the purpose of production work is usually to train advanced dancers as choreographers. In educational dance in public schools or private studios, the purpose of production work is usually to develop the learner's personal expression, critical and analytical thinking, and an understanding of aesthetic values for students who may be, for the most part, at the elementary level. What these two scenarios have in common is the development of *artistic process*: the process of discovery, experimentation, exploration, and shaping. It is important to remember that students at *any* age and level of ability are able to engage in artistic process. Teachers of children's creative dance classes often observe young children deeply engaged in this process of discovery, exploration and solution.

At this point we ask two important questions: *Why* do artists create, and *how* do they create? In answer to the first question, the main reward that artists receive from the work that they do is *knowledge*. Choreographers generally state the answer to this question in terms of *coming to understand* or *discovery*. It is by working in the medium of motion that the dance artist comes to a new understanding of the art of dance. Every new dance work reveals a new facet of the art of dance, reveals something new about the artist himself or herself, enables choreographers to know something new about their dancers. The knowledge received in the arts is an intuitive, existential, phenomenological, profound understanding of the artist in relation to other people, to other objects and events, and within the self. During the creation of art and even during the full appreciation of it, the artist and observer arrive at a state of one-ness, a state of "being at one" with the artwork.

The answer to the question of how works of art are produced is more difficult, because artists themselves are generally more involved in the doing than analytically describing the process. The process of producing art involves problem-solving, and the now-familiar concept of problem-solving has been applied to many areas including the arts, sciences, academia, and business management. However, Jacob Getzels and Mihaly Csikszentmihalyi (1976), in their extensive longitudinal study of the creative process, found that artists whose cognitive approach emphasizes problem finding over problem solving are more successful in their creative careers. In the previous chapter the difference between problems presented and problems discovered was introduced as an important factor in the difference between Style H: Divergent Discovery and Style I: LDIP. It is the step *before* solving the problem that is crucial, the step in which the artist *finds or identifies* the problem to be addressed. Thus *discovering* problems is the aspect of creative thinking and creative performance beyond merely solving a *given* problem, and we see that it is necessary to know how to *find* problems as well as how to *solve* them. This is the reason why Styles I: LDIP, J: Learner Initiated, and K: Self-Teaching are not for everyone, and must be initiated by the learner. However, application of the Spectrum will help teachers develop, in their students, the ability to initiate problem-finding.

> *The step before solving the problem is crucial: here the artist finds or identifies the problem to be addressed.*

The journey towards artistic process begins with discovery: learning how to discover answers. When students in the arts are studying aspects such as choreography, composition, and design, the teacher often gives the problem to be solved. Students start with *presented problem situations*, in which the problem has a known formulation, a method of solution, and a recognized solution (Guided Discovery, Convergent Discovery). However, artistic process involves *discovered problem situations*, where the *problem is yet to be identified*. There is as yet no solution, nor a routine method of solution (Divergent Discovery, Learner-Designed Individualized Program, Learner-Initiated, Self-Teaching); the teacher must then guide students to learn how to *find problems that they feel are intriguing and want to address*.

Thus the journey of discovery starts with the *responsibility for making decisions and choices*, moves to involve *discovering the known solutions to presented problems*, continues to *discovering unique or unknown solutions to presented problems*. Then, for artistic process, the journey must also include the ability to *discover problems* as well: *the problem solver must become a problem finder*. The Spectrum takes the teacher and learners from reproduction of existing ideas, to discovery of existing knowledge, to discovery in terms of problem-solving, to the artistic process of problem discovering.

> *For artistic process, the journey must also include the ability to discover problems.*

David Ecker (1963) described artistic process as a series of problems and their controlled resolutions. However, this description sounds too neat; artistic process is complex and, well, *messier*, than that. Creation in the arts is not merely a matter of the artist skillfully *manipulating* the medium. It is a much more involved process than simply reproducing or *expressing* an idea. One central issue of artistic activity is the ability to *interact* with the medium, allowing the problem to develop through the process of art making. Many artists, working in a variety of media, have likened the process of creation in art to a conversation between artist and material. According to Eisner (1982), it is an encounter between the artist, idea, and medium, a discovery-oriented activity in which the artist seeks solutions within the medium. Many artists say that the work itself gradually takes on a life of its own. It begins to "participate" in the process and suggest ideas that were not a part of the original idea. Through "qualitative negotiation", experimentation, investigation, and discovery, the artist learns about the work being created.

According to Getzels and Csikszentimihayli (1976), a creative problem or idea cannot be completely thought out in the mind's eye; it must be *discovered* duing an interaction with the elements that make it up. Central to artistic activity is the artist's *interacting* with the medium, allowing the problem to develop through the process of art-making. The researchers describe the process of artistic creativity as one in which an individual
1. Feels a **conflict** in perception, emotion, or thought,
2. Develops a **problem** articulating the conflict,
3. **Expresses** the problem in an appropriate form (i.e., visual, musical, movement, etc.), and
4. **Resolves** the conflict through symbolic means, thereby achieving a new emotional and cognitive balance.

John Dewey (1934) described the developing process as one in which *the problem itself* establishes a framework, and "as the experience of transforming subject-matter into the very substance of the work of art proceeds, incidents and scenes that figured at first may drop out and others take their place, being drawn in by the suction of the qualitative material that aroused the original excitement" (p. 111). Creation is often knotty, messy and confusing. It doesn't usually take a linear path right toward the culmination but is a process in which the artist must travel down many "blind alleys" and pursue unfruitful pathways in order to discover the solution.

In dance, the creative transactions which help to shape the idea are the result of a creative blend of interactions between the idea, the medium, the choreographer, and the dancers. It is this process of creative transaction which is referred to as interpretation. The interpretation of ideas leads the choreographer, the performer (and sometimes a director[29]) to single out that instance or qualitative aspect which is most intriguing. The dance performance is then a manifestation of the choices made by the artist during the creative transactions of artistic process.

> *A dictionary definition reveals that to interpret means to explain the meaning of something, to translate, to have or show one's own understanding of the meaning, to bring out the meaning, especially to give one's own conception of a work of art. Although the phrase "interpretative dance" often has a negative connotation for serious contemporary dancers, in this book "interpret" is used in the context of an artist conveying an understanding of the art form and the art work. When a choreographer or performer makes choices concerning presentation of a motional idea or concept, this is interpretation.*

The Parallel Processes of Choreography and Performance

Artistic process in dance is a multi-faceted course which comprises two parallel processes, choreography and performance. These two are each unique but interrelated; both important to the study and teaching of dance.

> The dancer and the choreographer both use similar processes to bring the work to the audience.

Dance is what is referred to as a "performer-mediated art form." Unlike painting or poetry, a performer brings the work of art to the audience. The artistic processes of choreography and performance are parallel, mutually interactive, and both contribute to the dance performance. During choreography or the development of the dance work, the choreographer is the primary creative force, generating the images with which the performers will work. However, the dancer is often argued to be a co-creator of the dance: without dancers, there is no dance. The performer is an artist who "brings" the dance to the audience by interpreting, presenting and "explaining" the work of art through intentive movement.

This involves several aspects of interaction between the dancer and the dance. First, the performer is a human being who has a unique background, training and point of view with which to form an understanding of the meaning of the work. Second, dancers use certain strategies to bring out the meaning of the work. The dancer, through the act of moving intentively, shapes the movement to convey that meaning or idea to the audience. Dancers are not, nor should they be, a clear glass or colorless vessel that is a mere conduit for the dance steps. Murray Louis (1980) wrote, seeing Balanchine's *Agon* just after it premiered, "I thought the dancers made the ballet. They were strong personality dancers then—clever, witty and hip, and they brought the piece to life. Today much of what those dancers added is part of the choreography of *Agon*...I think about this many times as I struggle with dancers to 'give' themselves to the choreography and not just do it as steps" (p. 25).

Audiences return, time after time, to experience familiar works anew because of the artistry of the dancer, because each performer brings a new understanding of the work to the performance. It is due to the artistry of dancers that dances continue to live: each new cast brings out new aspects of a dance. Seeing a new performance of a familiar dance is not like seeing the video of your favorite movie over and over: to see a new cast in Balanchine's *Diamonds* or Taylor's *Aureole* enables the audience to gain a new understanding of the dance and the dancers. Recognizing these aspects of artistic activity as belonging to the performer as well as to the choreographer recognizes the status of the performer as an *artist*.

Here it is important to dismiss the notion of dancers as "instruments", or refer to technique as "training the dancer's instrument." Performers in dance are not merely physical bodies trained in the motional habits of this or that school. It is impossible to separate the dancer-as-person from the dancer-as-body. Dancers are whole human beings, not a collection of dissected or disparate parts. Any discussion of teaching dance and especially artistic process applied to dance performance must refute this fallacy of mind-body dualism. Addressing only the "body" aspect of the performance artist prevents us from understanding performance as an active artistic process and strips the performer of the role of *artist*.

It is a mistake to think that dancers improve technique by sheer physical means, by simply repeating the movement over and over. If the movement were repeated endlessly in exactly the same way, nothing would be accomplished. However, through training—taking technique classes and receiving feedback—the dancer learns how to analyze performance, detect errors, make corrections, and develop an understanding of movement and meaning.

The source of dance is the intentive dancer, and understanding intentive movement is the key to understanding the artistic process aspect of the performer. The act of performing a dance involves dancers as artists finding and solving challenging movement problems. It is essential for the dance teacher to understand that choreography and performance are two parallel artistic processes which have many aspects in common. Let's take a look at a model for artistic process that incorporates creativity theory and aspects of the Spectrum.

Aspects of Artistic Process

The artistic process model will help us understand how dancers, as choreographers and as performers, create. The four layers of the artistic process model are:

1. *Disposition to act,*
2. *Schema,*
3. *Strategies,*
4. *Training and temperament.*

The core, the *disposition to act*, is central to artistic process, for without activity, there is no art. Disposition to act refers to the initiative to discover and solve artistic problems. *Schema* refers to how the individual artist conceptualizes the art form or medium; in dance this is referred to as "thinking in movement." *Strategies* are the rules or choces which the artist utilizes in decision-making. *Training and temperament* are the characteristic observable actions with which the artist works. The structure of this model does not necessarily mean that one layer forms first, with the others developing after the first is completed. The layers are interactive throughout the life and work of the artist; changes in training may lead to further development and evolution of schema and strategies.

Let's look at each of these in more detail. As you read through each of these aspects of artistic process, think of the Styles of the Spectrum which you, in your role as a teacher, can use to enhance them in your students.

Disposition to Act

> The disposition to act is the ability to seek, discover, formulate, and resolve problems in the medium.

Disposition to act is the *initiative to discover and solve* artistic problems. From the original idea, which may be somewhat vague at first, the task of the artist is to create the concrete statement of a problem. The problem is not foreseen or preconceived, but rather is found *in the situation itself.* The artist alone has ownership of the problem, and no other individual will perceive or resolve it in the same way. The ability to formulate problems is the essential difference between the artist and the craftsman or technician. Students at any age or level of ability are able to engage in artistic process.

The process of creation in art begins with an idea. This idea, which grows out of the artist's experience, undergoes several transformations on its way to becoming the final art product. The original idea doesn't become a work of art instantly in the artist's mind; it is a process in which the original idea, the artist, and the work-in-progress all undergo several transformations. The artist creates a framework, outline, or scaffolding, which creates boundaries or rules that help to shape the work. The work sometimes says to the artist, "No, that doesn't fit." Or, "Well, that seemed ike a good idea at first, but it's time to get rid of it." Like a river, it flows of its own accord and in its own direction. It is this ability to seek, discover, formilate, and resolve problems in the medium that constitutes the disposition to act.

Since formulating and solving a problem is a process that cannot be completely visualized in the mind's eye, the problem must be discovered during interaction with the elements that constitute it. In dance, this means that the artist works with the dance medium: motion. Creative activity in the arts is a heuristic process through which the artist learns by experimentation, investigation, and discovery; learns about the work being created, learns about the medium in general, and gains a deeper understanding of the self. During the creative process the artist is often blocked, inspired, frustrated and catapulted by the essential qualities of the idea or conflict

> Formulating and solving a problem cannot be visualized in the mind's eye. It is a process that must be discovered during interaction with it.

that produced that first irresistible urge to create the dance. Choosing a problem to be solved through choreography or performance means wrestling with that problem, exploring deeply all the possibilities and making choices, divergent discovery and PFD reduction, concerning what to keep and what to discard; thus creativity takes the artist on an odyssey of self-examination.

An aspect of artistic process that is unique to dance is the nature of the materials with which the dancer interacts. One of the entities with which the choreographer works when creating is movement as supplied by the intentive dancer. Dancers are not just clay, paint and metal that the artist manipulates. They have personalities, thoughts, ideas; they are changeable. For choreographers such as Paul Taylor and George Balanchine, the dancer is a primary source of inspiration for creation, and they want dancers to assert their personalities onstage.

> Often a choreographer creates for the abilities of a particular dancer, who is often referred to as a "muse." George Balanchine was one choreographer who often worked this way. The dancer for whom Balanchine created the most works was Suzanne Farrell. The paradigm of a Balanchine dancer, Farrell has said that the reason why Balanchine was so inspired by her was that she understood how to be "useful" to him as a dancer in the dancer/choreographer relationship (Daniel, 1979). She understood that choreography does not reside in the steps of a dance; the steps only serve as structure to show the dance. The performer must understand the essence of the dance, not just its steps, to be able to bring the dance to the audience.

In the relationship between dancer and choreographer, each contributes a different and necessary aspect of the total dance. However, dance students may be unaware of the process that the dancer as artist uses to develop a performance. The performer works with aspects such as stage space, relationship to other dancers, the quality of a jump, attack of an arm movement, the shape of a hand, when the focus goes out to the audience and when it is pulled in. The dancer as artist must be aware of this process and understand how to apply it in rehearsal.

The dance teacher must be very aware of this aspect of the interaction between choreographer and performer, between choreography and performance, for three important reasons. The first reason involves learning about and seeking the optimal experience of flow that was discussed earlier. The act of dancing will be more deeply fulfilling when dancers learn how to seek, find, and develop problems by working with the qualitative features of the medium of motion. Students will learn and understand more about themselves, the process of performance, and the process of choreography.

Second, frustration may occur when student choreographers think that a rehearsal is like a technique class, that the choreography should unfold sequentially like a technique class unfolds, or that they must have the entire dance choreographed in their minds and then simply teach it to the dancers. Making the cognitive "leap" from technique class protocol to artistic process in rehearsal takes guidance and practice—and this requires exposure to the various teaching Styles because each Style offers a different vista, emphasis on different human capacities and opportunities to develop different cognitive skills. All dancers must understand both sides of the dancer-choreographer relationship: as a dancer, how to become useful to a choreographer by developing a thorough understanding of the art form and how to bring the choreographer's image to life; as a choreographer, how to elicit from dancers cognitive abilities and qualities will be useful during the choreographic process. If the training of young dancers hasn't included experiences in artistic process, they will often be at a loss when a choreographer asks them to participate in the choreography. Accustomed to being a *moving body*, they may not know how to be a *thinking body*. On the flip side, a beginning choreographer may subconsciously expect all of their dancers to look or move exactly like himself or herself, and become frustrated when they don't. Students need to understand how the choreographer and dancers both contribute to the dance.

Third, teachers often choreograph using their students, whether in the school associated with a regional company; in the high school or university dance company, or in the company class for a nationally-recognized dance company. The choreographer/teacher who incorporates artistic process information and experiences in technique class, starting with the decision-making process inherent in the Spectrum, will be rewarded with performers as artists who are equipped to supply intentive movement, and the transition from class to rehearsal can be smoother. Thus dancers can learn to be most useful to the teacher as choreographer, useful to other choreographers, and gain the richest knowledge about the discipline of dance and personal satisfaction, by understanding artistic process as applied to the study of technique, improvisation and choreography.

> *Heuristic art: a dance choreographed for the dual purpose of creating art and educating the dancers.*

Teachers can provide such experiences by using the Spectrum in technique, choreography and improvisation classes as well as during repertory classes or rehearsals. One example is the choreographer creating a dance for the dual purpose called heuristic art: through the process of participating in the production of an art work, students learn new aspects of the discipline and the process of performance. Suzanne Farrell relates, "Remember how wonderful Mimi Paul was in Valse Fantasie? She didn't jump very well, so Mr. Balanchine choreographed a lot of jumps for her. Because she was willing, Balanchine brought out a facet of Mimi we had never seen before....When he did Don Quixote for me I had lousy bourées, and he wanted me to improve them. Consequently every act of Don Quixote contains a different problem in bourées" (Daniel, 1979, p. 12). Sometimes a work is created as a challenge for the entire group; often a role is created not only to exploit but also expand the abilities of a performer. Choreographers often create challenges in a dance for dancers who demonstrate willingness to dare or inventiveness.

Dance students must learn that the steps or movement vocabulary is *only one* of many elements with which the dancer interacts in order to convey the dance. Often, although the teacher stresses this in class, it is not until students have been out of school working on their own that they develop the professionalism of an artist.

The disposition to act is not something that simply happens to a dancer, it must be developed. An effective teacher understands this and guides students by designing deliberate episodes to develop this attribute. Performers who lack the disposition to act seem to work only with the surface texture; dancers who approach a role from the steps alone demonstrate this lack. Thus an important part of the development of this aspect of artistic process is the ability to interact with the entirety of the medium itself, not the surface texture or external characteristics ("doing the steps"). It is when the dancer, working in the medium of motion, experiences a conflict, formulates a problem, and succeeds in resolving the conflict thereby achieving a new emotional and cognitive balance that technique is improved. In addition, through this artistic problem-solving interaction with the medium, the performer matures as an artist.

Getting students to move from *doing the steps* to *dancing the dance* usually doesn't happen fully until the student has left the studio classroom: the gardener plants the seed and the flower blooms while the gardener is away on vacation. Our students will not become mature artists while they are under our tutelage. Maturation is a process; we must therefore equip students with the knowledge to develop artistically throughout their lives. Thus it is our careful attention to teaching methods that will enable students to develop as artists.

> *It is revealing that Suzanne Farrell seemed to develop most as a performer during her absence from Balanchine's company. Arlene Croce (1980) wrote that, upon Farrell's return to New York City Ballet, her performance style had matured markedly. Farrell related that during her absence from New York City Ballet, she would practice the Balanchine barre and ballets daily. In other words, she developed the disposition to act.*

Schema

| *Schema: how each artist conceptualizes art and the art form.* |

The second aspect of artistic process, schema refers to the manner in which an artist conceptualizes the art form.[30] In dance, each artist has a particular vision of art and the art form that helps to sculpt the developmental process. Each choreographer has a special conception of the dancing body, of dance, of the purpose of dance, of the purpose of art. "Conception" does not imply that the artist necessarily verbalizes the way that the medium is organized according to this personal framework. Dance involves qualitative thinking, thinking in the medium: the painter thinks in terms of line, hue, saturation of color; the musician in terms of tonal relationships and the timbres and durations of sounds; and the dancer in terms of the organic or geometric shapes of the body, the ineffable connotations of gestures, or the flow of movement. In dance this is known as "thinking in movement." The movements of a dancer are not simply a symbolic way of designating things or thoughts, but are the very *presence* of thought, the thoughts themselves. Thinking in movement does not mean that the choreographer or performer is thinking *about* movement or htat dance movement is symbolic of words. Dance movements *are the thoughts themselves* (Maxine Sheets-Johnstone 1981).

Curtis Carter (1983) discussed the mind as having a central role in the execution of a dance performance, stating that the mind is the controlling force which coordinates all of the various sources that a dancer may draw upon to create a performance. These sources include kinesthetic intelligence (spatial intelligence that operates through the muscles and includes muscle memory), feelings and ideas, as well as prior training and a sense of style to harmonize rhythmic spatial qualities of movement with expressive qualities and abstract ideas to create a sense of unity and order in a performance. Gardner (1993) identified bodily-kinesthetic as one of the seven intelligences and wrote that "the ability to use one's body to express an emotion (as in a dance)...is evidence of the cognitive features of body usage" (p. 19).

> Thinking in movement includes awareness of:
> 1. Abstract relations of space and time, of scale and proportion,
> 2. The movement phrases and body shapes in one part of the dance connecting with those in another part,
> 3. Relationships between various parts of the moving body,
> 4. Spatial relationships such as placement on stage and spatial relationship to other dancers.

Performance is more than an expression or output, it is an *information-gathering event* for the dancer. Through performing a dance, the dancer gathers information which includes developing an understanding of the entire dance work, its overall shape or purpose and the role of the parts as contributing to the whole. The choreographer establishes goals for the work, which must be internalized and given shape in the dancer's mind and body and are guided by the performer's own sense of the work. This leads the dancer to strive for the right movements to realize the dance in performance.

> Intentive moving is a cognitive activity. Dance movements are the thoughts themselves, and performing is a heuristic, information-gathering event.

The mental activities of the dance include an awareness of abstract relations of space and time, of scale and proportion, concrete awareness of the movement phrases and body shapes in one part of the dance connecting with those in another part, and heightened awareness of relationships between various parts of the moving body (Carter 1983). In addition, often a dancer will discover new relationships between movements in various parts of the body while performing. This qualitative thinking in the medium is as important to the choreographer's creation as it is to the director's interpretation and direction and to the performer's recreation of the work in the dance event.

Some choreographers and performers do research or reading during the artistic process, but what is important is not language or words but the qualitative thinking in movement. Reading about a role may provide useful information, but remember that dance is not a mere translation of words into movement, but the presence of thought in motion.

The creative dialog between the artist and the medium takes place at a level which supersedes the verbal. The dialog proceeds not by words but by the direct feeling-thoughts of the motions.

The dancer and choreographer may not be able to put it into words until after the work is completed, if at all. Furthermore, each dance can be seen as a unique world, with a unique set of rules and "language" all its own.

> *Application of the Spectrum will enable students to understand this analytical and artistic process in dance. By helping students understand aspects of dance such as phrasing, qualities, spatial relationships, and how to vary and control these, we help students become cognitively aware artists and enable students to develop the critical thinking skills specific to the medium of dance.*

Schema in dance genres

- *Ballet is often referred to as a system rooted in tradition.*
- *Modern dance has often been referred to as a point of view.*
- *Jazz is often characterized as highly skillful popular entertainment.*
- *Tap has roots in Irish clog dance and African rhythmic arts.*
- *Hip-hop started as improvisational and competitive street dance.*

One way of looking at schema in dance can be to recognize the genres of modern dance, ballet, jazz, tap, and hip-hop as general schemata in dance, from which each individual artist then forms a personal schema. Ballet is often referred to as a "system", and is

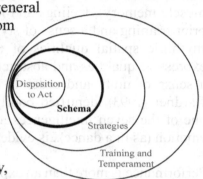

characterized by a sense of tradition, its relatively long and strong collective history, and a movement vocabulary, pedagogical system, and "rules" for choreography developed over centuries. Modern dance has often been referred to as "a point of view" and is characterized by its individualistic spirit and individual discoveries, creativity, will, and imagination. In the early days of modern dance in the first half of the 20th century, a dichotomy existed: Ballet dancers considered themselves disciplined instruments of precision whereas modern dancers felt themselves creative and self-expressive individuals (Cohen (1983). The motivation for movement was different, the movement was different. Ballet dancers tend to view themselves as part of a tradition dating back centuries, in which procedures for passing on knowledge about dance, and the knowledge or vocabulary of steps, are rigorously defined through technique class (Foster, 1986), whereas modern dancers saw themselves as iconoclastic.

The master jazz dancer and teacher Gus Giordano (1975) himself said that jazz is often characterized as highly skillful popular entertainment to be appreciated but not studied, dealing with the purely physical and sensual aspect of dance. Tap and hip-hop started as street dance performed by individuals without professional training but with a natural feel for movement. Tap evolved as a fusion of Irish clog dancing and African rhythmic arts, brought together by immigrants to the New World. Hip-hop began in New York City during the 1970s as a primarily improvisational, solo competitive dance form.

Dance genres exemplify but are not exclusively bound to these schemata. Performers or choreographers trained in any genre may conceptualize dance primarily as an individual point of view which is developed through individual discoveries, as a movement system embodying established ideals which is subject to stylistic interpretation, or as purely physical entertainment using highly skilled performers. Furthermore, a dancer's conceptualization of the art form may not necessarily be a *result* of training in a particular genre; individuals may *seek* training that closely resembles a personal schema. A beginning dance student may start training in one genre due to a pure joy of moving, only to find greater personal fulfillment and success in another genre. For example, a dancer might start taking ballet but feel truly "at home" in a modern class.

Furthermore, contemporary dancers generally study several different genres, and dancers often perform more than one genre, bringing a unique articulation to each. For example, Mikhail Baryshnikov has performed works of ballet, modern, and musical theatre genres. In addition, it is possible for a choreographer's *oeuvre* to include dances using more than one genre. Twyla Tharp has composed works specifically for dancers trained in each of several different genres of dance using the distinctive movement vocabularies of ballet, modern, and social dance, as well as ice skating.

It is important for students to learn as much as possible about each genre or "style" of dance, because such knowledge is useful in several ways. First, dancers who understand why certain dance genres grew and evolved will have a better understanding of the qualities for that genre. Knowing that ballet began as training in court behavior for the European royalty helps give students a distinct picture of the qualities for that movement style. Understanding that modern dance was originally a revolt against what had become the empty athleticism of classical ballet at the turn of the 20th century will enable students to comprehend this genre. Knowing that José Límon was a student of Doris Humphrey whose technique is based on strong use of weight will help students more fully apply weight in class and rehearsal. World, international or folk dances can be approached either as a series of steps, or as representative of a particular culture, revealing the worldview of a certain country.

> *I remember taking a modern dance class with a teacher who had been a partner of early modern dancer Erik Hawkins. In one combination she demonstrated a quick transfer of weight and there was a sudden buzz among the students of "what was that?" One student said, "Oh, it's a pas de boureé." The instructor whirled and indignantly corrected, "It is NOT a pas de boureé. Do NOT use ballet terms in this class!" While all the students could now understand the movement of the feet given the action associated with the ballet terminology, the teacher's point was important: the qualities typical of the ballet genre were inappropriate for the movement she was demonstrating. A ballet dancer, modern dancer, jazz dancer, and folk dancer will all do a pas de boureé in different ways; the qualities of each genre are as important, if not more so, as the specific step. Such qualities can be an essential part of the checklists used for Style C: Reciprocal and Style D: Self-Check and help students understand that dance is created with qualities as well as with movements.*

Strategies

| *Strategy involves two types of restrictions: the tacit set of rules imposed by the genre, and the self-imposed boundaries of the artist's choosing.* |

This third aspect of artistic process involves rules or choices for acting upon what is chosen. These rules may be tacity implied by the genre in which the artist works, or they may be impose by the artist according to a choreographic or aesthetic plan. The particular nature of these strategies and how they are applied involves slightly different elements for each of the interpretive processes of the choreographer and the performer. Choices are determined by the aspects of the medium with which the artist interacts at each level. The choreographer interacts with the original idea and overall plan for the dance; the performer will tend to be more concerned with bringing a unique understanding to one role in relation to the whole dance.

However, both choreographer and performer are concerned with perceiving and resolving an artistic problem or idea in a unique way through execution in the medium of motion.

The nature of the choices made during creation in the arts is complex. The constraints or rules suggested by society and history still leave an enormous number of possibilities open to the artist, who would find it impossible to accept all such possibilities; thus what is chosen can also be seen as the result of what is *not* chosen. For example, the sculptor Auguste Rodin, when asked about his sculpture of the head of Balzac,

> The artist learns to pare away everything that does not help to clarify the developing idea.

stated that he simply cut away everything that was not Balzac. During the heuristic process of creation that is the interaction between artist, idea, and medium, the artist learns to pare away everything that does not portray the developing idea.

> Dr. Linus Pauling was once asked, "How does one go about having a good idea?" He replied, "You have a lot of ideas and throw away the bad ones." To do that, you must understand what that particular discipline, field of study or medium is like and what constitutes "good" and "bad" ideas (Csikszentmihalyi 1996).

> Rules may be a tacitly imposed by the genre, delimitations imposed by the choreographer, or self- imposed by the performer.

Within a particular genre, each choreographer chooses to cut away anything that does not contribute to a particular artistic vision. If each dance utilized the entire vocabulary of movements or range of qualities available, there would be little except music and costumes to distinguish one dance from another. During the process of choreography, the choreographer discards original material because it doesn't "fit" with the idea as it is developing; thus the choreographer decides what to do by deciding what *not* to do (an example of PFD reduction).

The concept of strategies involves *restrictions or rules* on two levels. The first level is that a genre imposes a tacit set of rules on choreographers and performers that defines what is acceptable in that particular genre: What so shocked the audience attending the first performance of Nijinsky's ballet, Rite of Spring (Sacre du Printemps) that they were moved to riot, was that it didn't *look like ballet*. The second level concerns rules as personally imposed delimitations, the self-imposed boundaries that the artist has chosen. Thus working within existing rules is one strategy; breaking rules and creating new rules is another strategy. In general the ballet genre, with its strong tradition, encourages strategists, whereas the modern, contemporary or post-modern genres are characterized by iconoclasts who sought (and seek) to break established rules as well as to create new strategies.

> Just breaking the rules is not enough; anarchy alone doesn't make art. Well-known modern choreographers, such as Merce Cunningham and Martha Graham, have been those who were able to establish a consistent, stable style by breaking old rules, developing new rules and strategies, and then becoming strategists within their own well-established rules. Overall, successful choreographers in any genre are those who have employed, in new ways, the forms and procedures established by themselves or others.

Performers employ a similar process in applying strategies. For the performer, conveying the dance image is a more complex process than simply "expressing" oneself or "reacting to the music." While a performer may sometimes produce an effect that wasn't planned, the performer-artist is aware of the effect and will analyze it via PFD reduction, using criteria, which may be unspoken and intuitive, to decide if it is appropriate for that dance. Dancers who grow as artists are able to experiment to produce a wide range of possibilities for a particular phrase, analyze each, work on how to attenuate it, and make it part of a personal artistic palette.

> *Rehearsal is a transformative, heuristic process for the dancer and the dance: in rehearsals the dancer gradually transforms the subject matter into the very substance of the work of art.*

Conveying the dance work to the audience necessitates conveying an understanding of the dance work. In order to do so, one must first develop an understanding of the work, and must make choices about how to best convey that understanding. Each dancer approaches the art of performing differently, and will find unique qualitative problems of interpretation and realization. Like the choreographer, the performer as artist must find a way to express a particular idea through movement.

However, the performer may be given the work as movements or "steps" and must work with this in a developing process to come to know the dance through the structure of the movements. Rehearsals represent a series of successive transformations during which the dancer transforms the subject matter into the very substance of the work of art. The dancer may experiment with making the arm movements bold and strong or gentle and flowing, may restrain or involve the shoulders and torso in an arm extension, may make a step delicate and soft or deliberate. Students usually need to be guided in this process, and using the Spectrum to enable your students to make choices via PFD reduction will provide them with experience in the process of assessing, experimenting, choosing, transforming.

> **To Do**: *Develop a phrase for a class of your choice, using the Style you think is appropriate for that phrase and the objective of making choices to develop artistic process. Consider what choices students are being asked to make and how this will contribute to artistic process.*

Whether the dancer is improvising and working with the dance in terms of qualities or ideas, or working with the choreography as prescribed movements or steps, the same process applies. The parameters and possibilities for improvisation and for performance are of different degrees, but are no less existent in one type of performance than the other.

Training and Temperament

> *Training and temperament refer to how the artist conceives the act of moving, how movement is motivated, and the qualitative features of motion.*

The fourth aspect of artistic process involves the interweaving of training and temperament. Training in the form of technique class is more than simply exercising the body to increase speed, flexibility and endurance. Training also helps to shape how the dancer conceives the act of moving and initiates or motivates movement. For example, a port de bras may be seen as a geometric shape, an arm framing the body, or as a spatial investigation. Each teacher and choreographer will define technical competence differently. For some it means an understanding of the *qualities* of the movement, for others it refers to producing clarity in body *design*. Training also develops a dancer's view of the relationship between the studio educative process and the dance performance. In addition artists interact with a particular movement style (such as Límon, Cecchetti, or Fosse); the dancer formulates an external model of the dance movement as a cohesive style. For example, to be told that a teacher's movement is "fundamentally Graham," or is in the Vaganova style, is to be provided with information that makes it possible to execute the movement that is demonstrated. Dancers come to know the fundamental characteristics of the vocabularies of the major dance genres. Students come to understand the general movement style in the process of understanding implementation and interpretation of a movement phrase.

This is one purpose and pitfall of technique: to present students with one model of, and motivation for, movement. Technique in dance not only enables the student to build a wider "movement vocabulary" but also to learn to *motivate* movement or *conceive* of movement in new and different ways. The pitfall is that some beginning dancers, or accomplished dancers who begin to study a new genre or style, may approach the new style in terms of its shapes or steps without understanding that a new viewpoint is needed. Renowned dance writer Marcia Siegel recognized the need for performers to understand the style of the work that they perform, when she wrote, of the Joffrey Ballet's 1977 revival of José Límon's The Moor's Pavane, that it was "performed for its top layer only." According to Siegel, the dancers achieved the shape and intensity of the choreography, but "they never got it to look like a modern dance….The Moor's Pavane is first-rate storytelling, but it must have weight, amplitude in space, incisively controlled and balanced tensions among the four characters in order to be Límon" (Siegel, 1977, pp. 45-46).

> *Observers may say of certain performers that they look like a ballet dancer doing modern or vice versa; a folk dance teacher was once overheard correcting a student's performance, saying "Don't do it like a dancer!" At the Cunningham studio, even accomplished dancers are required to start at the elementary level in order to learn the basic qualities, weight shifts and features of Cunningham technique.*

Training and temperament also involve the characteristic use of the body. Susan Foster (1986) has characterized the choreographic style of four contemporary choreographers according to their use of parts of the body. According to this analysis, ballet choreographer George Balanchine *fits body parts to geometric designs*, modern dance choreographer Martha Graham *arranges the movement of body parts in an organic sequence* (often from center to periphery), while contemporary choreographers Merce Cunningham and Deborah Hay *use body parts randomly.*

Each dancer, through training and temperament, develops a unique movement style, like a fingerprint. The movement idiom that the dancer prefers to adopt is related to the dancer's temperament or personality. Foster (1986) refers to a dancer's performance "persona," or the dance version of the dancer's personality. A dancer will choose to study a general style that "fits" his or her personal temperament, and the interaction of training and temperament will shape the dancer's personal movement style. If a dancer's movement propensities are not in accord with or are not fulfilled by one movement style, the dancer will tend to leave that style to study another. Professional performers have remarked that they switched companies when they felt "unfulfilled" performing a certain movement style. Artists tend to seek a style that matches their own temperamental proclivities.

Efforts (dynamic qualities)

Dynamic qualities are an important aspect of training and temperament in the artistic process. The work of the early 20th century movement theorist and choreographer Rudolf Laban offers a comprehensive systematization of quality in movement. Qualities, which are called Efforts, are divided into four basic components: space, time, weight, and flow. Each of these comprises two opposite dimensions—sustained and sudden for time, fine and firm (or light and strong) for weight, free and bound for flow, direct and flexible (or indirect) for space. According to Laban, all human movement exhibits constellations of these factors that form certain identifiable textures of movement.

Efforts: Dynamic Qualities	
Time Sudden vs. Sustained	**Weight** Strong vs. Light
Space Direct vs. Flexible	**Flow** Bound vs. Free

Most people have predilections for certain Effort elements, and their movements tend to reflect some Effort elements or ranges of elements, sometimes to the exclusion of others. Use of each of the Efforts, which may range from neutral to exaggerated, give qualitative shading to movement. This is rather like having an accent when speaking: the southern drawl, the mid-western twang, the Scottish burr; each accent has particular qualities that characterize the speech of an individual.

The style of a particular dancer can be analyzed in terms of these qualitative shadings. For example, the style of Mikhail Baryshnikov, especially in his performance of the classical ballets, has been characterized as exhibiting direct space, quick time, light weight, and bound flow (Foster 1987). Critic Marcia Siegel has identified distinct qualities in the performances of Swan Lake by Cynthia Gregory and Natalia Makarova, suggesting that Gregory's Swan Queen was characterized as exhibiting firmness or strength, suddenness, and direct focus; while Makarova's swan Queen exhibited fine or light touch, sustainment, and flexible focus (Siegel 1977).

Try to recognize temperamental proclivities within your students so that you can help guide each student toward appropriate dance styles or genres, or help each student understand how and where they "fit." When I was an undergraduate dance major, the upper-level modern dance class was in Graham technique. It was taught by Dorothy Silver, who was a wonderful teacher and performer, but I remember disliking it intensely: I struggled not so much with the movements per se but with putting myself completely in the quality or style of it--it seemed to be based on so much suffering and angst. I could only smile when Dorothy finally told me, "You'll never make a good Graham dancer; you're too happy!"

This statement was important to both teacher and student: she and I both recognized that, although I was struggling with this type of dance, it didn't mean that I wasn't a good dancer. If this had been my first or only exposure to dance, I might have become discouraged, given up and majored in English or music.

Years later I took class from Ethel Winter; it may have been the more joyful aspect of the Graham technique that she articulated or the changes in my life in the intervening ten years, but I felt much more comfortable with it—it was still a bit foreign, but more understandable. When you and your students understand the many facets of artistic process, you will gain a deeper understanding of the breadth and depth of the art of dance.

When a choreographer articulates time, space, weight, and flow in a distinctive manner, uses these distinctive qualities to train performers, and characteristically employs them in works, they become more than an individual constellation of effort factors, they become a choreographic dynamic. For example, Daniel Lewis (1984) wrote of José Límon, "He developed a series of exercises that isolated the different parts of the body, so that he could learn how to control the weight within each body part as he moved. This consciousness of weight, and the sense of power behind it, was remarked upon by critics throughout José's career and became a trademark of his style" (p. 18). On the other hand, in the middle of the 20th century, a time when most modern choreographers were exploring and using weight, Merce Cunningham's use of lightness was considered unusual. However, his articulation of it, through the years, continued to be very different from the way in which ballet choreographers use it. Arlene Croce (1968) suggested that instead of the aerial steps associated with ballet, he substituted "incredibly rapid shifts of weight and direction, and packed staccato changes of pace on the ground" (p. 25).

Bringing together the Spectrum and Artistic Process

The role of the teacher, and eventually the role of the learner, is to design a problem or series of problems that will serve as the stimulus that invites the learner to engage in the discovery or artistic process. For example, each of the statements below might be used in a class, but as such they do not invite the learner to move beyond memory to discovery. How might each be re-worked or expanded in Divergent Discovery with PFD reduction?

1. "Design three preparations for a pirouette en dehors."
2. "Develop four ways to get from the first action to the second action in the phrase we're doing in class."
3. "Create a phrase which presents a spatial progression from right side low to left side high."
4. "Compose a study exhibiting the extremes of bound and free flow."
5. "Design a locomotor sequence which uses all five basic elevations."

Initiating the discovery process is a challenge which involves:
- Understanding the nature of discovery in dance,

- Designing tasks conducive to discovery and artistic process,
- Highlighting specific aspects of artistic process,
- Learning and applying deliberate teaching behaviors that are appropriate for this process,
- Monitoring the learning behaviors that are unique to this process,
- Knowing your goal or objectives.

Armed with the tool belt of the Spectrum, an understanding of flow and artistic process in dance, and your own personal passion and artistic vision, you will be well-equipped to face the many challenges of dance pedagogy.

Applying the Spectrum in Every Class
The following are examples of using Styles A-H in a variety of activity classes; find ways to apply the Spectrum to *every* class you teach.

Aerobic Dance
- Cued Response: Everyone follows the teacher and does the same steps and moves.
- Practice: Set up a Circuit which includes stations with specific tasks such as curls or flys with weights, resistance bands, steps, and jump ropes.
- Reciprocal: To acquire proper form in push-ups and sit-ups (or similar exercises): Have students work in pairs, while one partner practices the proper form for the push-ups and sit-ups the other partner offers feedback using the teacher-provided criteria.
- Self-Check: Have students work with weights in Circuits using criteria for proper form
- Inclusion: Have students choose high/low impact, high/low intensity, include or delete turns, etc.
- Guided Discovery: Guide students to discover proper form for sit-ups.
- Convergent Discovery: Have each student create their own combination which uses five different steps; have each student lead the class doing their combo. Students use logic to choose steps which use a variety of muscle groups and smooth transitions from one step or move to the next.
- Divergent Discovery: Have each student design three different movements or actions to use their arms in a basic step such as the grapevine.

International or Multicultural Folk Dance
- Cued Response: Demonstrate a dance phrase and take the class through it step by step.
- Practice: Demonstrate the basic steps of a dance such as Misirlou then have learners practice it using task sheets
- Reciprocal: Have learners work with partners to check each other for accuracy of footwork in a complex dance such as the Rumunsko Kolo using teacher-provided criteria.
- Self-Check: Learners use a criteria sheet to practice a dance such as Hora Pe Gheata.
- Inclusion: Design different practice levels for intricate or physically demanding steps or moves (such as a two-step instead of polka) for learners to select the level they perform.
- Guided Discovery: Develop a target answer to the question, "How does dress or costume affect dance and vice versa?"
- Convergent Discovery: Choose a dance which has variations such as Tcherkessiya. After practicing several existing variations in class, divide students into small groups. Each

group designs a variation which is in the movement characteristics of the dance (criteria provided by the teacher).
- Divergent Discovery: Have students work in pairs to design a "never before seen!" pattern for partner turns as variations on a basic grapevine step: hand-holds, arm movements.

Ballroom or Social Dance
- Cued Response: Demonstrate a dance step or maneuver and take students through it step by step.
- Practice: Demonstrate the basic step then have learners practice it, such as the waltz box step or box turn.
- Reciprocal: Work in partners to check each other (using criteria which you supply) for accuracy of footwork, frame or carriage.
- Self-Check: Develop a checklist from the list of elements from *Dance A While* or other textbook.
- Inclusion: First, have the class brainstorm on entry levels for certain steps (this is Style B: Practice). Then have students choose their entry levels.
- Guided Discovery: Guide students to discover how to lead from closed to open position and from open to closed position.
- Convergent Discovery: Have pairs "discover" the barrel roll (dishrag) by stating that they will both turn simultaneously one full turn, keeping both hands joined and without either person doing an aerial.
- Divergent Discovery: After working with the group to "get past the roadblock", have each pair work divergently, then use PFD reduction to create a swing dance sequence which includes at least one new release, one new turn, an elevation or aerial, and a 2-4 count freeze.

Ballet, Modern, Jazz, Tap, Hip-Hop Technique
- Cued Response: Demonstrate a phrase, have the class perform it in unison.
- Practice: Have students individually practice a warm-up or barre sequence.
- Reciprocal: Have students work in pairs on a new and/or longer sequence, using teacher criteria, to enhance retention and precision of the phrase.
- Self-Check: Have students practice and self-check as a review for a movement mid- term or final exam.
- Inclusion: Develop a phrase that includes four degrees of complexity using turns or elevations. For example, in arabesque, using a relevé (level 1), sauté (level 2) or cabriole (level 3) in first arabesque.
- Guided Discovery: Choose a specific concept from *The Physics of Dance* such as torque in turning, that has a target answer, develop and deliver the question sequence.
- Convergent Discovery: Teach a phrase (Style A), then have students analyze and notate it (using vocabulary, Motif writing, Benesh notation or Labanotation).
- Divergent Discovery: With a previously-introduced and -practiced locomotor phrase, have each student produce a unique ending (having worked first to get past the initial "roadblock" and using PFD reduction).

Creative Dance for Children
- Cued Response: Have children follow a simple port de bras sequence.

- Practice: Set up "stations" and pathways in the studio such as walking a foam "balance beam," jumping from spot to spot, turning to a designated corner, and have students individually practice.
- Reciprocal: (about age 9 and up): Work in partners to provide feedback on aspects of student-generated dance phrases such as limb position, overall sequence, qualities of movement, etc.
- Self-Check: (about age 9 and up): After students have generated their own dance sequence, have them develop a criteria list of about 3 items that are important.
    - Inclusion: In a class dance phrase, children choose whether they will jump (level 1), hop (level 2), or leap (level 3).
    - Guided Discovery: Discover principles of balance (refer to the previous examples of dialectics).
    - Convergent Discovery: Discover the number of different elevations (refer to previous example of Convergent Discovery).
    - Divergent Discovery: "Design a different sitting shape every time you hear the drum beat—one you haven't seen before" (after working with the class to get "past the roadblock").

Chapter Summary

This chapter examines the nature of discovery, creativity, and artistic process in dance, and how the Spectrum can be applied to enable students to discover ideas, concepts, and joy in dance. The word "creativity" can be overly vague and sometimes intimidating; however, discovery is a pleasurable experience that all students can engage in.

When studying discovery and production in dance as an art form, we must understand *artistic process*. The purpose of production work may vary according to the age group, style of dance or skill level. However, most dance classes are generally involved with producing dances of some kind whether they are teacher-produced phrases, choreographic studies, repertory, or improvisation. The common thread is that of *artistic process*: the process of discovery, experimentation, exploration, and shaping.

The four aspects of artistic process are disposition to act, schema, strategies, and training and temperament, and the key to artistic process is problem-finding. The artist, whether as choreographer or performer, works with a deliberate set of restrictions and choices. A personal schema, and the choices made, are fueled and guided by a disposition to act, to discover and solve artistic problems. The schema, disposition to act, and choices will all be consonant with the artist's personal temperament and chosen training. The layers of artistic process are interactive throughout the life and work of the artist; changes in training may lead to further evolution in schema and strategies.

Getting students to move from *doing the steps* to *dancing the dance* is an essential part of dance study. Although this process may take time, it can begin in dance class by deliberately exposing students to a variety of experiences, to develop a range of attributes, by using the Spectrum. Sometimes this doesn't happen fully until the student has left the studio; our students generally will not become mature artists while they are under our tutelage but will use the tools we have given them to grow and mature. Maturation is a process; we must therefore equip students with the knowledge to develop artistically throughout their lives. Thus it is your careful attention to teaching methods that will enable your students to have opportunities to develop as artists, eventually, if not immediately. Dance students may understand the direction in which they are to go, even if they are only at the beginning of the journey. The Spectrum will provide them with the tools they will need on their journey.

<u>Ahead</u>

As teachers, we can become so focused on our students that we neglect taking care of ourselves. However, caring for mind, body, and spirit are a priority. Creating an environment—both within and around ourselves—that is productive and calming takes the same thoughtful attention as planning and implementing lessons.

> ***To Do***: *Read an autobiography or biography of a dancer you admire, or read articles about their life and work. If possible, view performances and/or videotapes of their work in choreography or performance. Try to identify the layers of artistic process in the work of this artist.*

Questions for Reflection and Discussion

1. Identify how *you* define **creativity**.

2. Have you experienced "**flow**?" When, and how did it feel?

3. Discuss how **artistic process** functions for the choreographer, for the performer, for the director or reconstructor.

4. Reflect on the threads from Dewey to Divergent Discovery, Convegent Discovery, and PFD reduction.

5. Discuss the nature of choreographing as an information-**gathering event**, and the nature of performing as an information-gathering event.

6. Identify and discuss the **material** with which the choreographer creates in the art of dance.

7. Define "**heuristic**" and "heuristic art."

8. Identify the difference between **presented and discovered problems**, and discuss how this is important in artistic process.

9. Discuss the difference between the **artist and the craftsman** and personal experiences with each.

10. Define **intentive** moving.

11. Identify and discuss aspects of the **medium of motion** that the dancer-as-artist works with to develop a performance.

12. Discuss where, when and how should students should learn this process.

13. Discuss why the dance teacher needs to be aware of, and make students aware of, the **relationship** between choreography and performance, between the choreographer and the performer.

14. Discuss the difference between *doing the steps* and *performing the dance*.

15. Define **schema** in dance, and give examples of personal schema and schema of genres.

16. Identify your schema; and with which dance genre you feel most "at home."

17. Identify the **mental activities of the dancer** listed, and discuss additional possibilities.

18. Reflect on **strategies** and rules and how they feed into application of PFD reduction during choreography and performance.

19. Discuss how **rules** function in strategies and what can happen when rules are broken.

20. Discuss how individual **training and temperament** interact in dance.

21. Identify and give examples of the four **Efforts** identified by Rudolf Laban.

22. Reflect on your training and temperament: what genres or styles of dance feel good for you, what are your qualitative movement proclivities?

23. Reflect on and discuss PFD reduction in reference to John Dewey, Curtis Carter, Linus Pauling, Auguste Rodin, and choreographers such as Paul Taylor and George Balanchine.

10 Self-Care for the Dance Teacher

Recipe for Iced Coffee:
1. Become a dance teacher.
2. Bring hot coffee to the studio.
3. Start doing a million things.
4. Forget you brought coffee.
5. Drink it cold.

Hopefully teaching is a creative act that is emotionally rewarding, financially viable and spiritually uplifting. But let's face it, teaching dance can also be exhausting and emotionally draining. Whether your teaching includes a lot of demonstration and dancing, or mostly circulating around the room correcting and encouraging, you're often on your feet, giving and nurturing. Recognize that you need to balance the outward giving with the inward receiving. To be a better teacher, take care of yourself physically, mentally, emotionally, and spiritually.

Body Care
We should all have a personal massage therapist, on call at all hours, who works for nothing more than the delight of our smile and the crumbs at the bottom of our fridge. However, until that person knocks on the door, we'll have to take care of ourselves.

First be sure to warm up yourself prior to teaching. If you have the time to do a full personal class prior to teaching, that's wonderful. Demonstrating isn't the same as taking class. While you may be able to physically warm your muscles, focus is also an important aspect of a warm-up. While we may think of ourselves as first-class multi-taskers, it is impossible to focus on yourself and on students at the same time. Also remember that what you need as a warm-up will be different from what your students need. A four-year-old child, an advanced teenager, and a mature dancer will each need a different warm-up.

Second be sure to plan activities that support and balance your teaching. Nautilus or other weight-training, Pilates, yoga and other activities use muscles which are different from what we typically use in most dance classes. If you teach mostly ballet and other dance forms which use primarily turned-out positions, be sure to include activities which use parallel positions. Core, upper-body strengthening, and cardio are also important to include.

Be pro-active when it comes to taking care of muscle fatigue and injury recovery. Remember "RICE" for an injury: Rest, Ice, Compression, Elevation. Ice is the cheapest and easiest body-care modality; keep a bag of frozen peas or corn, used only for this purpose, in your freezer, to pop onto a sore spot. Isopropyl alcohol and water in a baggie also makes a good ice pack. Put the ice where it hurts, wrap snugly in an Ace or other elastic wrap, elevate it, and try to stay off of it or allow it to rest as often as possible. Remember that it's perfectly OK to let students see you taking care of your body; this isn't weakness, it's wisdom.

Take vharge when it comes to nutrition, body care, stress, muscle fatigue and injury recovery.
- *Having a professional massage, chiropractor visits, and other body care isn't a luxury, it's essential. Prevention and maintenance are key.*
- *Balance your body. If you spend most of your day teaching ballet and other genres that use outward rotation, be sure to use your parallel stabilizers, too.*
- *Dance technique isn't typically aerobic, so get cardio training in your day. Cardio helps increase stamina and reduce stress.*
- *Know when and how to take a break. Yes you* **can** *muscle through a bad day but you don't have to. Have ideas in your "dance teacher's bag of tricks" that you can pull out when needed: something that will be pertinent to class and educational. Don't be afraid to use it.*

Here are a few "tips from the trenches" from fellow teachers:
Kristine A. Izak: Nautilus weights machines for major muscle groups at the gym at least three times of week. Added some Pilates to my jazz warm ups with the students, so we both benefit.
Jenny Gudmundsen Griffes: Regular personal workouts daily, chiropractor, and healthy eating. Do something not dance-related at least once a week.
Cathy Wind: Core power yoga a few times a week, essential oils, reflexology, acupuncture for any inflammation. I have a lovely acupressure massage at the mall by me that takes walk ins for that day I wake up with muscle fatigue.
Leann Garth: Instant ice packs and frozen peas in a bag. Extra vitamin C helps the body clear itself of the acids and waste products from muscle over-use which helps reduce soreness faster. After a long night teaching drink a glass of citrus juice or lemonade.

Spread Joy, Not Germs

Let's face it, in the dance studio, everyone touches everyone and everything, and as teachers we can become vectors for disease. Take a tip from doctors and nurses: wash your hands before and after every class, and keep antibacterial foam or gel with you at all times. Avoid touching your face, especially mouth and eyes. Have students wash their hands before and after class (especially children; their parents will appreciate it). Keep boxes of tissue in several places in the studio.

Massage, Mindfulness, Meditation

Sometimes it feels great to stop moving! Massage, self-massage, acupuncture, acupressure, chiropractic, reflexology and other modalities are yummy. Also, be sure to include activities other than dance at least once a week: reading fiction, cooking (not the gotta-throw-something-together-fast but really taking time to be engaged with all your senses in the aroma, sound, and textures of the food you are preparing), taking a warm bath with essential oils, knitting, getting together with friends, re-establishing special time with family.

Meditation doesn't have to involve 30 minutes in a darkened room; it can be loosely defined as any activity that involves focusing and controlling your attention, or mindfulness; in other words, about focusing on your senses in the moment. Seems easy, but this can be a challenge when we are being pulled in a dozen directions, especially when we are worried about an upcoming event or need to remember to do something.

Does this sound familiar?
> "5-two-three" (Did I remember to order tights?),
> "6-two-three" (Forgot to go to the bathroom at the last class break, oh, well, gotta hold it now),
> "7-two-three" (Drat, there goes that 'problem child' again),
> "Ready-and-ah" (Gee, I could use coffee right now. . . .)

It's not a matter of emptying your mind, but rather of filling your attention with your focus on only one thing. It might start with just paying attention to your breath for one minute. First notice your breathing, without judging or changing it. Simply notice whatever you notice; there is no "good" or "bad"; an itch is just an itch, the pressure of your butt on the chair is just pressure. Next, scan your body. If you are holding tension anywhere, send your breath to that part of your body with an inhalation, and release the tension with an exhalation. From the inside, observe how it feels to inhale, and how it feels to exhale—the coolness or warmth of the air, expansion and relaxation of the ribcage, release of any tension in shoulders, neck, hands. Each time you notice your attention wandering, gently bring it back to focus on your breathing again. When you're ready to finish, take a moment to recognize that you've taken time to calm and center yourself, with an affirmation such as, "I am calm, I am serene. I will share this with everyone I contact today." Then engage with the world again as a centered individual!

To Do: A wonderful mindfulness experience is Mindful Walking, which you can do in just a minute to two.
From https://www.eomega.org/article/walking-meditation-for-kids Jennifer Cohen Harper.

- *Stand in a tall and strong but also comfortable and relaxing position, with your feet hip-width apart.*
- *Make sure your shoulders are relaxed and take a few deep breaths.*
- *Notice how your feet feel on the ground. Move your weight around a little to see how it feels. Lean forward and backward, then side to side. Now find the center—the place where you are balanced and most strong.*
- *Take a slow walk. It can be as short as walking to the end of a yoga mat and back. You can walk a short path in any room and then turn around and walk back to where you started.*
- *Notice how your feet feel as you walk. What is the sensation like in your heels? In your toes?*
- *Notice what walking feels like in the rest of your body. What happens in your legs and hips when you walk? What about your arms? Can you feel walking in your neck and your face?*
- *If your mind starts to wander while you are walking, notice where it is wandering to, then gently bring it back to how your body is feeling during your walk.*
- *Come to stillness, take a deep breath, and send a thank-you thought to your feet.*

(My thanks to Shari Dowburd Williams for sharing this with me!)

Relaxation

I love to do relaxation for each class periodically—not only does it help connect with students in a different way, it is relaxing for me as well. Here are a few different kinds of relaxation.

These can be done in separate sessions, or together as an introduction to different types of relaxation.

- <u>Deep diaphragmatic breathing</u>: Have students lie in Constructive Rest Position (CRP): on the back, with knees bent so the soles of the feet rest on the floor, feet about hip width apart and knees gently supporting each other. Let the hands rest on the belly, between the navel and pubic bone. Allowing the breathing to slow and deepen, feel the belly rise with each inhalation and hollow with each exhalation. The goal is to breathe diaphragmatically ("belly breathing") rather than just costally (into the ribs).
- <u>Progressive contraction/release</u>: Sometimes we don't realize we are holding tension until we contract a muscle and then release it. Guide students to contract and release muscle groups sequentially (i.e., hands, arms, feet, calves, thighs, etc).
- <u>Guided visualization</u>. Some people don't have a view of inhabiting a wonderful, three-dimensional physical body with length, breadth, depth, with internal and external connections. In addition to relaxing, guided visualization can also help create greater understanding of the musculo-skeletal home we inhabit. Develop a "journey" through the body, for yourself or students, which might include taking a boat trip through the canals of your body from the top of your head to along the arms and legs, or visualizing opening pathways of air along your spine and limbs, or gradually filling your body with a tide of warm ocean.

At the end of the relaxation, include directives for students to gently move arms, spine, legs, or head. This achieves two purposes: it brings them back into the present, and enables you to see if anyone has actually fallen asleep, so you can gently wake them. Some students enter a very deep state of relaxation and may be disoriented, so be as comforting and nurturing as possible.

<u>Breathing</u>

Mindful breathing helps reduce tension, focus attention, and increase the oxygen that your muscles need to combat fatigue. Yawning means that your body is starved for oxygen and is trying to get more, so if you (or a student) yawns, it may not be exhaustion but that you're holding your breath because you're stressed and have forgotten to breathe.

Take a moment to inhale completely and exhale completely before starting class. Take a moment to inhale completely and exhale completely before you start that first warm-up. Take a moment to inhale and exhale completely when you finish a demonstration or an exercise. If students see you practicing mindful breath, they will see it as important and begin to do it, too. Finally, take a moment to inhale and exhale completely when you leave the studio at the end of the day, to delineates that time when you're "off duty."

Mindful breathing can include more than just remembering to exhale. Pranayama is the formal yoga practice of controlling breath. The following is a brief list of different pranayama exercises:

- Breath retention (kumbhaka) can involve retaining breath after an inhale (antara) and after an exhale (bahya).
- Alternate nostril breathing involves the sympathetic and parasympathetic systems, and is said to synchronize the two hemispheres of the brain.
- Conqueror breath (ujjayi breath) is known as the ocean-like sound made as breaths are directed over the back of the throat. It is good for quieting the mind.

- Skull shining breath (kapalabhati) consists of alternating forceful exhales with longer passive inhales.
- Breath of fire (bhastrika) involves rapid and forceful inhalations and exhalations.

Your Voice

I've learned over the years that I can teach a class perched on a stool when nursing a foot or leg injury, but if my voice is gone, I'm sunk. Preserving your voice involves prevention and maintenance.

1. Warming up. You wouldn't think of doing jumps and leaps before warming up, so don't expect your voice to do that either. Think of a quick vocal warm-up as tendus and pliés for your throat. The vocal folds are the smallest muscles in your body and they need to be warmed up too. Simple warm-up exercises include yawning, which lifts the palate, and humming while relaxing your jaw and wiggling it back and forth. Warm up your lips and tongue by doing a "lion's face": inhale deeply, then open your eyes wide, open your mouth as wide as possible and stick out your tongue as far as you can as if you're trying to touch your chin with it. Hold this pose for the length of your exhalation. Relax and repeat. Look at yourself in the mirror as you do it, and nothing else that happens during the day will embarrass you!
2. Humming is a great way to warm up your voice.
3. Hydrate, hydrate, hydrate. Lozenges and chewing gum during class look tacky and are distracting, you also don't want to aspirate an object while you're teaching. So sip water throughout the day. Yes, you may need to zip to the restroom between classes, but your body needs water anyway. Dance teachers especially need more water, as we not only lose water through perspiration but also through our mouths during constant cueing and giving feedback.
4. Keep your environment hydrated. Plants are possibly one of the best things to have in your studio: they clean the air and return an enormous amount of water to the room. See the section on "Plants in the studio" for more suggestions.
5. Avoid irritants. Alcohol, smoke, and sugar are three big irritants. So is (sigh) caffeine.
6. Avoid clearing your throat, which is hard on your vocal cords. Sip water or warm liquids.
7. When your voice is tired, let it rest. On those days when you have to talk a lot or loudly, or if you're sick and feel laryngitis coming on, allow someone else to do the talking and have it be part of the learning process.
8. Never try to be heard over the class. If things are getting out of hand in class, use the "If you can hear me, clap once" technique: Say, in a moderate-to-quiet voice, "If you can hear me, clap once." The clap will get the attention of those who aren't paying attention. If some students are still talking, go on to, "If you can hear me, clap twice." You'll probably never need to go to three claps. This gets everyone's attention without compromising your voice.

Haley Mathiot Smelcer says, "I find the quieter I am in my classes, the quieter my kids are. It's amazing how kids will step up to the proverbial plate. You'll be amazed. Literally pretend you have lost your voice, watch what happens." (Dance Teacher Network, Oct. 20, 2016).

9. <u>Avoid whispering</u>, which is actually harder on your vocal cords than talking. If your voice is gone, don't speak at all. Use gestures, facial expressions, and other non-verbal communication. While studying American Sign Language might not be feasible, learn a few signs for concepts you use frequently, such as "wait," "practice," "again," "listen," "watch," "everyone all together."

10. <u>Don't smoke</u>. Just don't. It not only wrecks your voice, it also gives you wrinkles, reduces the oxygen to your body, and stinks.

11. <u>Breathe and speak from your diaphragm</u>. When your throat is relaxed and open, and you support from your diaphragm, your voice will be stronger and you won't have to strain to be heard.

12. <u>Relax</u>. When you're anxious or nervous, it is reflected in your voice, and it undermines your authority. Lift from the crown of your head (not your chin), lengthen your spine to stand tall, inhale and exhale as you reach your arms out wide. This is "power posture", and also makes you feel more confident.

13. <u>Acid reflux can damage the vocal folds</u>. Avoid foods and situations (lying down after eating) that cause acid reflux. If you have a bad taste in your mouth in the morning, frequent bloating, burping, heartburn, or a lump in the back of your throat, see a throat specialist.

14. <u>Be Well.</u> Easier said than done, but realize that a cold, flu or other virus will wreck your voice and sap your energy. Wash your hands often, keep a bottle of waterless hand cleaner handy at all times, and avoid touching your face during the day.

(Thanks to Dr. Margaret Ball, of the Theatre Dept. of East Stroudsburg University, for many of these suggestions.)

Nutrition

<u>Make your food work twice as hard</u>. Think in terms of nutritionally-productive foods, ones that do "double duty": bananas provide both potassium and carbs; blueberries and strawberries provide fiber, slow-release carbs, and antioxidants; kale and spinach have fiber, antioxidants, calcium; baked potatoes provide potassium and surprisingly, lots of water. Whole grains such as brown rice, quinoa and barley also provide iron and, when you mix in curry spices such as cumin, turmeric, and ginger, help regulate the release of their carbohydrates to last throughout a long teaching day. Egg whites and tofu are low in fat and excellent sources of protein. Whole fruits (better than juice) are high in vitamin C and provide fiber and water, and help prevent muscle soreness.

- <u>Prepare "Grab N Go" packs:</u> When time is tight, it's easy to fall back on packaged prepared foods such as granola bars which tend to be notoriously heavy in sugar and empty calories. Put together baggies of sliced raw veggies like carrots, red sweet bell peppers, and cucumbers, for a quick snack which provides fiber and a deliciously satisfying "crunch". Prepared fresh fruit such as apple or pear slices with a splash of lemon juice; kumquats, and berries also give complex carbs and fiber for quick energy and a zip of flavor which can revive you. Take control of your nutrition and plan meals as if you were planning a class: in advance, with careful thought for your objectives.

<u>Once a week, do food prep</u> for the rest of the week.

- I make huge pots of soup—mixed garden vegetable, creamy butternut squash, zippy zucchini bisque—then ladle into single-serving containers and freeze. Every day I take a frozen container (easier to transport, less chance of spillage) of soup to work, then heat it in the microwave at the studio or office. Put up your feet with your hands around a warm bowl of soup and feel stress melt away; you can even sip it from a thermos during class.

- You can do the same with casseroles (divide into single-serving containers), or complex salads of greens and raw veggies seasoned with lemon juice and/or herbs such as dill, basil, and oregano (oregano can also be grown as a hanging plant in the studio or office).

- Chop or shred a variety of veggies such as zucchini, carrots, red cabbage, asparagus, bell peppers, and spinach, and keep each in a separate container in the fridge. Then you can pull together a quick meal: microwave with chicken vegetable stock for soup; toss together raw for a salad; microwave with pre-cooked couscous, rice, quinoa or other grain for a quick hot meal, or toss into a wok to stir-fry quickly when you get home exhausted and might otherwise be tempted to call a glass of white wine your dinner.

Be a student. Have some time during the week when you turn off the giver or teacher-self, and focus on your own emotional/physical/spiritual/mental needs. In order to maintain health and wellness as a dancer, you need cardio, strengthening, stretching, and technique, so find a way to be a student for at least one of those: If you teach technique and cardio, take a yoga class; if you teach technique and yoga, take a cardio or weight training class. Especially when you spend a lot of your day teaching, being in charge of and generally giving unto others, there is something absolutely delicious about turning off the "teach and judge" part of your brain to take someone else's class, allow yourself to be a student and just *receive*.

Do less to do more. The less you dance in class, the more you observe. The less you demonstrate, the better your students become at visualizing the movement. The less you talk, the more they hear. Give students the opportunity to demonstrate in class, and boost their confidence and performance skills.

Clean and Green
If, like many dance teachers, you spend most of your day in a dance studio, it helps to have the healthiest environment possible. In addition to reducing the dust around your electrical equipment, plants can help clean the air, reduce dryness, absorb noise, reduce stress, and give life to your indoor environment.

Plants Clean the Air
Indoor plants can remove up 80 percent of air toxins, such those in paints, varnishes, car exhaust fumes and tobacco smoke in 24 hours. It is recommended to have 1 potted plant per 100 square feet, so a studio which is about 30' x 30' should have about 8 plants in 6-to-10 inch containers. Hanging plants keeps them out of the way and away from children.

In addition to cleaning the air, plants help people feel calmer and more optimistic. Studies have shown that hospital patients who face a window with a garden view recovered more quickly than those who had to look at a wall. Other

> **Best Indoor Plants for Cleaning the Air**
>
> - Dragon tree or dracaena*
> - Ivy or hedera helix
> - Ficus
> - Philodendrons*
> - Spider plants
> - Peace lilies
> - Ferns
> - Chrysanthemums
> - Palms
>
> *May be harmful if ingested, so keep up and out of reach of children and pets.

studies show that indoor plants can reduce fatigue, coughs sore throats and other cold-related illnesses by more than 30 percent, partially by increasing humidity levels and decreasing dust. If you don't have expansive windows with glorious views of a wooded forest, create that sense of verdant calm with plants.

> *Dust was wreaking havoc with the sound system in the dance studio. The electrical fields around equipment, and the static electricity which is more prevalent in dry air, can attract dust. Increasing humidity reduces static electricity, but when I looked into purchasing a humidifier of the size needed for the dance studio, the expense was prohibitive. I've always been a plant person, so my second thought was to start propogating some of my green friends. Philodendron, pothos, and spider plants propagate readily from cuttings, so I soon had plenty of "free" plants, all from my own house plants. Problem solved!*

<u>Plants Help Control Humidity Indoors</u>. Humidity helps prevent the air from becoming too dry. Dry air and the electrical activity around your sound system can attract dust which can create problems with sound equipment. Humidity tends to drop during winter. In addition to supplying moisture to the air, plants may warn you when humidity becomes low by displaying brown tips on their leaves.

<u>Plants Help to Reduce Noise</u>. This can be important near a highway or a busy area. Random noise can raise stress levels. Placing some plants near windows can help absorb noise and keep it from penetrating your educational and creative environment.

<u>Plants Improve Quality of Life</u>. Numerous studies have found that spending time in the company of plants can provide measurable stress relief. In addition to plants in the dance studio, consider adding a plant to your office desk, the bathroom, and reception area of your studio.

<u>And Sometimes They're Edible</u>
Oregano and thyme make lovely hanging plants (but need a sunny location by a window), and you can snip some into the salad that you bring from home for lunch or dinner. Push unpeeled cloves of garlic halfway into dirt and watch them grow; snip shoots into soups, salads and stir-fry. Chives grow prolifically. Lemongrass can be grown just in a container of water. Rosemary can make a miniature bush.

<u>Care of Plants</u>
Plants generally need nothing more than air and water. While they are usually grown in dirt, some plants thrive just in water. Most plants enjoy the sunshine near a window, but philodendrons and pothos are generally fine in low-light corners. You can also rotate plants every couple of months from low-light areas to brighter spots near windows.

Plants in containers with self-watering reservoirs or systems can reduce the time it takes to care for them. Putting a pot with a drainage hole in the bottom into a low bowl enables you to add water to the bowl (the soil will absorb it, and when the plant stops drinking, it's full) rather than pouring it over the top of the soil. Hanging planters with self-watering reservoirs keep water off the floor.

I find that plants are a reflection of my own stress; if I'm too busy to care for my plants, I'm just too darned busy! Taking a few minutes to water, pinch off dead leaves, and sing to the plants helps reduce stress. Or, give the job for plant care to a scholarship student, work-study, or parent in exchange for tuition.

> **_To Do:_**
> _Create a brief guided de-stressing sequence. It could be for meditation while seated or lying or even walking and stretching. Include imagery and cues for breathing and body awareness._

Ahead

The work of many dancers and educators supports the concepts on which the Spectrum is based. The Spectrum is an educational tool that can not only improve your teaching, but can help you understand yourself, your students, and the art of dance. Let's look back over the concepts presented and discussed to reflect on the what, why, and how of teaching.

Questions for Reflection and Discussion

1. Identify 2-3 self-care messages that speak to you—what would you like to do more, or less, to feel better, healthier, more organized?
2. Identify one tip or bit of advice you would like to share with others concerning nutrition, body care, or mindfulness.
3. Think of an environment in your life that you would like to make more productive and/or calming. Identify 3 areas, factors, or qualities that you can change, and create a plan to make those changes.

11 Summary

When the student is
ready the teacher appears.
When the student is
truly ready the teacher
disappears.
~Lao Tzu

The individual Styles and clusters of Styles can be applied to the many subjects in the dance curriculum. Styles A-E are designed for the acquisition of fixed or codified information, such as in classes in dance technique, international or ethnic dance, aerobics, ballroom, and dance notation, and provide a bridge to the discovery cluster by gradually shifting specific decisions from the teacher to the learner. Styles F-G are options that foster discovery of single correct concepts, principles and guiding rules, and can be used in children's dance classes, technique, ethnic dance, ballroom dance, and notation as well as other courses such as dance kinesiology and dance history; in any course to deliver concepts and principles. Styles H-K are options that invite discovery of multiple alternatives, new ideas, providing an environment for expressing creativity. These Styles can be implemented in the previously mentioned courses plus creative movement, choreography, composition, and improvisation. Styles F-K engage the student in reasoning, inventing, and problem-solving activities that invite the learner to go beyond given information. Style K is in a class by itself, or rather, outside of the physical class.

All subjects can employ the entire range of the Spectrum, depending on what you want students to accomplish: acquire information and principles, discover single correct concepts, or discover and invent new concepts. You can develop mobility along the Spectrum by applying teaching strategies appropriate to the task at hand.

Your students can develop mobility along the Spectrum and take class more productively. For example, when taking technique class, I may engage in Divergent Discovery to explore different Efforts in the combination given by the instructor.

Reasons to Apply the Spectrum

The reasons for implementing the Spectrum are numerous. Let's revisit and elaborate on the reasons to apply the Spectrum that were presented in the second chapter.

First, objectives in the dance curriculum (which may be determined by you, by the owner of a private studio, by a school board, or by standards set on a state or national level) may include skill acquisition, aesthetic sensitivity, artistic process, and cognitive reasoning. The National Assessment of Educational Progress (NAEP) has set standards for assessment of students' dance achievement. The Arts Education Consensus Project has sought to establish objectives for assessing arts instruction in the nation's elementary and secondary schools. The guidelines for dance assessment include concepts such as affirming dance as a way of knowing which integrate intellectual, emotional, and physical skills; addressing processes and products; addressing the social domain, and utilizing a comprehensive vision of dance education from the viewpoint of what dance education *should be* rather than simply recognizing current dance education.

Second, the task sheets, criteria and checklists used in Styles B-F provide concrete examples of the academic rigor of dance as a field of study equal to the other arts and sciences. The virtual, temporal nature of dance sometimes creates problems for dance faculty who must

> *Five reasons for using the Spectrum:*
> 1. *Multiple objectives of education*
> 2. *Tangible examples of rigors of dance as an academic field*
> 3. *Assessment of student progress*
> 4. *Diversity of student population;*
> 5. *The need for an integrated framework for teaching;*
> 6. *Active learners make for future artists.*

provide documentation of teaching excellence. Examples of checklists utilized in classes can be useful for dance faculty in applications and interviews for new jobs, dossiers for retention, tenure and promotion.

Third, the checklists used in Styles B (Practice), C (Reciprocal) and D (Self-Check) can be used for assessing students, providing "hard copy" or written documentation of a student's progress in class. Checklists can also be used to explain to students exactly what is expected of them during class, as documentation of progress, as motivation for excellence. Checklists can thus be a tool to let students know what is important, what is being graded, what is being assessed; to help students visualize and understand the parts and sequences in performing a movement or phrase and thus give students specific directives for learning.

All of the above needs, objectives, standards and guidelines are addressed very well by the Spectrum. The Spectrum provides an integrated, comprehensive framework that can benefit educators in any subject including theory or lecture classes as well as technique or activity classes; children's creative movement, advanced technique in a college dance major's program, or recreational social dance. This framework can be utilized in all dance classes including ballet, modern, jazz, tap, ballroom, international folk or character dance, aerobics, improvisation, composition, notation, and history classes. You can use the Spectrum to address artistic, physical, cognitive, social, emotional concerns of dance depending on your background and focus. Once you develop facility with the Spectrum, new applications evolve rapidly and easily. Once students develop familiarity with the Spectrum and making decisions, little explanation is needed beyond stating the Style to be used; then students know what is expected of them and how to proceed.

> *Michael Goldberger wrote that the Spectrum is best described by the word* elegant. *"It is a simple concept, yet it becomes infinitely more complex as one studies it more closely. I have been studying the Spectrum for years and am still only a beginning student in fully comprehending its myriad of intricacies and insights"* *(Simri pp. 153-154).*

Accommodating cultural diversity, individual modality preferences, and the special needs of students with documented learning disabilities of all kinds are not merely the current academic buzzwords, they are always essential. Students come from diverse cultural backgrounds, have diverse needs and goals, and learn in different ways. Individual differences have a great impact on how students are best able to learn in an educational setting, and the Spectrum can be a valuable tool for you to use in addressing the many challenges of teaching dance.

Students also have many different emotional, cognitive and physical needs that affect learning. The impact of the dance class on students is more profound than just the student learning steps or movements. Years after taking a particular class, students may remember the experience and associate it with feelings of joy, empowerment, or dread. Applying the various Styles, especially Style E (Inclusion), can provide you with a variety of approaches to teaching, whether your students are primarily visual, auditory, or kinesthetic, whether they learn best with a peer, from a teacher, or individually. Thus, sensitivity to learner needs may drive your pursuit of facility with the Spectrum.

> *After completing an elementary modern dance class for non-dance majors at the university, a junior-year student told me that this was the only course she had taken in which she interacted with and was encouraged to learn the names of other students. For a lonely or overwhelmed freshman college student, for a teenager struggling with developing a sense of self, for a young child in a new town, for an older adult who wants to learn more about themselves or meet people, the social or affective domain can be the most important aspect of a dance class.*

Finally, it is the hope of every teacher that students become active learners who take the initiative to analyze, question, develop alternatives, and learn how to learn on their own. We would all like our students to become self-directed learners. Educational research has demonstrated the importance of developing self-directed learners but also that this goal has not yet been translated into curricular content. Knowles (1975) defined self-directed learning as learner-controlled instruction, a process in which individuals take the initiative in identifying learning needs, formulating goals, identifying human and material resources, and evaluating learning outcomes.

There are many degrees of self-directed learning. Style B: Practice is the beginning of self-directed behavior—learners who are not used to making decisions have their first experience in making the nine decisions. Each subsequent Style shifts more opportunities to learners for them to become more independent. The truly independent person is the one who can demonstrate mobility ability among the various Styles, and the truly gifted dancer can not only replicate movement accurately but can also produce subtle nuances by choosing variations appropriate to the task, and discover new ideas. However, Kreber (1998) indicated that while self-directed learning has been proposed as a goal for higher education by administrators and faculty, higher education teaching has not yet translated this into changes in the process of teaching. It appears that teachers assume that somehow, over the course of their studies, students are responsible for picking up the necessary skills for lifelong learning, but may never thoughtfully direct students in this pursuit. That's why it is essential that teachers (and students) become familiar with the objectives of each Style, because these objectives are also necessary lifelong human skills.

It is important to understand that self-directed learning is not only a *goal* but a *process* as well. P. C. Candy (1991) distinguished two aspects of self-directed learning: personal autonomy, a personal attribute as a desired goal of education, and autodidaxy, the independent pursuit of learning outside formal institutional settings. The self-management of learning tasks is not an end in itself but a means toward self-directed learning or autodidaxy. According to Kreber, educators can foster competence in autodidaxy by providing opportunities for students to develop both intuition and logical reasoning. Thus we see that it is beneficial for students to learn the skills necessary for the *process* and *goal* of self-directed learning. Self-assessment is an essential step if your students are to continue learning once they leave a formal school setting, and the Spectrum provides a powerful teaching and learning tool for students to learn self-assessment.

Teaching as Profession, as Personal Expression, as Learning, as Artistry

"Open your arms to change, but don't let go of your values."
H. Jackson Brown, Jr.

When you start teaching, even though you may have extensive content knowledge, you still have a relatively limited amount of pedagogical knowledge. Through knowledge acquisition, you develop an overall philosophy based on this collected knowledge base. Just as the style of a performer or choreographer will evolve over time, so will your style of teaching. You will approach teaching as a profession and regard teaching Styles differently at various stages of your development as a teacher and as an artist. Ronnie Lidor writes, "Probably, when you are young and uncertain, you prefer to use the conservative approach to teaching. However, when you gain some knowledge and experience, you prefer to shift your attention to more 'freedom oriented' teaching style. The Spectrum provided a clear direction to be followed. It gave me the first theoretical as well as practical guidance to establish my own philosophy of teaching" (Simri, p. 125).

Dance is first and foremost a performing art. You are an artist and a teacher, and these two are intimately intertwined in the dance studio when you face a class. Teaching is fed and shaped by your artistic sensibilities and aesthetic sense. Like the quote by H. Jackson Brown, Jr., "Open your arms to change, but don't let go of your values," incorporating the Spectrum doesn't mean that you let go of the artistic values which you hold; rather, it gives you more possibilities for implementing these values in the studio classroom. And, Anna Pavlova's quote, "Master technique and then forget about it and be natural" can refer to teaching as well as to performing: master the Spectrum, then let it become part of you and let your teaching become as natural as possible.

"Rather than view a class as a group to be taught en masse, [Muska] treated learning as the personal experience it is. He artfully used the Spectrum to empower each student to think, create and gain efficacy" (Mueller in Simri, p. 138).

Most dance teachers will work with students whose talents lie in a number of the intelligences. Knowing who has what sort of intelligence is not important: You don't need to know or remember that Tiffany is primarily linguistic, Adam is spatial and Kelsey is mathematical. What *is* important is to recognize that students will have different preferences and will deal with information in individual ways. Being able to present information using a variety of approaches will invite more students to participate, to reap the benefits of the dance experience, and to develop in the learning process.

According to Janice Ross (200b), the arts have the capacity to be "portals to the processes of cognition" (p. 32). The Spectrum can be your guide and inspiration in this journey.

Questions for Reflection and Discussion

1. Identify and discuss ways in which you can begin **applying** the Spectrum, as a learner and as a teacher.

2. Discuss learning, whether alone or in a class, as a **personal** experience.

3. Identify and discuss how the Spectrum can **empower** teachers and learners.

Resources

A full list of resources for teaching all types of dance would be an impossible task. However, the following are resources that I have found valuable for use with the Spectrum (some available online, some have updated editions).

Bartenieff, Irmgard. 1965. *Effort-Shape Analysis of Movement: The Unity of Expression and Function,* Albert Einstein College of Medicine, Yeshiva University.

Blom, Lynn, and Chaplin, L. Tarin. 1982. *The Intimate Act of Choreography.* Pittsburgh: University of Pittsburgh Press.

Blom, Lynn, and Chaplin, L. Tarin. 1988. *The Moment of Movement: Dance Improvisation.* Pittsburgh: University of Pittsburgh Press.

Dell, Cecily. 1970. *Primer for Movement Description Using Effort/Shape.* Dance Notation Bureau, Center for Movement Research and Analysis.

Dell, Cecily and Crow, Aileen. 1977. *Space Harmony: Basic Terms.* Dance Notation Bureau.

Dowd, Irene. 1995. *Taking Root to Fly: Articles on Functional Anatomy.* Published by the author.

Fitt, Sally. 1996. *Dance Kinesiology (2nd Ed.).* New York: Schirmer Books.

Gilbert, Anne Green. 2015. *Creative Dance For All Ages (2nd Ed.)* Champaign, IL: Human Kinetics.

Guest, Ann Hutchinson and Curran, Tina. 2007. *Your Move (2nd Ed.)* New York: Routledge.

Joyce, Mary 1994. *First Steps in Teaching Creative Dance to Children.* Mountain View, CA: Mayfield Publishing

Joyce, Mary 1983. *Creative Dance Technique.* Mountain View, CA: Mayfield Publishing.

Laban, Rudolf. 1974. *Effort: Economy in Body Movement.* Plays, Inc.

Laban, Rudolf. 1974. *The Language of Movement: A Guidebook to Choreutics.* Plays, Inc.

Laban, Rudolf. 1980. *The Mastery of Movement.* McDonald and Evans.

Laban, Rudolf. 1986. *Modern Educational Dance*. Princeton: Princeton Book Company Publishers.

Lange, Roderyk. 1960. *Philosophic Foundations and Laban's Theory of Movement*. Laban Art of Movement Centre.

Laws, Kenneth, and Swope, Martha. 2005. *Physics and the Art of Dance: Understanding Movement*. Oxford University Press.

Maletic, Vera. 1987. *Body, Space, Expression: The Development of Rudolf Laban's Movement and Dance Concepts*. Amsterdam: Mouton De Gruyter.

Minton, Sandra. 2007. *Choreography: A Basic Approach Using Improvisation (4th Ed.)*. Champaign, IL: Human Kinetics.

Pittman, Anne; and Waller, Marlys. 2015. *Dance a While: Handbook for Folk, Square, Contra and Social Dance (10th Ed.)*. Long Grove, IL: Waveland Press.

Preston-Dunlop, Valerie. 1967. *Readers in Kinetography Laban, Series B: Motif Writing for Dance*. Macdonald & Evans.

Preston-Dunlop, Valerie. 1984. *Point of Departure: The Dancer's Space*. Published by the author.

Stinson, Sue. 1997. *Dance for Young Children: Finding the Magic in Movement*. Reston, VA: National Dance Association.

Sweigard, Lulu. 1974. *Human Movement Potential: Its Ideokinetic Facilitation*. New York: Harper & Row, Publishers, Inc.

<u>Major publications by Muska Mosston</u>

(1965). *Developmental Movement*. Columbus OH: Merrill.

(1972). *Teaching: From Command to Discovery*. Belmont, CA: Wadsworth.

(1990). *The Spectrum of Teaching Styles: From Command to Discovery*. Co-authored with Sara Ashworth. New York: Longman.

(1994). *Teaching Physical Education*. Co-authored with Sara Ashworth. New York: Macmillan College Publishing Company.

CLASSROOM CHARTS (SA)[31]

The following are suggestions for classroom charts. You may wish to enlarge the font as desired, and make them into classroom posters.

STYLE A:
CUED RESPONSE

The purpose of this Style is to perform the task(s) accurately and within a short period of time, following the decisions of the teacher.

ROLE OF THE LEARNER

- To perform the task when and as described, following the pace and rhythm.

ROLE OF THE TEACHER

- To make subject matter decisions,
- To make decisions about how to perform the task,
- To make logistical decisions,
- To provide feedback.

STYLE B: PRACTICE

The purposes of this Style are to offer the learner time to work individually and privately, and to provide the teacher with time to offer the learner individual and private feedback.

ROLE OF THE LEARNER
- To perform the task
- To make the following nine decisions:
    - Order of the task(s),
    - Starting time,
    - Pace and rhythm,
    - Starting time,
    - Stopping time,
    - Interval,
    - Location,
    - Posture,
    - Attire and appearance.

ROLE OF THE TEACHER
- To be available to answer learner's questions,
- To gather information about the learner's performance and offer individual and private feedback.

Style C: Reciprocal

The purposes of this Style are to work with a partner in a reciprocal relationship, and to offer feedback to the partner based on criteria prepared by the teacher.

ROLE OF THE LEARNER
- To select the roles of Doer and Observer:
  - As D*oer*, to perform task (as in Style B),
  - As *Observer*, to compare the Doer's work with the criteria, draw conclusions and offer feedback to the Doer,
- At the completion of the task, to switch roles.

ROLE OF THE TEACHER
- To monitor the Observers,
- To give feedback to the Observers,
- To answer the Observers' questions.

Style D: Self-Check

The purpose of this Style is for students to perform the task and to check their own work.

ROLE OF THE LEARNER
- To perform the task,
- To check own work,
- To make the nine decisions of the Practice Style.

ROLE OF THE TEACHER
- To prepare the subject matter and criteria,
- To answer questions by the learner,
- To initiate communication with the learner.

STYLE E: INCLUSION

The purposes of this Style are to participate in a task and learn to select a level of difficulty at which you can perform the task and to check your own work.

ROLE OF THE LEARNER
- To make the nine decisions of Practice Style,
- To examine the different levels of the task,
- To select the personally appropriate level,
- To perform the task,
- To check own work against criteria prepared by the teacher,
- To ask the teacher questions for clarification.

ROLE OF THE TEACHER
- To prepare the task and levels within the task,
- To prepare the criteria for the task levels,
- To answer the learners' questions,
- To initiate communication with the learner.

Style F:
Guided Discovery

The purpose of this Style is to discover a predetermined concept by answering a sequence of logically designed questions.

ROLE OF THE LEARNER
- To listen to the questions, or clues,
- To discover the answer for each question in the sequence,
- To discover the final answer which constitutes the targeted concept.

ROLE OF THE TEACHER
- To design the sequence of questions, each resulting in a small discovery by the learner,
- To provide periodic feedback to the learner,
- To acknowledge the discovery of the concept by the learner.

Style G: Convergent Discovery

The purpose of this Style is to discover the solution to a problem by employing logic and reasoning skills and by constructing and linking questions, which lead to the anticipated response.

ROLE OF THE LEARNER
- To examine the problem or issue,
- To evolve a procedure toward a solution or conclusion,
- To develop a sequence that will lead to the solution or conclusion,
- To verify the process and the solution by checking them against appropriate content criteria.

ROLE OF THE TEACHER
- To present the problem or issue,
- To follow the learner's process of thinking,
- To offer feedback or clues (if necessary), without providing the solution.

Style H: Divergent Discovery

The purpose of this Style is to engage in producing (discovering) multiple (divergent) responses in a specific cognitive operation.

ROLE OF THE LEARNER
- To make the nine Impact decisions of Style B,
- To discover divergent responses (multiple responses to the same questions),
- To ascertain the validity of the responses,
- To verify responses in particular subject matter tasks.

ROLE OF THE TEACHER
- To make the decision about the question to be asked,
- To accept the responses,
- To serve as source of verification in particular subject matter tasks.

Style I: Learner-Designed Individual Program

The purpose of this Style is for the learner to design, develop and present a series of tasks that are organized into a personal program.

ROLE OF THE LEARNER
- To select the topic that will be the focus of the study,
- To identify questions and issues appropriate for the topic,
- To organize the questions, to organize the task, and design a personal program—a course of action,
- To collect data about the topic, to answer the questions and organize the answers into a reasonable framework,
- To verify the procedures and solutions based on criteria intrinsic to the subject matter at hand.

ROLE OF THE TEACHER
- To select the general subject matter area from which the learners will select their topics,
- To observe the learner's progress,
- To listen to the learner's periodic presentation of questions and answers.

Style J:
Learner-Initiated

The purpose of this Style is to provide the learner with the opportunity to initiate his/her learning experience.

ROLE OF THE LEARNER
- To initiate the Style,
- To design the program,
- To perform it,
- To evaluate it,
- To decide when and/or how to consult with the teacher.

ROLE OF THE TEACHER
- To accept the learner's decision to initiate his/her own learning experience,
- To provide the general conditions required for the learner's plans,
- To accept the learner's procedures and products,
- To alert the learner to any discrepancies between intent and action.

Style K: Self-Teaching

Style K does not have a chart since it is not a classroom experience.

Bibliography

Brand, Paul and Yancey, Philip. 1987. *Fearfully and Wonderfully Made*. Grand Rapids, Michigan: Zondervan Publishing House.

Brown, H. Jackson, Jr. 1997. *The Complete Life's Little Instruction Book*. Nashville, Tennessee: Rutledge Hill Press.

Candy, Philip. C. 1991. *Self-Direction for Lifelong Learning*. San Francisco, CA: Jossey-Bass.

Carrol, Lewis. (nd). *Alice's Adventures in Wonderland*. Chicago: The Goldsmith Publishing Co.

Carter, Curtis. 1983. "Arts and cognition: Performance, criticism, and aesthetics." *Art Education*. 36(2), 61-67

Clark, Dawn. 2003. "Developing observation strategies to enhance teaching effectiveness in the dance class." *Journal of Physical Education, Recreation and Dance*. Vol. 74, No. 9, pp. 33-36, 47.

Cohen, Selma Jean. 1972. *Doris Humphrey: An Artist First*. Middletown: Wesleyan University Press.

Cohen, Selma Jean. 1982. *Next week, Swan Lake. Reflections on Dance and Dances*. Connecticut: Wesleyan University Press.

Cohen, Selma Jean. 1983. "Problems of definition. In Copeland, R. & Cohen, M. (Eds.), *What is Dance* (pp. 339-354). New York: Oxford University Press.

Cook, Ray. 1977. *The Dance Director*. (published by the author).

Copeland, Misty. 2014. *Life in Motion: An Unlikely Ballerina*. New York: Simon & Schuster.

Croce, Arlene. 1968. Untitled contribution in Merce Cunningham et al., "Time to walk in space," *Dance Perspectives*. 34, pp. 24-38.

Croce, Arlene. 1980. "Suzanne Farrell." In Steinberg, C. (Ed.), *The Dance Anthology* (pp. 112-119). New York: The New American Library.

Csikszentmihalyi, Mihaly. 1996. *Flow*. New York: HarperCollins, Publishers.

Thirteen WNET in association with RM Arts and BBC-TV. 1992. *Dancing*. Videotape, *The Power of Dance: Program 1*.

Daniel, David. 1979. "A Conversation with Suzanne Farrell". *Ballet Review*, 7, pp. 1-15.

DeBono, Edward. 1970. *Lateral Thinking: Creativity Step By Step*. New York: Harper & Row.

Dewey, John. 1934. *Art as Experience*. New York: Capricorn Books, G. P. Putnam's Sons.

Ecker, David. 1963. "The artistic process as qualitative problem solving." *The Journal of Aesthetics and Art Criticism*, 21, 283-290.

Elia, Susan. 2000. "Simonson says." *Dance Teacher*, Vol. 22 No. 10, 51-54.

Fitt, Sally. 1988. *Dance Kinesiology*. New York: Schirmer Books.

Foster, Susan Leigh. 1986. *Reading Dancing: Bodies and Subjects in Contemporary American Dance*. Berkeley: University of California Press.

Fraleigh, Sondra. 1987. *Dance and the Lived Body*. Pittsburg: University of Pittsburg Press.

Gardner, Howard. 1971. "Problem solving in the arts." *Journal of Aesthetic Education,* 5, 93-114.

Gardner, Howard. 1993. *Multiple Intelligences*. New York: Basic Books, Inc.

Getzels, Jacob., & Csikszentmihalyi, Mihaly. 1976. *The Creative Vision: A Longitudinal Study of Problem Finding in Art*. New York: John Wiley and Sons.

Gibbons, Elizabeth Goodling. 1989. *A Prismatic Approach to the Analysis of Style in Dance* (Texas Woman's University doctoral dissertation, available through University Microforms).

Gilbert, Anne Green. 1992. *Creative Dance for All Ages*. Reston, VA: American Alliance for Health Physical Education Recreation and Dance.

Giordano, Gus. 1975. *Anthology of American Jazz Dance*. Evanston, Illinois: Orion Publishing House.

Grant, Gail. 1982. *Technical Manual and Dictionary of Classical Ballet*. Dover Publications.

Guest, Ann Hutchinson and Curran, Tina. 2007. *Your Move (2nd Ed.)* New York: Routledge.

Hodgson, Moira. 1976. *Quintet: Five American Dance Companies*. New York: William Morrow and Company, Inc.

Humphrey, Doris. 1959. *The Art of Making Dances*. New York: Grove Press.

Joyce, Mary. 1994. *First Steps in Teaching Creative Dance to Children*. Mountain View, CA: Mayfield Publishing Company.

Kerollis, Barry. 2017. http://www.dance-teacher.com/from-the-male-teachers-perspective-should-i-teach-hands-on-2517738954.html

Knowles, Malcolm. 1975. *Self-Directed Learning: A Guide For Learners and Educators*. New York: Cambridge Books.

Kreber, Caroline. 1998. *Studies in Higher Education*. March 98, vol. 23 Issue 1, p. 71.

Laws, Kenneth, and Swope, Martha. 2005. *Physics and the Art of Dance: Understanding Movement*. Oxford University Press.

Lewis, Daniel. 1984. *The Illustrated Dance Technique of José Limón*. New York: Harper & Row Publishers, Inc.

Louis, Murray. 1981. *Inside Dance*. New York: St. Martins Press.

Mosston, Muska. and Ashworth, Sara. 1994. *Teaching Physical Education*. New York: Macmillan College Publishing Company.

Mosston, Muska. and Ashworth, Sara. 1990. *The Spectrum of Teaching Styles: From Command to Discovery*. New York: Longman.

Mosston, Muska. 1965. *Developmental Movement*. Columbus OH: Merrill.

Mosston, Muska. 1972. *Teaching: From Command to Discovery*. Belmont, CA: Wadsworth.

Nordin-Bates, Sanna. 2015. IADMS Education Committee. *http://www.iadms.org/ blogpost/1177934/233854/Using-imagery-to-optimise-dance-training-and-performance*

Pittman, Anne; and Waller, Marlys. 2015. *Dance a While: Handbook for Folk, Square, Contra and Social Dance (10th Ed.)*. Long Grove, IL: Waveland Press.

Preston-Dunlop, Valerie. 1981. *The Nature of the Embodiment of Choreographic Units in Contemporary Choreography*. Unpublished doctoral dissertation, University of London, Goldsmith's College, Great Britain.

Purcell, Theresa. 1994. *Teaching Children Dance: Becoming a Master Teacher*. Champaign, Illinois: Human Kinetics.

Ross, Janice. 2000(a). *Dance Magazine* Vol. 74, issue 1, p. 50.

Ross, Janice. 2000(b). "Arts Education in the Information Age: A New Place for Somatic Wisdom." *Arts Education Policy Review*, July/Aug.2000, Vol. 101 Issue 6, p27, 6p.

Sheets-Johnstone, Maxine. 1981. "Thinking in Movement." *The Journal of Aesthetics and Art Criticism*, 39, 399-407

Siegel, Marcia. 1977. *Watching the Dance Go By*. Boston: Houghton Mifflin Company.

Simri, Uriel. (n.d.). *Muska: A Biography of Dr. Muska Mosston*. Tel-Aviv: Maor.

Sirridge, Mary & Armelagos, Adina. 1977. "The In's and Out's of Dance: Expression As an Aspect of Style. *The Journal of Aesthetics and Art Criticism*, vol. 36, issue 1, pp. 15-24.

Sparshott, Francis. 1995. *A Measured Pace: Toward a Philosophical Understanding of Dance*. University of Toronto Press.

Stinson, Sue. 1997. *Dance for Young Children: Finding the Magic In Movement*. Reston, VA: The American Alliance for Health, Physical Education, Recreation and Dance.

Stinson, Sue. https://libres.uncg.edu/ir/uncg/f/S_Stinson_Piaget_1985.pdf.

Index

Outevsky, David, 105

P

parameter feedback, 97, 102, 118
Parkinson's, 54
Pauling, Linus, 230, 239
Pavlova, Anna, 254
pedagogical agility, 9, 31, 32, 38, 39
pedagogical unit, 55, 65, 66, 92, 93
Pilates, 48, 241, 242
Pilobolus, 42, 137
Preston-Dunlop, Valerie, 202, 256, 270
problem solving, 20, 26, 79, 103, 192, 212, 217, 220, 226, 251, 268, 269
program feedback, 97, 102, 115
proprioception, 42, 54, 55, 96, 105

R

reinforcement, 21, 98, 100, 101, 116, 181, 183, 230
relaxation, 86, 243, 244
Rite of Spring (Sacre de Printemps), 230
Rodin, Auguste, 230, 239
roles, 11, 13, 14, 15, 16, 17, 19, 55, 65, 66, 72, 73, 78, 79, 86, 93, 113, 129, 141, 142, 143, 144, 146, 147, 151, 154, 157, 163, 212, 213, 214, 247, 259
Ross, Janice, 31, 34, 254, 270, 273

S

schema, 150, 209, 210, 223, 224, 226, 228, 229, 230, 237, 238
Schmidt, Richard, 98, 99
Sheets-Johnstone, Maxine, 227, 270
Shulman, Lee S., 29
Siegel, Marcia, 232, 233, 270
Silver, Dorothy, 233
Simri,Uriel, 183, 252, 254, 270
slanted rope, 18, 19, 155, 156, 157
Smelcer, Haley Mathiot, 245
social, socialization, x, 2, 7, 14, 15, 34, 41, 44, 47, 49, 52, 54, 71, 74, 78, 79, 84, 104, 108, 113, 117, 122, 125, 136, 138, 139, 142, 145, 146, 147, 148, 155, 161, 229, 235, 252, 253, 256, 270
Steiner, Pete, 31
strategies, 3, 8, 25, 29, 31, 32, 55, 65, 81, 93, 108, 109, 126, 143, 144, 186, 196, 212, 222, 223, 228, 229, 230, 231, 237, 238, 239, 251, 268

T

tap, 5, 7, 10, 12, 19, 23, 30, 38, 41, 44, 46, 48, 49, 52, 56, 58, 67, 71, 83, 96, 97, 106, 122, 127, 130, 131, 198, 201, 228, 236, 252
Taylor, Paul, 218, 224, 239
Teacher-Observer-Doer Triad, 15, 16, 113
telesis, 36, 39, 77, 90, 93
terminal feedback, 97, 118
Tharp, Twyla, 229
torque, 81, 96, 116, 179, 193, 194, 236
training and temperament, 223, 224, 228, 230, 231, 232, 233, 237, 239
transfer 47, 48, 49, 55, 58, 130, 157, 203, 229
transposition, 126
Triano, Maria, 64

V

verbal, 11, 23, 41, 42, 43, 55, 71, 72, 73, 74, 75, 76, 84, 97, 99, 100, 101, 102, 104, 109, 114, 115, 125, 129, 130, 136, 145, 146, 151, 152, 154, 180, 181, 183, 186, 191, 226, 227
visual, 11, 13, 31, 33, 45, 46, 76, 84, 97, 100, 103, 109, 111, 118, 119, 125, 130, 131, 133, 144, 221, 224, 244, 247, 252, 253
vocabulary, 3, 20, 29, 30, 33, 38, 39, 41, 42, 44, 45, 47, 48, 49, 54, 55, 58, 80, 86, 110, 121, 125, 128, 226, 228, 230, 232, 236

W

warm-up, 3, 47, 48, 49, 50, 54, 55, 64, 76, 78, 79, 80, 81, 83, 86, 88, 89, 107, 112, 122, 183, 236, 241, 244, 245
Williams, Shari Dowburd, 243
Wind, Cathy, 242
Winter, Ethel, 233

Y

yoga, 34, 44, 48, 51, 71, 86, 105, 241, 242, 243, 244, 247

Z

Zen garden, 8, 178
Zygorski, Noelle Martin, 23

End Notes

1 MM/SA

2 Briefly, these seven intelligences are: Linguistic, logical-mathematical, spatial, musical, bodily-kinesthetic, interpersonal, and intrapersonal.

3 Two juvenile jails in California, San Jose's Juvenile Hall and San Mateo's Hillcrest Juvenile Hall, offer weekly dance classes to male and female teen inmates taught by Israeli jazz dancer Ehud Krauss. Interviews with several students in these classes reveal that the first benefit that many students list, what affects them most profoundly, is the supportive and patient attention of a caring adult (Ross, Janice, Arts Education in the Information Age: A New Place for Somatic Wisdom, *Arts Education Policy Review*, Jul/Aug2000, Vol. 101 Issue 6, p27, 6p.

4 The Spectrum was published in *Teaching Physical Education* by Mosston and Ashworth. The phrase "Spectrum of Teaching Styles" was coined in the mid 1960s. The term, "Teaching Style" was selected to refer to specific teaching behaviors and to distinguish it from terms such as method, approach, model, and strategy that are used in many different ways by different teachers, researchers and writers. The term "style" is often used to refer to a personal, idiosyncratic style. However, in this book, as in other publications by Mosston and Ashworth, the term "teaching style" refers to a structure that is independent of one teacher's idiosyncrasies. Style, with a capital S, will be used in this text to denote one of the eleven landmark Styles of the Spectrum.

5 MM/SA

6 Gail Grant's *Technical Manual and Dictionary of Classical Ballet* is one of many excellent resources, as is the Video *Dictionary of Ballet*.

7 Ann Hutchinson Guest's *Your Move* is also an excellent resource for detailing and clarifying dance terminology.

8 *Dance A While* (various editions) is a very comprehensive yet accessible resource for folk and social dance steps, positions, formations, concepts, and history.

9 Sally Fitt's *Dance Kinesiology* is an excellent resource for more information on dance kinesiology.

10 Arabesques in each of the ballet "schools" are termed differently; see Grant's *Technical Manual and Dictionary of Classical Ballet* for more detail.

11 MM/SA

12 My diagrams here are developed from the "O-T-L-O relationships" and diagrams of MM/SA.

13 Sara Ashworth clarifies this further, "Accuracy, self-assessment, and artistic expression are human attributes that can be accomplished in any dance class. The Styles are also a way of developing *people as people*, in addition to being a way to approach subject matter" (personal correspondence, 2006).

14 Developed from MM/SA.

15 MM/SA

16 *Alice's Adventures in Wonderland*, Lewis Carrol. Chicago: The Goldsmith Publishing Co. (nd)

17 See Joyce, *First Steps in Teaching Creative Dance for Children*.

18 Developed from MM/SA

19 Gardner (1993) suggests that there is no single, across-the-board process or ability called critical thinking. "The kind of thinking required to analyze a fugue is simply different from that involved in observing and categorizing different animal species, or scrutinizing a poem, or debugging a program, or choreographing and analyzing a new dance. There is little reason to think that training of critical thinking in one of these domains provides significant 'savings' when one enters another domain. Rather, one needs to develop the forms of critical thinking that are relevant to that particular domain: on closer analysis each domain exhibits its own particular *logic of implications*" (p. 43). Thus dance students must learn the form of critical thinking that is relevant to *dance*.

20 Edward DeBono, *Lateral Thinking*.

21 MM/SA

22 Sara Ashworth, unpublished manuscript, 2007

23 MM/SA.

24 Mosston & Ashworth 4th edition p. 195.

25 Theoretically this question and its answer apply to any and all rotations or turns, but it is a good idea to put limiters or parameters on your questions, otherwise the number of variables can be overwhelming:

use of arms and other limbs, direction of turn, even (more in the case of gymnastics) axis of rotation as in cartwheels and forward rolls. In this case I chose pirouettes en dehors, because they represent a task that has both limits (standard ballet pirouettes) and variations (can be done from 4th, 5th, and 2nd position). The information gained from this question could then be applied to other types of turns.

26 Developed from Mosston & Ashworth, 5th Ed.

27 Betsy Blair, personal correspondence, July 17, 2001.

28 This section on Flow is developed from the work of Mihalyi Csikszentmihalyi.

29 Artistic process may also include the interpretative process of the reconstructor or director who mediates the work between the score and the dancers. The choreographer, performer, and reconstructor each use parallel operations that have many aspects in common; however, each individual works with slightly different aspects of the dance medium. Since most dance pedagogy is concerned with choreography and performance, these two will be addressed. For more information on the processes of the reconstructor, refer to Ray Cook's *The Dance Director.*

30 Until almost the 17th century, creation in art was considered the craftsman's technique of making pictures and statues "correctly" according to established methods. The Greeks considered the artist to be divinely inspired, guided by the hand of God and creating art using the model of eternal archetypes. The artist was thus seen as an *imitator* rather than a creative agent, and as such was expected to be able to use different modes of representation according to the character of the subject matter or the patron for whom the work was being created. These modes, dictated by their purpose, were thought of as independent of the character of the artist. Personal choice, character or temperament, it was believed, had nothing to do with creating art. However, even in the work of Michelangelo, it had already become apparent that the changes in his style over time were due not to variations of subject matter or to the taste of the patrons by whom he was commissioned; it was due to the ripening and maturation process of his own thinking and feeling as an artist.

31 Sara Ashworth, personal correspondence, 2006.

Printed in the United States
By Bookmasters